She Persisted

THIRTY TEN-MINUTE PLAYS BY WOMEN OVER FORTY

She Persisted

THIRTY TEN-MINUTE PLAYS BY WOMEN OVER FORTY

Preface by Jacquelyn Reingold
Introduction by Theresa Rebeck

Edited by Lawrence Harbison

THEATRE & CINEMA BOOKS

Guilford, Connecticut

Applause Theatre and Cinema Books
An imprint of Globe Pequot,
the trade division of The Rowman & Littlefield Publishing Group, Inc.
4501 Forbes Blvd., Ste. 200
Lanham, MD 20706
www.rowman.com

Distributed by NATIONAL BOOK NETWORK

British Library Cataloguing in Publication Information available

Library of Congress Cataloging-in-Publication Data

Names: Harbison, Lawrence, editor. | Reingold, Jacquelyn, writer of preface. | Rebeck, Theresa, writer of introduction.
Title: She persisted : 30 10-minute plays by women over forty / edited by Lawrence Harbison ; preface by Jacquelyn Reingold ; introduction by Theresa Rebeck.
Description: Guilford, Connecticut : Applause, [2021] | Series: Applause acting series | Summary: "A collection of ten-minute plays by women over forty" —Provided by publisher.
Identifiers: LCCN 2021040481 (print) | LCCN 2021040482 (ebook) | ISBN 9781493061297 (paperback) | ISBN 9781493061303 (epub)
Subjects: LCSH: American drama—Women authors. | American drama—21st century. | One-act plays, American. | LCGFT: One-act plays.
Classification: LCC PS628.W6 S44 2021 (print) | LCC PS628.W6 (ebook) | DDC 812/.60809287—dc23
LC record available at https://lccn.loc.gov/2021040481
LC ebook record available at https://lccn.loc.gov/2021040482

♾™ The paper used in this publication meets the minimum requirements of American National Standard for Information Sciences—Permanence of Paper for Printed Library Materials, ANSI/NISO Z39.48-1992

Contents

Preface

On June 5, 2018, Brooke Berman posted on Facebook "WARNING. RANT . . . Composing an Op-Ed in my mind about the generation of female playwrights sandwiched between the Baby Boomers and the Pussy Grabs generation. Because I fear we will be forgotten."

Within hours there were forty pages filled with four hundred comments. "It's true." "OH MY GOD YES." "a sandwiched generation." "submerged writers." "Now that young female playwrights are paid attention to, we're told we're old." "We were told to pay our dues and hopefully we'd earn a place at the table. THEN THEY MOVED THE FUCKING TABLE."

Playwrights were named. "You are on the list." Everyone had their favorites. "You are on the list." Women in their 40s, 50s, 60s. "You are on the list." Pages of names. "You are on the list." I was on the list. But what good was being on a list of the soon-to-be forgotten? What if we did something to get those playwrights and their plays into—theaters?

Theresa Rebeck invited some of us to her house. We ate, drank, and wailed. We felt better, but we still weren't getting produced. Months later, after noticing a highly touted list of women/nonbinary playwrights barely included us, Susan Miller invited more of us to her place. We ate and drank, but instead of just wailing, we began to . . . organize. We kept meeting. And organizing. We no longer ate and drank at meetings, since, thanks to Yvette Heyliger, we were now at the Dramatists Guild, where we focused on actions. We formed an Executive Committee: Cynthia Cooper, Cheryl Davis, Yvette Heyliger, Olga Humphrey, Jacquelyn Reingold, Sarah Tuft, Lucy Wang. We wrote, and rewrote (hey, we're writers), our mission statement:

Honor Roll! is an advocacy and action group of women+ playwrights over forty—and our allies—whose goal is our inclusion in theater. The term "women+" refers to a spectrum of gender identification that includes women, non-binary identifiers, and trans. We are the generation excluded at the outset of our careers because of sexism, now overlooked because of ageism. We celebrate diversity in theater, and work to call attention to the negative impact of age discrimination alongside gender, race, ethnicity, faith, socioeconomic status, disability, and sexual orientation in the American Theater and beyond.

We are, at the time of this writing, thirteen hundred members and growing.

Some of us started writing plays later in life, and though early in our career, we're excluded from emerging writer programs. Some of us landed productions while young, but learned if we weren't famous by forty, theaters closed their doors. Some of us found more success in TV, fiction, film, teaching. Some of us were waylaid by mentors who savaged our plays, while others were traumatized when those mentors sexually harassed us. Some of us, in addition to sexism, faced racism and homophobia. Lately, most of us delight in cheering on our younger sisters who are, finally, getting productions, but we puzzle over theaters that consistently confuse "fresh voices" with "young voices." All of us know the odds are against us getting produced by high-profile theaters, but we keep doing what we love: writing plays.

Honor Roll! is a grassroots group of self-initiated actions. Sarah Tuft helms a campaign to redefine "Emerging/Early Career" to include women who are forty plus. Claudia Catania, Cindy Cooper, and I have a program to feature members in "Playing on Air" podcast recordings. Betsy Howie and Catherine Castellani host our monthly NYC Happy Hour. Yvette Heyliger wrote a personal essay for *The Dramatist Blog*. Kathy Anderson, Liz Amadio, and Betsy Howie compiled extensive statistical research. Stephanie Alison Walker created a portal for members interested in TV. Jacqueline E. Lawton, Lucy Wang, Winter Miller, and Sarah Tuft honed our language to reflect intersectionality. Jacqueline Goldfinger started a play reading exchange via NPX. Bayla Travis organized a Musical Theater Panel. Barbara Kahn, Jean Hartley Sidden, and Saviana Stanescu all planned theater events. To name just *some* of our actions.

This book began, full circle, with a post on the Honor Roll! Facebook page on November 7, 2019, about publishing our short plays and monologues. It wasn't a rant. It was an action. I contacted prominent theater editor Lawrence Harbison and pitched the idea over a New York diner breakfast. His face lit up. Not only was he enthused, he persuaded John Cerullo, the head of Applause Theatre and Cinema Books, to publish two books, one of ten-minute plays and one of monologues. Larry edited and selected the work, while the Publishing Committee (Suzanne Bradbeer, Cheryl Davis, Lucy Wang, and I) worked tirelessly on our end. It was way harder than we ever imagined. Yet worth it. It is a thrill to introduce the Honor Roll's first books. I hope there will be many more. Thank you to the Publishing Committee, the Executive Committee, Lawrence Harbison, John Cerullo, Theresa Rebeck, and most of all to the no-longer-forgotten, submerged, or sandwiched playwrights in Honor Roll! Now we need to see productions of these writers *onstage*.

Jacquelyn Reingold
Playwright and founding member of Honor Roll!
June 1, 2020

Introduction

Years and years ago, when I was a young playwright who happened to be a woman, I was issued plenty of warnings about what that might end up looking like. One of my teachers, who positioned himself as my mentor, thought I was really talented, but he told me I needed to be careful not to let myself get "ghettoized" as a woman playwright. Idealistic and passionate (and did I mention young?), I replied: It's a great thing to be a woman playwright! It's a new world! They are waiting to hear from us! We share the planet! People want to receive our stories!

It turned out to be a little more complicated than that.

Few people thought of the appearance of female playwrights as a "Wow! We haven't heard from the women!" kind of moment. It was a deeply painful time, even a terrifying time, to be a woman playwright. It was like you were being deselected even before they'd read your play. There were many different ways to explain why theaters were not interested in producing plays written by women, but none of them were, I'm sorry to say, very persuasive. The primary reason being thrown around was that our plays were just "not good enough." If you got anyone to explain what "not good enough" meant, they gave you nothing, really. It was like the idea that a woman had written this made it bad before you even got past the set description. Female playwrights were trapped in kindergarten, also known as the underground reading series, for far too long, while frankly a lot of guys who were actually "not good enough" got handed the keys to the kingdom.

That went on for quite a long time. And it's not as if people didn't know this was happening. Allies—often, powerful male allies—told us to rethink our names, to go by our initials, to use a male pseudonym. The problem, it seemed, was the gendered name, right there on the title page. If you could somehow scrub that gender out of the name of the playwright, you'd have a much better shot at a fair read. This move had already led to a sea change in orchestra auditions: Once the auditions were held behind screens, so that no one could see the gender of the auditioner, orchestras went from being utterly lopsided, in terms of gender representation, to being pretty much evenly balanced. The theater just needed to somehow figure that bit out. So concerned friends everywhere tried to kindly explain to us: Equalize the playing field. Make yourself a man.

If you pointed out that this was appalling and that women are every bit as good as men, and our stories are just as important, and what's more the planet hadn't really heard them yet, you were branded as "difficult."

If you tried to point out that playwrights are supposed to be "difficult," well, you see where this is going.

There was seemingly something essentially wrong with the idea of a Woman Playwright. Women are not supposed to speak up like that. If you're going to write a play, it should be more like an Emily Dickinson poem. Women who wrote plays unfortunately seemed too loud by definition. If you were a woman writing about what you knew—women's lives—that meant you had a "feminist agenda." Which was bad, even though men were at the same time being wildly celebrated for having misogynist agendas.

This wasn't that long ago. It was much more recent than it should have been. Still, it went on for a long, long time, and frankly it was ridiculous.

And then we rose up.

In 2002, the great Susan Jonas was our John the Baptist, with Suzanne Bennett spearheading and publishing a powerful NYSCA report which went into damning detail about how female creatives in the theater had been systemically discriminated against for decades. In the 90s, we discovered, there were fewer new plays on Broadway than there had been in the 1920s. We were going backward. Julia Jordan, Sarah Schulman, and New Dramatists held a town hall, inviting artistic directors to come and explain why their programming systematically excluded women directors and playwrights. That got covered by the press, and slowly but surely this ridiculous situation was observed and acknowledged. Opportunities for women started to appear, a small trickle and then a small stream. The numbers—which were being tracked by the Dramatists Guild—started to change. More plays by women were being produced, and there was more than one woman playwright at a time.

Sadly, we were still excluded from the awards season, so we started our own awards, The Lillys. And then the Kilroys were born, an organization which put together lists of wonderful new plays by female playwrights, so that artistic directors who wanted to know where those plays were, had a place to look. The Guerrilla Girls stepped up and left messages *everywhere* about the importance of women artists and audiences. (Women make up about 75 percent of our audience, which is partially why we can't figure out why this wasn't addressed years ago.)

And then Me Too happened. And another shocking window opened, revealing the systemic discrimination against women in show business. The focus of #MeToo very much centered on the sexual abuse of women in the workplace, and how impossible it was for women to find a legal remedy to predatory and bullying behavior from men in power. But alongside that, women knew there were other behaviors that went hand in glove with sexual abuse. Women were still being excluded or suppressed in the corporate boys' clubs behind the scenes, and women's writing was not being promoted or included in the front lines of storytelling in television and film, as well as in the theater.

The NYSCA Report. The Guerrilla Girls. The Lillys. The Kilroys. #MeToo. We are moving ahead. Progress has been made.

And yet. There were many plays written during those decades of struggle. We're not there yet, and the plays are being written still. Women are not yet seen as full partners in this mighty enterprise, the theater. And yet plays are being written. We still have a long way to go. And plays are being written.

And they're being written by many of the same writers who fought through all those years to be heard. These women are in their forties and fifties and sixties, and they have been writing a long time, and they are at the height of their craft. These are tight, complex, nuanced pieces of writing, which no one has seen because for too long they weren't looking.

These are important writers, and important plays.

History has not yet caught up or even had the thought that maybe we should go take a look at those plays that stand as witnesses to human nature and joy and suffering, which tell the story of women fighting for the rights of all women storytellers to be heard. It's time to look at what was silenced, during those years of lost writing. The plays are still here, because all these women persisted.

Theresa Rebeck
Playwright
May 19, 2020

ARTS AND SCIENCES

by Sheri Wilner

Original Production, May 20, 2012
Boston Theatre Marathon, XIV
Produced by Boston Playwrights' Theatre, Artistic Director
Sponsored by Vaquero Playground
Directed by John J. King

MEGAN: Lynn R. Guerra
AARON: Bob Mussett

Arts and Sciences was originally commissioned by the Cornell University Department of Theatre, Film and Dance, Bruce Levitt, Professor and former Chair and was presented at the Snapple Theatre Center, New York City, June 2, 2011.

Sheri Wilner's plays include *Kingdom City, Father Joy, Hunger, The End, A Tall Order, Equilibrium, Relative Strangers, Little Death of a Salesman, The Bushesteia, The Unknown Part of the Ocean,* and *Joan of Arkansas,* and have been performed and developed at major American theaters including the La Jolla Playhouse, Actors Theatre of Louisville, Eugene O'Neill Playwrights Conference, Guthrie Theater, and the Williamstown Theatre Festival. She cowrote the libretto for her first musical, *Cake Off* (based on her ten-minute award-winning play *Bake Off*), which was produced by the Signature Theatre in Washington, D.C. (nominated for a Helen Hayes Award for Outstanding Original Musical Adaptation); workshopped at the Old Globe in San Diego; and produced by the Bucks County Playhouse this past September. Her work has been published in over a dozen anthologies, and Playscripts has published twelve of her one-acts, which have received over three hundred productions across the United States as well as in Australia, Denmark, Germany, Ireland, Japan, the United Kingdom, and India. She served as the Director of the Dramatists Guild Fellows Program. Her playwriting awards include a Howard Foundation Fellowship in Playwriting, a Bush Artist Fellowship, and two Playwrights' Center Jerome Fellowships. Also a playwriting teacher, Sheri was the 2016–17 Rev. J. Donald Monan S.J. Professor of Theatre Arts. She was Master Playwright for the Miami-Dade Department of Cultural 2013–15 Playwrights Development Program. Previously, she was the Fred Coe Visiting Playwright-in-Residence at Vanderbilt University and a Visiting Assistant Professor in Playwriting at Florida State University's MFA Dramatic Writing Program. She attended Cornell University and received her MFA in Playwriting from Columbia University. She lives in New York City.

CHARACTERS

AARON REYNOLDS: 21, a college junior majoring in biology. He's introverted and defensive but also very empathetic.

MEGAN RICE: 18–20, a college undergrad majoring in art. She is horribly homesick and lonely.

SETTING

Harvard Yard, Harvard University. In between Weld and University Halls, there are two American sweet gum trees facing each other across a walking path. This play takes place in between those two trees.

TIME

Any year between 2002–2019.

Playwright's Note

Although the setting specifies a location on the Harvard University campus, the script can be adjusted so that it is set at a different college or university; either a specific school of the producer's choice, or one located closer to the producing theater. Please contact me at shw221@gmail.com to request this change, which I would be happy to make.

• • •

MEGAN, *a Harvard undergrad art major, sits by one of the trees and attempts to sketch it. Her work is not going well, which clearly upsets her. She tries to calm herself and begins again—perhaps ripping a page out of her sketchbook and starting over. She repeats this process of frustration, attempted relaxation, and beginning again a few times, during which* AARON, *a junior biology major, enters and walks to the tree she is sketching. When they make eye contact, he nods to her in acknowledgment. He then retrieves a digital camera from his backpack. Before he aims it at the tree, he turns to her.*

AARON: Do you mind if I . . . ?

   (She shakes her head 'no'.)

Thanks. I think it's just this tree.
   (He examines the bark on the other side of the tree.)
Oh shit! That's gotta hurt, right?

   (She does not respond and returns to her drawing. He takes pictures of the tree's bark.)

Are you in Holbrook's FREC class?

MEGAN: Freck?

AARON: Field Research in Ecology and Conservation?

MEGAN: No.

AARON: Biology of Plants?

   (She shakes her head 'no.')

Physiology of Plants?

   (She shakes her head 'no.')

Life Cycles of Plants?

   (She holds up her sketchpad and pencil.)

MEGAN: Painting. I'm in a painting class.

AARON: For real? What's the assignment?

MEGAN: (*Rote.*) Render something from the natural world and infuse it with a human emotion.

AARON: What's the emotion? Despair?

MEGAN: Joy. Why would you say / despair?

AARON: Joy?! You picked this tree to depict . . . ? It's got . . . This is the worst case of *botryosphaeria disrupta* ever. You didn't see this?

MEGAN: No.

AARON: It's a huge . . . gaping wound. How could you not . . . ? Come over here and look.

MEGAN: I don't want to.

AARON: You can't walk five feet to / see . . . ?

MEGAN: I said I don't want to.
    (She starts packing up her things.)
How long are you going to be? I'll come back.

AARON: What's the point? You're barking up the . . . Or I guess painting up the wrong bark. There's no joy here. It's dying.

MEGAN: Shit! Are you sure?

AARON: Yeah. I'm sure. Will you just look at this?

   (She walks around to the other side of the tree and is shocked to see a huge "wound.")

MEGAN: Oh my god. What is that?

AARON: I told you *botryosphaeria / disrupta*.

MEGAN: In English.

AARON: A bleeding canker.

MEGAN: Bleeding?
    (Beat. She stares at the "wound.")

AARON: It's fungal.

MEGAN: And you can't . . . ?

AARON: Incurable.

   (They both look at the "wound.")

Not for lack of trying though. We've attempted bark drenches, soil drenches, trunk injections, but . . .

MEGAN: How much longer does it . . . ?

AARON: I'm not sure. A couple of months. Maybe. It definitely won't be here next spring. (*Beat.*) All we can do now is try to keep it comfortable.

(She looks to see if he's joking. He is. She's not amused and walks briskly toward her things.)

That one is healthy.
(He points across the path. She looks.)

MEGAN: And it's the same kind, right? Sweet gum?

AARON: Yeah. I'm impressed.

MEGAN: You're sure it's healthy? It's not bleeding?

AARON: It's fine. Its proximity is troubling, / but . . .

MEGAN: Thanks.
(She moves to sit near the healthy tree and then starts sketching it. He watches her for a moment. When he sees that she's now totally focused on the new tree, he becomes angry.)

AARON: That's cold. You've literally turned your back / on . . .

MEGAN: On you. This is due tomorrow.

AARON: You've already started that one. Instead of changing trees, why not change emotions?

(She ignores him.)

I see. You have to paint "happy trees." Who's your professor? Walt Disney?

(This pisses her off, but she does not respond and begins sketching the healthy tree. He takes some pruning tools out of his backpack and begins pruning the bark. After a moment, she looks back and is alarmed to see him scraping the tree.)

MEGAN: What are you doing? You're making it worse!

AARON: I'm removing the . . . *Why* would I make it worse? Jesus. You didn't even notice this huge . . . necrosis, and now you're its protector? Who knows more than . . . ?! God! That is so frickin' typical.

MEGAN: Typical of what?

AARON: Of . . . nothing. Go . . . paint joy. I need to help the tree.

MEGAN: You said it was incurable.

AARON: We're working on it. A cure. My professor. She needs samples. Plus, this stops it from spreading. So . . . chill. I'm not making it worse.
    (*He returns to his work. She stands in between both trees now, unsure what to do next. He notices her looking at the sick tree.*)
It won't look so bad when I'm done. If you want to paint joy here.

    (*She shakes her head 'no,' but does not return to the healthy tree. She looks up at the sick tree's leaves.*)

How'd you know this was a sweet gum? Most BAs don't know the difference between an oak / and a eucalyptus . . .

MEGAN: We have them at home. We called them gumball trees because/ of . . .

AARON: Of the fruit. That's pretty common. I mean, a lot of people call them that.
(*He hands her a round, spiked fruit.*)
Sorry. You didn't think you were the only . . .

    (*She looks at the fruit, quickly pockets it and then starts to walk away.*)

So, if you have sweet gum at home, you live somewhere south of Connecticut but east of Texas. Same here. Culpeper, Virginia. You?

MEGAN: Are there any others on campus? Any . . . disease-free, nonbleeding . . . Anywhere?

AARON: Yeah. There are two more right over there.
    (*He points.*)
In front of Thayer.

MEGAN: Are they healthy? One hundred percent healthy?

AARON: Well, no tree is one hundred percent healthy. Especially not this year after that freak Halloween snow / storm . . .

MEGAN: Is it healthier than that?

AARON: Yeah. It's a lot healthier than that.

(She starts gathering up her things.)

Why do you have to paint joyful sweet gum trees? That's a really oddly specific assignment.

(She looks in the direction where he pointed.)

MEGAN: Is anyone from your "FREAK" class over there?

AARON: *FREC.* No.

(She continues to gather up her stuff.)

Just happy-go-lucky gumball trees. And maybe some singing and dancing bluebirds to sit on your shoulder.

(She grabs her sketchbook and storms over to him. She opens to a page that depicts very disturbing images—such as a tormented face or a bleak burnt-out landscape—and holds it up to his face.)

MEGAN: I've mastered despair. I can paint despair. If I bring in any more despair, I'll probably get sent to Health Services. So screw you for accusing me of . . . whatever the hell it is you're accusing me of!
(She starts to withdraw the sketchbook, but he takes hold of it and moves it so that he can get a better look at her picture. He looks at her and then starts to turn to another page in the book. She grabs the book back and starts to leave.)

AARON: I'm sorry. Don't go. Wait. Wait.
(He grabs the book to prevent her from leaving. She grabs at it frantically.)
Whoa. Calm down.

(She grabs for it again.)
I'm sorry. I'm sorry. Hold on. Let me apologize.

MEGAN: Forget it.

AARON: I was mad you didn't notice. I was an asshole because you didn't notice. I'm sorry.

MEGAN: Give it to me!

AARON: No one here ever notices. Not just this. There are dozens of sick trees all over campus, and no one ever notices. Or no one here, I should say. Up in front of the Bio Labs it's a whole different story. A prematurely brown leaf sends us all out there like first responders. But over here, on the Holy Ground of Harvard Yard—where you'd think people would give a shit . . . And, OK, maybe that's too much to expect, but you're a *painter*. So, I thought if anyone would see and . . . *care* . . .

MEGAN: Give me my book.

   (He doesn't.)

Give it back!

AARON: I said I'm sorry.

MEGAN: NOW!

AARON: Are you alright? You seem . . .

MEGAN: What? I seem what?

AARON: Very, very upset.

MEGAN: What a genius. The Tree Whisperer understands people too.

AARON: No. Actually, I don't. I tend to give people way too much credit.
   (He returns to the tree.)

MEGAN: Yeah, all of us BAs are just . . . spoiled blue bloods who are too narcissistic and . . . superficial to notice tree cankers. Yeah, that's giving us *way* too much credit.

AARON: It won't happen again.

MEGAN: I bet it won't.

AARON: Pretty ironic. You're trying to infuse trees with human emotion, and I keep trying to infuse *humans* with human /emotion . . .

MEGAN: I showed you my drawings. What else do you want me to do? Hang myself from that tree? Would that be enough notice for you? I'm sorry it's dying. I'm sorry you can't cure it. Now, how about you feel sorry that a fellow human being is miserable? How about you notice . . . I mean, here I am at "The Greatest School in the World" surrounded by history and genius and every resource and opportunity known to mankind and I can't be happy. These trees used to make me happy. At least . . . the ones at home did. I used to paint them and . . . No. Screw you. Stay at the fucking Bio Lab if you think everyone's so superior over there.

(He takes a picture of her with his digital camera.)

What the hell?!

AARON: I don't know why I did that. I'm sorry. I
(He looks at the picture. She scowls at him and then storms off. Calling out)
Wait! WAIT! My name's Aaron. Reynolds. There are three of us here, but I'm the only one concentrating in Organismic and Evolutionary Biology. (*Beat.*) And I'm miserable too!

(But she's gone. He looks at the tree. Then looks at her picture on his camera. He studies it closely, not noticing when she returns. He looks up and sees her, and their eyes meet. They stare into each other's eyes for several seconds.)

MEGAN: Megan Rice. Edgewater, Maryland.

(He smiles. She almost does too.)

END OF PLAY

AT THE TRAIN STATION IN MUNICH
Based On the Real-Life Story
of Gisa Peiper Konopka
by Cynthia L. Cooper

Original production:
Remember the Women Institute at the Center for Jewish History, April 2017

Cast:
GISA: Sarah Baskin
ADRIANA: Abby Royle

Directed by Ludovica Villar-Hauser

Cynthia L. Cooper's plays have been performed in New York at Primary Stages, The Women's Project (*How She Played the Game*), Wings (*Slow Burn, Sisters of Sisters*), Lincoln Center Clark Studio (Starfish—*Beyond Stone*), Town Hall, Promenade (Theatreworks, *The World at Your Fingertips*), Museum of Tolerance, Anne Frank Center USA (*Silence Not, A Love Story*), EST New Works, Manhattan Theatre Source, WOW Café, MultiStages, Actor's Temple, Guild Hall, Judson Church, Union Seminary, HBO, Center for Jewish History, Urban Stages, New Circle Theatre Company, Chain Theatre, Art and Work Ensemble, Museum of Jewish Heritage, Riverside-Goddard Center, Ronald Feldman Gallery, and in Chicago (*Strange Light*), Minneapolis, DC, Philadelphia, Los Angeles, Reno, Richmond, Maryland, Texas, Alabama, Florida, Indiana, Tennessee, North Carolina, as well as London, Budapest, Jerusalem, Montreal, Vancouver, Helsinki, and more. She has fourteen produced full-length plays, and thirty-five short plays. Her plays are in sixteen publications including by Smith and Kraus, the New Press (*Frontlines*), Applause, Henry Holt, Heinemann, and others. She has won awards from Pen and Brush, Samuel French Play Festival, Malibu International Playwriting Festival, Nantucket Theatre, Northwest Area Foundation, Rimon, City of Providence, Quixote Foundation, and more. A journalist and author, her book *Mockery of Justice* was made into a CBS movie. She is a two-time Jerome Fellow and an Affiliate writer at the Playwrights Center. She lives in New York City. www.cyncooperwriter.net.

CHARACTERS

GISA PEIPER, born in 1910, Gisa is a young Jewish woman who moves from Berlin to Hambin in 1929 at age nineteen to join the efforts of labor and political activists, part of a small liberal organization. The members are young idealists who wish to create a more equitable society in the new German democracy created after World War I, despite combustible economic and political circumstances.

ADRIANA KUEHN, seen throughout the entire play, Adriana is the same person as GISA, above. She is twenty-eight years old and is using false papers as she sits in the Munich train station during a layover from Vienna to Paris. All of her dialogue is her inner thinking.

TIME

March 1938.

PLACE

A train station in Munich, Germany.

Notes

The play is written as a stylized memory scene in which two actors play one character—an inner and outer monologue. One actor plays Gisa; the other plays Adriana, an assumed name that Gisa has been forced to take.

Note on the formatting

Italics within a speech indicate that the character is repeating the words of someone else.

• • •

March 12, 1938: On the day that Hitler announces Austria has agreed to come under German rule—the "Anschluss." The raucous sound of a railway station with trains coming and going, clacking of signs and schedules, the announcement of trains, people walking, talking. In the station, Nazi soldiers are celebrating and cheering everywhere, yelling "Heil Hitler," raising steins of beer as they sing patriotic songs. ADRIANA enters, coming off a train from Salzburg, Austria. Wearing white gloves and carrying a suitcase, she looks around at a sign that says 'Munich.' The words she speaks are internal thoughts.

ADRIANA: Munich! No! Why must we come through Germany? And . . . look . . . that officer, that Nazi, is giving me a look. A hateful look. A smirking look.

(*GISA enters. A second woman, younger, also wearing white gloves, she is, in fact, a younger version of Adriana.*)

GISA: Quiet! Shhh. We mustn't say anything.

ADRIANA: Oh! And there they go hoisting their beers and raising their arms in the Nazi salute. All because of Austria! Can you believe—Austria . . . gave . . . in . . . to . . . the . . . Nazis! CAP-IT-U-LATED! (*As if imitating the soldiers, toasting and boasting.*) "*To Anschluss: to the Union! March 12, 1938—today and forever!*"

GISA: Sit.

ADRIANA: It's enough to make you want to SCREAM!

GISA: Say nothing.

ADRIANA and GISA: Don't laugh. Don't cry. Don't smile.

GISA: Don't joke. Don't wink. Don't wince. Don't blink. DON'T!

ADRIANA: And now you—telling me what to do!

GISA: We get through, together. When we were questioned. When we were arrested. When we fled from Germany.

ADRIANA: You can't help! You make me think all sanity has fled! Another me talking to me? We must be going crazy. Here. In Munich.

GISA: We know how to handle these situations. We've done it before!

ADRIANA: Not LIKE THIS! Don't look over there! A guard is eyeing us. He's coming our way.

GISA: Don't grimace. Don't shake your head. Don't nod. Don't make a face.

ADRIANA: The handlers wouldn't listen. A train through Germany is out of the question. Even on a layover. *"Austria is no longer safe for you. We have a train ticket to Paris. Only one layover. In Munich."* Our friends told me this! Friends in the underground! "What if they ask travelers if they are Jewish? What if they check files for people who've been in prison in Germany? What if, what if my sanity fails?" *"You are not the same person who lived there! No more Gisa. Remember the name on your new visa! Your parents are different. Your birthdate is different. Your hair is different. Now you're Adriana. Please. It's to protect everyone in the underground."*

GISA: We're disciplined. Trained! Let's think about something else! Keep the mind occupied. That's rule number one. Stories!

ADRIANA: No stories from Germany.

GISA: Good ones! 1927. Remember that? The big rally in Berlin to support labor? Only nine years ago.

ADRIANA: The world was different. We were young and full of ideals . . .

GISA: Remember!
    (She claps loudly. She reenacts the moment when she hands out literature.)
"Information." "Information you need." "Please take one."

ADRIANA: "Information you need."

GISA: All the political clubs from school are attending. "Hello! *Guten tag!* I have literature supporting fair wages for all!" "Read a statement on safe working conditions in Germany!" "Support justice for workers!"

ADRIANA: (*Remembering.*) "Justice for workers."

GISA: We weave through the crowd on the plaza, handing out literature to everyone. And there she is. Käthe Kollwitz! The same face in the bookstore, posted next to her famous etching, "The March of the Weavers!" Her woodcuts! Her posters! Showing the suffering of laborers! She takes a leaflet from me. And then we can't help it.

ADRIANA and GISA: We burst out . . . "Excuse me, Miss Kollwitz—I am only a high school student in Berlin. But I must tell you how much your art means to me."

ADRIANA: She turns her head up from the leaflet and looks from under her eyelids, heavy and wide.

GISA: *"You are young and full of ideals. Promise me you will remember this also when you are old."*

ADRIANA: They aged us. When they took us in for questioning, when they closed the gates at the prison, when they terrorized. They left a knife on the table. *"Do us a favor and spare us the trouble. You can end your pathetic woes."*

GISA: *"Promise me,"* she said. And we said, "I promise, Miss Kollowitz. I WILL remember."

ADRIANA and GISA: "I promise, Miss Kollowitz. I WILL remember."

ADRIANA: And now, this! A layover in Munich with false documents and a new hairstyle. That one over there—he's watching us.

GISA: Shhh. Say nothing.

ADRIANA: We should have stayed in Austria! We should have . . .

(GISA claps loudly, as if trying to get ADRIANA to snap out of her train of thought.)

GINA: And then when we graduated, Rudy, dear dear Rudy, brought over, as a gift, a Käthe Kollwitz print—*Never Again War."*

ADRIANA: Father didn't like him: *"A rich boy and a Communist, too. A Jew and a boy who likes boys, too."*

GISA: Rudy attached a card to the print: "Art and poetry and friendship. Hunting the truth will keep us alive."

ADRIANA: And where is he now? One day they came knocking on his door and . . .

GISA: *"Never Again War."* Signed by the artist! It was the first thing Hilde saw when she met us in Hamburg in 1929. We had it laid flat with baker's paper covering it. *"What's that?"* she said.

ADRIANA and GISA: "My most precious possession."

ADRIANA: (*As if she is Hilde.*) *"An art print? What a strange duck you are."*

GISA: No, she didn't say that. She said, *"Welcome! We have a room for you. And a job in the bottle factory—you can organize the workers into a women's union. And since you have a high school degree, we're going to make you the editor of our newsletter for workers!"*

ADRIANA and GISA: "What's the newsletter called?"

GISA: *"We don't have a newsletter yet. But if you are the editor, we will! And you can name it!"*

ADRIANA and GISA: And she laughed.

GISA: Her wonderful laugh!

ADRIANA: "Take a copy of our newsletter, 'The Spark.' Information you can use. A decent wage. Safe working conditions. We're holding a big rally, right here, tomorrow!"

GISA: More and more people are finding their way to the rallies! "Information you can use." Workers from the factories and the shipyards— all our efforts are paying off!

ADRIANA: Until . . .

GISA: Yes.

ADRIANA: Brutes. Thugs. Like that one standing over there boasting about Anschluss! Pushing their way into our rallies. Like the one by the town hall, 1931. Men and boys, punching and kicking, bloodying noses and breaking arms. Brown shirts. National Socialists. Hitler's men.

GISA: We fight back! "The Spark" sent a team to investigate. We went to Nazi territory to see for ourselves! To Munich!

ADRIANA: Munich!

GISA: (*She claps loudly.*) "Hilde! The next issue of 'The Spark' has an eyewitness account of a Nazi rally in Munich. We saw it all. 100,000 people. Flags waving. Military music. Free uniforms to anyone who will listen. Speeches about the righteous place of Germans. They're out to eradicate the trade unions—that's all of us. To 'rid' Europe of the Jewish 'race'—that's me. And they're arming themselves with weapons in secret. Using money from the big factory owners. This is information people can use! We can resist. In the morning, I'll take the north end of the Elbe Tunnel. You'll take the south, Hilde. Others will cover the park. We should be able to reach all of the stevedores on their way to work. The goons are everywhere, but we're living in the light. Just like Käthe Kollwitz: art and truth will keep us alive!"

ADRIANA: You should be more careful. You should watch yourself every step of the way.

GISA: "Life, I wrote on my banner. My first skin is made out of leather. But my second is made out of steel." (*Handing out literature.*) "Information you can use. Take a newsletter. Read about the Nazis in Munich. We can stop them in their tracks. Information you can use!"

ADRIANA: They could beat you up. They could follow you home. They could go into your room . . .

GISA: There are good people everywhere. We mustn't forget! "Far away the twilight of something new, moves slowly at first . . . miraculous. Spirit alone cannot be action. Action needs body and hand."

ADRIANA: How do you explain what happened in the boarding house?

GISA: Perhaps we've gone far enough. Perhaps the train will be announced soon. Let's sit quietly.

ADRIANA: In 1932?

GISA: (*Clapping.*) We can think of different stories. Hiking? Swimming! Camping in the forest! How we loved to pitch a tent and sit under the leafy boughs?

ADRIANA: How did they get into our room?

GISA: We don't know.

ADRIANA: Or, we know! You can't believe everything people say.

GISA: The landlady told us right away. *"Some men were here. They went into your room. They took some things. Books."*

ADRIANA and GISA: "Men? Men can't just come into my room! Men can't take away my books.

GISA: "A book is a book. A book is to read."

ADRIANA: She said . . .

GISA: *"I don't want trouble. I'm only one person. I have a daughter to support. What could I do?"*

ADRIANA: (*Clapping loudly.*) Signs you must watch! Signs all around. Don't blink. Don't nod. Don't frown.

GISA: We are not afraid.

ADRIANA: You should have known better! You should have seen the signs. Knocking on Hilde's door was a sign! 1932!

GISA: That's so long ago. I can't think about it.

ADRIANA: (*Knocking on Hilde's door.*) "Hilde! I know it's early. We're supposed to get to the Elbe Tunnel before the dockworkers start arriving."

GISA: I arrived earlier than usual, I think.

ADRIANA: *"I'm too tired today."*

GISA: We have the latest news—a report from Dessau. The Nazis forced the Bauhaus design school to close and banned all of its art—even the furniture. It's famous all over the world! And they're calling it "degenerate"—in this day and age! 1932! And they're setting up Nazi youth groups to go hunt down more. It's all in the newsletter: They banned a CHAIR and they are making children join Nazi groups. Käthe Kollwitz issued a Call to Action. It's not too late! We can do something.

ADRIANA: *"My mother is sick."* *"The morning air is bad for me."*

GISA: (*Clapping; leaving the memory.*) Let's stand! Let's check the train schedules. It must be close to the time.

ADRIANA: She said: *"Men came to our house yesterday."*

GISA: We don't want to dwell on that! There are good people everywhere.

ADRIANA: And you said . . .

GISA: "If we don't speak out, who will? The signs are all around us! If we don't act now, everything could come tumbling down on our heads! Of course, it's not convenient. We are but a small bulwark against . . ."

ADRIANA: No! That's not what you said. You said: "I understand, dear Hilde. I imagine it does not help your mother's health to be seen handing out literature with a Jew at the Elbe Tunnel at five o'clock in the morning."

ADRIANA and GISA: "I can do it on my own. It is, perhaps, a foolish thing to do."

LISA: But there were many others who stood with us. Several.

ADRIANA: Yes, there were others. Other than Hilde. There were. And there were not. And now here we are in Munich! Six years later. Enough memories to come crashing down on the mind. Hitler to power. The boycott of Jewish businesses. The Reichstag fire. Suspension of Parliament. Martial law. The Gestapo. The order to Käthe Kollwitz to stop displaying her art. The racial segregation laws stripping Jews of civil rights. The months we spent in prison.

GISA: They let us out.

ADRIANA: The disappearances. The detentions. Of the agitators. Of the gypsies. Of the labor activists. Of the Communists. Of the homosexuals. Of . . .

GISA: WHERE IS RUDY? "Art and poetry and friendship. Hunting the truth will keep us alive." (*Covering her face.*) It really is too much to bear.

ADRIANA: No! We are NOT allowed to give up. We got out of prison. We escaped. We've come this far! "When they grinned and spat. And left us weeping. And left us all alone. And left no love." Get up. Move around! Remember who you are . . .

GISA: (*Standing timidly. handing out literature.*) "Information." "Information you can use." "Information you need."

ADRIANA: "You, who then must have seen us from above. bear testimony. That we were not sleeping. If you are there at all, bear witness, God! We were not sleeping."

> (*Voiceover. An announcer is heard: "Now arriving on lower level, track twenty-six. Express train to Paris."*)

GISA: It's our train! It's the call for Paris! Steady now. Steady.

ADRIANA: Of course. We know what to do. We're experienced. It's only a layover, and now it's almost over.

GISA: Don't laugh. Don't cry. Don't nod. Be safe. Be safe. Be safe.

ADRIANA: Remember this . . .

GISA: Remember this also when you are old.

END OF PLAY

THE BARDO STATE

by Susan Cinoman

The Bardo State was produced February 20–23, 2020, by Stagebites Theatre, Westbrook, Connecticut.

SIB: Joanna Keylock
BEN/CAL: Eddie Varley
Director: Susan Cinoman

Susan Cinoman is a playwright and screenwriter whose work is published and produced internationally. Her one-act play, *Fitting Rooms*, is featured in Applause Theatre and Cinema Books *Best Short Plays of 1996*. Off-Broadway plays include *Cinoman and Rebeck* at the Miranda Theatre and *Gin and Bitters*. She has had numerous workshop productions at Ensemble Studio Theatre and Naked Angels. Prizes and awards include: The Best Narrative Film at New England Film and Video Festival, Official Selection by The International Berkshire Film Festival, The Maxwell Anderson Playwrights Prize, The Aristos Award, Guilford Performing Arts Prize in Drama, Circle of Excellence Award. She is also the creator of the recurring character of Ms. Cinoman on ABC-TV's *The Goldbergs* and is a frequent contributor to the show.

CHARACTERS

SIB, 30–older.
BEN/CAL, 20–older.

TIME

Present.

PLACE

A cheerful room.

•   •   •

Cream-colored curtains wafting gently on long French doors. Through the door, the sky is pink and blue, placid, bright. A chaise lounge is in the room, plush, tasteful. A bed, a night table, a desk complete with papers, pens—some ballpoints, some quills. A tea set is seen on another small table by the bed. On the chair near the chaise lounge, reading, sits SIB. She is long-limbed, with reddish-brown hair pulled up with some strands loosely framing her face. She's in a robe, lounging pajamas underneath, simple, refined. A timid-sounding knock is heard at the door of the room. She glances, gets up, unlocks it, and sits back down in the chair by the chaise. A younger man, BEN, cautiously enters.

BEN: Oh, excuse me. God, I'm sorry.

SIB: No, no. Please, come in. Sit.

BEN: Uh . . . I really, I should go.

SIB: Where?

BEN: Uh . . .

SIB: How about some tea?

BEN: Oh. That always sounds nice, doesn't it? Tea.

SIB: It is nice.

BEN: Tea. And milk.

SIB: I have that.

BEN: All right. I'll have some.

SIB: I'll be happy to give it to you. It's been steeping.

BEN: Oh yeah? Let me take a look at that.

SIB: At the steeping?

BEN: Is that okay?

SIB: I can't see a problem with it.

BEN: The tea is rushing out a little.

SIB: Steepage.

BEN: Look delicious.

SIB: It's nice.

BEN: I feel sort of . . .

SIB: Light?

BEN: Yes. But also sad. But it passes.

SIB: It does. Like a breeze, right, Ben?

BEN: What?

SIB: Here you are.

BEN: Did you know I was coming? I mean, did I have an appointment?

SIB: Did you know I was with you?

BEN: Uh . . . I don't mean to be rude. But I don't recognize you. Am I supposed to? Is this like a virtual reality or something?

SIB: Oh. Is that what you thought it was?

BEN: I'm sorry. I didn't mean to hurt your feelings. I . . .

SIB: It's all right. I know you don't mean to. You never mean to. But then, why do you?

BEN: Oh, okay. Uh . . . So, this tea is great. And the room, and the light. And you are very pretty. But I really think I should go. I should be getting back.

SIB: Don't do that.

BEN: Don't go back?

SIB: It never works out. It can get scary and sad. Painful even, sometimes. I don't mean to sound so controlling. But, guess it's just in my nature.

BEN: Look . . . uh . . .

SIB: Sib.

BEN: I have a life, okay. And I don't exactly remember what that is right now. But I know I had it around here someplace. So, I should go and find it and get back in it. So can you please, please help me to just find my way back to where I'm supposed to be. Do you have my phone?

SIB: No. Did you check your pocket?

BEN: I feel flushed.

SIB: You don't want to leave and try the next room, do you?

BEN: Uh . . . no. I don't want to try any rooms. I'm flushed. My face feels hot. It's not really comfortable.

SIB: There were a few times you made things pretty uncomfortable for me. But I guess I wasn't supposed to say anything about that.

BEN: Are you angry? Have I done something to you?

SIB: Yes. You've made me incredibly happy. Don't you know that? And proud.

BEN: I want to remember more about how I got here.

SIB: (*Assuring him.*) You do.

BEN: (*Remembering.*) Oh, I do. Oh, that part . . . that part was amazing. That . . . part. Oh God, that part was so good.

SIB: You know how much we've loved you, don't you?

BEN: We?

SIB: Your father and I. Cal and me.

BEN: My father, Cal. He's been dead for years and years. He's been dead for so long I can't remember the sound of his voice. I don't think I'd recognize it, if I heard it. I don't remember anything about him. Barely. Some flashes of things, but maybe that's just remembering photographs, you know?

SIB: I know. Oh, here's your phone!

BEN: Thanks. Uh . . .

SIB: Did you want to check your messages?

BEN: Not really. Which is weird. I think I want to lie down.
(He starts to take off his shirt, his pants. He's undressed now, he goes under the sheets.)

SIB: I think you should.

BEN: Wow.

SIB: Those are great sheets, aren't they?

BEN: Outrageously good. I'd better not get used to this level of luxury. You know, the room, the tea, the curtains. Everything is so nice.

SIB: Kind of soothing.

BEN: Kind of bougie.

SIB: What you want to do now, is hover.

BEN: I don't want to hover. A nap sounds good.

SIB: Ben, please.

BEN: I've offended you.

SIB: No, you haven't.

BEN: It's the last thing I wanted to do. You're so kind. And sweet.
(Something dawns on him.)
And you'll always be so good to me.

SIB: I'll try, Ben. I'll try so hard. I won't always be able to understand you.

BEN: I know. I know. I don't want to be mean. I can't help it sometimes.

SIB: I don't take it that way. I barely listen to you.

BEN: That's good. That's very good. That makes me feel a lot better.

SIB: Get in the bed. Go on.

BEN: All right.

SIB: Okay.

BEN: *(He begins to sound younger.)* Okay.

SIB: Alright.

BEN: Okey-dokey.

SIB: Ben, now you're just being silly.

BEN: (*A little boy.*) I know. Tuck me in.

SIB: (*Tucking him in.*) Now, like I told you, it's time to hover.

BEN: But I don't want to hover. I want to stay here with you, Mom.

SIB: (*A lump in her throat.*) Maybe you do and maybe you don't. But it's time to find that out. Hover.

(BEN *turns around in the sheets. He goes underneath the sheets until he is completely covered, can't be seen at all. He comes out from under the sheets at the bottom of the bed as* CAL. *Older, sterner, maturity in his voice.*)

CAL: I'm sorry, Sib.

SIB: You're sorry. I was so happy. Ben was with me. Now he's gone.

CAL: You'll see him again someday.

SIB: How do I know that?

CAL: Have faith.

SIB: Oh, faith. How stupid is that. What does it mean?

CAL: It means you have to believe that something will happen and that it will all work out fine.

SIB: Well, why in God's name should I ever be that stupid.

CAL: Yes, exactly.

SIB: Oh, in God's name. You're so clever. Why would I ever care about any of that. That's all you, Cal. That's you and your Pollyanna-Cincinnati thinking.

CAL: I'm not from Cincinnati.

SIB: I know where you're from.

CAL: Say it then.

SIB: Pittsburgh. Okay, Pittsburgh. What's the difference if you're from Pittsburgh or Cincinnati? You're not a New Yorker. And if you were, you'd know that faith is great once a year when Macy's does its windows.

CAL: Why are you talking to me like we just met? I know all of your thoughts, Sib. And all of your fears. Lie down with me.

SIB: Cal, I don't have any more fears. Okay? They're gone. No fears, no more shame. My dogs are all buried. All of them. I'm just simply bereft, Cal. Just bereft.

(She sits at the nearby desk chair and cries.)

CAL: Oh, Sib. Honey . . .

SIB: I should be past all this.

CAL: It's just seeing Ben.

SIB: Yeah, I guess you're right.

CAL: How does it feel to have it back?

SIB: You mean the longing? The pain of grief? Feeling like you love your son more than anything you've ever loved or known but you have no idea who he is?

CAL: Yes.

SIB: It feels great!

CAL: Really?

SIB: Oh, yeah. Really good.

CAL: Even the pain?

SIB: I guess, especially the pain. Because it's raw. You know, you're not covering it up with a joke or a drink or a cupcake. And you know . . . it's life.

CAL: Yeah, you really liked life.

SIB: Of course, I did. Why? Didn't you?

CAL: Eh.

SIB: Eh? What do you mean, eh? You didn't like life? What about when you met me?

CAL: Oh, well, you know . . . I was a lucky bastard. You're a gorgeous, exciting woman. You let me marry you and go to bed with you. We had Ben.

SIB: I understand. It was after Ben was grown up. Life became too painful.

CAL: Well, it was before that. I just . . . I never really liked any of it that much. I'm not saying I hated it. It just wasn't . . . you know . . . amazing.

SIB: Oh, well, I didn't realize.

CAL: It wasn't you, Sib.

SIB: Did Ben pick up your . . . ennui? Did he, Cal? If he chooses another couple because of some spoiled emotion of yours . . . I'll kill you!

CAL: Sib.

SIB: Yes. Too late. I know. Oh, Cal! I want our Ben. Don't you?

CAL: I do. But he has to choose. He has to want to go through it all with us again. Try to avoid the same mistakes. The same pain.

SIB: This time we'll help him more. We'll pay more attention.

CAL: How could we have paid more attention to him?

SIB: We'll pay more attention to each other, then. And that will make him happier this time. Please, Cal.

CAL: I'd do anything for you. The first time I saw you, you put on your gloves. One finger at a time. It was very delicate. A very delicate gesture. You were so beautiful in your dark kindness. I loved you so much, Sib. So much.

SIB: I still love you, Cal. Maybe that will bring Ben back.

CAL: If not now, another time.

SIB: But I so want it to be this time. Can I send him a message?

CAL: How?

SIB: Stationery! See? I've got stationery. And envelopes. It must be there for a reason. Everything is for a reason. Right?
   (*She rushes to the writing table. She chooses a fountain pen and writes.*)
Dearest Ben, I'm sorry that we're all dead. (*Pause.*) That our *bodies* are all dead. Don't shake your head at me like that. It's patronizing.

CAL: I don't mean it that way. You always get that confused.

SIB: So? So I get it confused. Nobody's perfect. If we were—we wouldn't have to keep going through this ridiculous churning cycle over and over again, would we?

CAL: Sib, I'm sorry.

SIB: Cal, I'm sorry. Oh, Cal, if we're not good, Ben won't choose us. It's just so much pressure. I'm taking it out on you, I know I am.

CAL: That's a good start for us. Ben's hovering. He'll take note of that.

SIB: Will he?

CAL: Maybe just finish the letter.

SIB: Ben, we're your mom and dad. We're in this Bardo state, after the life that we all just left. Different times, it's strange. But we're up for the next one. All of us. As you hover, and look down on us, how about giving Mom and Dad one more chance? Don't hover on to the next couple, okay? The grass is always greener on another parent's playground, honey. (*To* CAL.) Oh! I don't mean that. It makes it sound like I'm saying he's immature . . . Cal, it's not letting me erase.

CAL: Then go with it.

SIB: Ben, no parents could love a child more than we loved you. For all the mistakes, the games we forgot, the conversations we were distracted from, the way we never listened to you sing. How we treated each other . . . stingingly. Choose us again in the next life, Ben. Because . . . because . . . ?

CAL: Because nobody makes us laugh like you did. No one made us laugh like you.

SIB: Oh, that's good! He'll like that!

CAL: Sign it, "With All Our Love, Mom and Dad." Sib, what else can we really ever offer?

SIB: You're right, Cal. It's all we really have, isn't it? . . . With all our love, Mom and Dad.

(*Blackout.*)

END OF PLAY

BLOOD TIES

by Michael Angel Johnson

Inspired by the lives of Edmonia Wildfire Lewis, c.1845–1917: the first woman of African American heritage and Native American heritage to earn an international reputation as a visual artist, and Lydia Maria Child, a white abolitionist, 1802–1880.

Original Production:
November 12, 2012. The Workshop Theater.
Producer: Yvette Heyliger
Director: Gail Kriegel

Cast:
EDMONIA WILDFIRE LEWIS: Natalie Wachen
LYDIA MARIA CHILD: Ivy Austin

Ms. Michael Angel Johnson's plays have been produced in New York, Los Angeles, Chicago, Cleveland, Amherst, New Haven, and other places across the United States. *The Price of Solitude* was a finalist in the National Ten-Minute Play Contest at Actors Theatre of Louisville. *The Apartment* earned Michael Angel the honor of special participant at the O'Neill Theatre Centre. Her screenplays: *Seasons* (semi-finalist in The Chesterfield Film/Writer's Project), *The Letters* (semi-finalist Writemovies.com), *The Tower* (Honorable Mention Los Angeles Film and Script Festival), and *Wild Fires* (finalist at the Hollywood Black Film Festival). Her stories and essays: "The African American Woman Who Shaped the Future of Art" (*On The Issues Magazine*), "The Echo" (*Persimmon Tree*), and "A Basket of Biscuits" (*On The Issues*

Magazine). Michael Angel has worked with the 52nd Street Project as a director, writer, and dramaturge. She is a member of The League of Professional Theatre Women and a member of New York Women in Film and Television. She is an Associate Professor at New York University and the Fashion Institute of Technology (New York) where she developed and teaches their African American Literature course. She is a graduate of The Yale School of Drama in Playwriting.

CHARACTERS

(Based on real people)

EDMONIA WILDFIRE LEWIS, 19. (c.1845–1917): an African American
    woman-sculptor.
LYDIA MARIA CHILD, 62. (1802–1880): a white abolitionist.

TIME

1864.

PLACE

Edmonia's Studio, Boston, Massachusetts.

• • •

It is 1864. Boston, Massachusetts. EDMONIA's studio: there is a table with books on it and another table near the window that has clay on it. EDMONIA is molding the clay into a man's face. She pulls her fingers out of the clay and wipes them. She then picks up a photograph and stares at it. There's a knock at the door.

EDMONIA: Come in.

> *(MRS. CHILD enters stage left. EDMONIA cannot see her.)*

It's like my fingers no longer have the ability to see. Whenever I close my eyes, I hear screams, which must be part of my nightmares, so I don't sleep at night; I just work. But look at this, his face is so empty; there's no soul. It's like those screams and shadows have covered—tied my hands.
    (She turns around and sees MRS. CHILD.)
Mrs. Child, I thought you were Anne . . .

MRS. CHILD: I have never heard you speak with such honesty—such passion . . .

EDMONIA: What are you doing here?

MRS. CHILD: You missed the lecture by Mr. Peterson, who came all the way from London, and who also spoke with passion, but about the evil of slavery . . .

EDMONIA: I told you yesterday that I wasn't sure that I would be there . . .

MRS. CHILD: And I told everyone that you were going to introduce Mr. Peterson.

EDMONIA: I'll introduce the speaker at the next lecture.

(MRS. CHILD walks over to the table and picks up a book, reading the title.)

MRS. CHILD: "An Appeal in Favor of That Class of Americans Called Africans." Where did you . . . ?

EDMONIA: One of my teachers at Oberlin gave me your book.

MRS. CHILD: I was not allowed to continue my education, but my brother Convers studied law at Harvard. And the abolitionists helped pay for you to attend Oberlin College.

EDMONIA: But you did manage to write that book, Mrs. Child, and many others. And since you reached your goals, please, let me return to my work.

MRS. CHILD: But I did not reach my goal, Miss Lewis. I did not study at Harvard or at Oberlin College as you did.

EDMONIA: Such rules—restrictions are not of my making, Mrs. Child. And you, who wrote that book, should understand that—none of it is of my making.

MRS. CHILD: Of course, I didn't mean to imply . . .

EDMONIA: Well, now that that's settled, I really do need to return to my work.

(MRS. CHILD picks up another book from the table.)

MRS. CHILD: How did you . . . ?

EDMONIA: Anne gave me your collection of letters the other day, but I haven't had a chance to read them. I really need to work now.

MRS. CHILD: What are you working on over there?

EDMONIA: A bust of John Brown.
    (MRS. CHILD looks at the book of letters.)
When John Brown was here in Boston did you meet him? Can you tell me anything about him?

MRS. CHILD: No!

EDMONIA: Why are you upset?

MRS. CHILD: I am not upset, but I am concerned about you.

EDMONIA: I don't need you to be.

MRS. CHILD: Mr. Brackett told me that you stopped taking lessons with him.

EDMONIA: My clay will dry out if I don't.

MRS. CHILD: Mr. Brackett has no problem working when I am in his studio.

EDMONIA: Suit yourself, Mrs. Child.
    (She returns to working on the clay.)

MRS. CHILD: Why did you stop taking art lessons from Mr. Brackett? Don't you think Mr. Brackett is a talented sculptor? Why do you intentionally give those who support slavery ammunition to use against you?

EDMONIA: Intentionally? I don't give them ammunition; they don't need that from me.

MRS. CHILD: I suppose that is true.

EDMONIA: You can be certain of that.

MRS. CHILD: Who is that a picture of that you keep looking at?

EDMONIA: John Brown.

    (MRS. CHILD looks at the picture.)
A lot of abolitionists are still upset with Mr. Brown for using violence at Harpers Ferry. I know you are against violence, Mrs. Child.

MRS. CHILD: The South pushed us into this bloody Civil War, and there's no way around that. But now we are discussing you and your situation.

EDMONIA: What situation?

MRS. CHILD: When Mr. Brackett expressed to me that you had talent as a sculptor. I was pleased to help you pay for this studio.

EDMONIA: Oh, yes, I owe you so much.

MRS. CHILD: As usual, you are twisting . . .

EDMONIA: My point is that I learned to sketch at Oberlin before coming to . . .

MRS. CHILD: The less said about Oberlin and art . . .

EDMONIA: Yes, they accused me of stealing those brushes, but they did find them. Twice I was found innocent, but they still wouldn't let me graduate from Oberlin. And you complain to me because you couldn't go to college.

MRS. CHILD: The point is that when you came to me, you wanted to become a sculptor; something you knew nothing about before coming to Boston.

EDMONIA: And over the past year, I have learned a lot.

(*MRS. CHILD is looking at the picture of Mr. Brown and at the clay.*)

MRS. CHILD: (*Meaning the clay face.*) I must confess that there is some resemblance to the photograph, but you have not captured . . .

EDMONIA: Which shows that . . .

MRS. CHILD: Mr. Brackett is a good teacher.

EDMONIA: But I don't need a teacher anymore. I need to work.

MRS. CHILD: But when I came in, you were obviously frustrated with your work.

EDMONIA: Maybe it's not the work that's frustrating me.

MRS. CHILD: Do you believe that being an artist is as simple as just re-creating an image?

EDMONIA: I know there's more, but that doesn't mean I need more lessons in sculpting.

MRS. CHILD: At times, you are very difficult to talk to, Miss Lewis.

EDMONIA: Thank you, Mrs. Child.

MRS. CHILD: I am here to help you.

EDMONIA: Help? There are many folks who believe that Mr. Brown didn't help the abolitionist cause by using violence at Harpers Ferry.

MRS. CHILD: This is not the time to debate Mr. Brown's philosophy.

EDMONIA: To truly understand Mr. Brown's philosophy, you needed to have experienced . . .

MRS. CHILD: And experience is something that you do not have as an artist, but I do have as a writer. And that's why I can guide . . .

EDMONIA: It's important for an artist to see the pictures in her own head. And I have seen atrocities, and those images are branded onto my brain, which means I have experience.

MRS. CHILD: And I have devoted years to fighting—without violence—to remove such images from our society, to help free . . .

EDMONIA: Do you really believe that your words are so powerful that they can free . . . ?

MRS. CHILD: You were born free, as I was born a free . . .

EDMONIA: White woman.

MRS. CHILD: . . . Who understands that if we do not use—express our individual indignation about the chains that have been clamped on Black slaves—none of us will remain free.

EDMONIA: Sounds like your concern is for yourself.

MRS. CHILD: And you sound like a child who is too stubborn.

EDMONIA: And you're too proud to admit that I'm right.

MRS. CHILD: And you're too proud to acknowledge my experience.

EDMONIA: You say that because I won't do what you want me to do.

MRS. CHILD: I only want to remind you of your responsibilities as a free black woman.

EDMONIA: And like John Brown, I'm going to do things for the cause in my own way.

MRS. CHILD: If you had what John Brown had, you would be able to capture that in his face, which you have not done, my dear.

EDMONIA: Did you meet . . . ?

MRS. CHILD: Men followed Captain Brown, willingly to their death. There was something in him that encouraged that; whatever "that" was, I would recognize it in his reflection.

EDMONIA: How dare you come in here like some general.

MRS. CHILD: This is not a battle.

EDMONIA: Of course, it is. And I've learned how to fight since Oberlin, Mrs. Child.

MRS. CHILD: I did not come here to . . .

EDMONIA: You are fighting by trying to make me do what you think is best for me. You're like that mob at Oberlin; only they used fists, and you use . . .

(Both women go into their own memories.)

MRS. CHILD: When working in New York, I saw the potential of such a mob. I am not one of them.

EDMONIA: I didn't see them coming, but I see you pretending . . .

MRS. CHILD: Pretending? I didn't pretend to go to New York to protest the atrocities of slavery.

EDMONIA: The abolitionists begged me to go to Oberlin College as a way of protesting, showing white people that a black woman could go to a college and accomplish . . .

MRS. CHILD: That mob in New York accomplished nothing by calling the women horrible names. I'd never heard such words spoken out loud before.

EDMONIA: I'm used to words being thrown at me, but that night . . .

MRS. CHILD: As I made my way through their words, I found my way to a hotel.

EDMONIA: There were no rooms for me to hide in.

MRS. CHILD: I stayed in that hotel room for three days and three nights, trying to understand the arrogance of that mob.

EDMONIA: I felt so trapped while in that jail cell.

(MRS. CHILD goes to the table and picks up her book of letters.)

MRS. CHILD: While in that hotel room, I thought about John Brown being in jail.

EDMONIA: When the sheriff released me from jail, he said that some folks in Oberlin would be very angry. But at last, I was out of jail, standing on the porch, gazing up at the stars.

(MRS. CHILD reads from the book of letters.)

MRS. CHILD: "Dear Captain Brown: Believing in peace principles, I cannot sympathize with the method you chose to advance the cause of freedom. But I honor your generous intentions. I admire your courage, moral and physical."

EDMONIA: I look at the stars, trying to understand how my life had brought me to a place where I was accused of attempted murder of two white girls.

MRS. CHILD: "Thousands of hearts are throbbing with sympathy as warm as mine, Captain Brown. I think of you night and day, bleeding in prison, surrounded by hostile faces, sustained only by trust in God and your own strong heart."

EDMONIA: Suddenly, there are piercing sounds that aren't a natural part of the night.

MRS. CHILD: "Captain Brown, I long to nurse you—to speak to you sisterly words of sympathy and consolation."

EDMONIA: There's a bevy of unattached bloodshot eyes circling me. Those bloodshot eyes turn into forms. I'm taken—abducted—as my father's people were taken from Africa. The cries of his people echo through my mind as this enraged group of white men, wearing masks, drags me to a field where they rip off my clothes, as my father's people had been ripped from their families, their beliefs, their accomplishments, and their own land. With each blow, these men say that I'm too proud; that I shouldn't be at Oberlin College. But it's their pride that's behind each blow. Eventually, they leave me in a field, which refuses to act as my deathbed. The earth—Mother Earth forces me to my feet. A cluster of stars guides me back.

MRS. CHILD: "Mr. Brown, may you be strengthened by the conviction that no honest man ever sheds blood for freedom in vain.

Yours, with heartfelt respect, sympathy and affection.

L. Maria Child."

> *(She sits, holding her book as EDMONIA limps over to the clay and begins to work.)*

EDMONIA: Captain Brown, now, let my fingers wash the blood from your face.

END OF PLAY

BRUCE

by C. Denby Swanson

Originally produced in August 2005 by The Drilling Company, Hamilton Clancy producing artistic director.

Directed by Richard Harden

GAIL: Kim Donovan
DEAN: Dave Marantz
LAWYER: Colleen Cosgrove

C. Denby Swanson is a graduate of HSPVA, Smith College, NTI, and the Michener Center for Writers at the University of Texas at Austin. She is a former Jerome Fellow, McKnight Advancement Grant recipient, William Inge Playwright in Residence, and resident playwright through the NEA/TCG National Theater Residency Program for Playwrights. Her "killer comedy" *The Norwegians* premiered at The Drilling Company and is published by Dramatists Play Service. Her EST/Sloan Commission play *Nutshell*, inspired by "the mother of forensic science" Frances Glessner Lee, was included in the First Light Festival, Austin New Play Festival, and the Alley Theater's All New Festival. Her other work is published by Smith and Kraus, Heineman, and Playscripts.

CHARACTERS

GAIL, 30s.
LAWYER, 30s–40s.
DEAN, 30s.

TIME

The present.

PLACE

A house and a courtroom.

• • •

SCENE: A house.

LAWYER: I wish you had come to my office.

GAIL: We have to make up a story.

LAWYER: Gail, I can't make up a story.

GAIL: He will be home from work.

LAWYER: Gail . . .

GAIL: We have to have a story.

LAWYER: Next time, will you come to my office?

GAIL: No, I can't—I can't be gone when he gets home.

LAWYER: Jesus.

GAIL: We'll just tell him you're a long-lost friend from college.

LAWYER: A long-lost friend from college who has come by to show off some fancy legal filings?

GAIL: What do I need to sign? I'll sign it and—I'll sign whatever I have to, just . . .

LAWYER: Gail . . .

GAIL: He can't know.

LAWYER: Are you that scared of him?

GAIL: He just can't know.

LAWYER: We'll file for the divorce and get an order of protection.

GAIL: No, it's just . . .

LAWYER: I can take you someplace. He won't be able to find you.

GAIL: No . . .

LAWYER: I have lots of experience in this field, Gail, I know people. Trust me to help you.

GAIL: He doesn't . . .

LAWYER: What?

GAIL: He . . .

LAWYER: What?
    (Pause.)

GAIL: If I leave, he'll do something to the pig.

LAWYER: The pig.

GAIL: Yes.

LAWYER: He'll do something to the pig?

GAIL: We had three, but . . .

LAWYER: But?

GAIL: Well.

LAWYER: I don't think I fully understand.

GAIL: He'll do something to it.

LAWYER: I think you should be worried about your own safety, Gail, that's what I think. The pig . . .

GAIL: I am. I am.

LAWYER: Alright. So, we file based on a record of physical abuse.

GAIL: Abuse.

LAWYER: Yes.

GAIL: Not abuse, but, um . . .

LAWYER: Gail.

GAIL: It's not that.
   (*Silence.*)
He's going to be back soon.

   (*LAWYER stuffs her briefcase full of papers.*)

I don't have any proof, but . . .

LAWYER: But what?

GAIL: I think he's given me something.

LAWYER: Given you something?

GAIL: Yes.

LAWYER: Like a disease?

GAIL: Um . . .

LAWYER: He's been unfaithful?

GAIL: He has . . .

LAWYER: Gail, come with me to a shelter. You don't need to bring anything. Just let me get you out of this house. I'll take you to a doctor, you'll get treated . . .

GAIL: If I'm not home when he gets back, he has gone out there and done— something with the pigs—he used to when there were three of them . . .

LAWYER: What?

GAIL: Done something . . .

LAWYER: Something . . .

GAIL: And then he brings it back in to me.

   (*A moment of silence.*)

LAWYER: Oh.

GAIL: I think—I think he is turning me into one of them. I think that is the result.

LAWYER: What?

GAIL: I think. I am turning. Into a pig.

LAWYER: Oh.

> *(They regard each other for a moment. A car door slams. GAIL jumps. She makes a pig snorting sound. It just comes out.)*

GAIL: Oh, no.
> *(She snorts again. She is overwhelmed by snorting.)*
Oh, no. Oh, no.

LAWYER: It's alright, it's alright . . .

GAIL: Oh, no. Oh, no. Oh, no.
> *(She panics. She continues to snort. She gets very upset. The LAWYER tries to comfort her. Snorting. Crying. It's a mess.)*

> *(DEAN enters.)*

DEAN: Honey?

> *(GAIL freezes. DEAN stares at the LAWYER.)*

> *(Silence.)*

LAWYER: I am a long-lost friend from college.

Dinner.

> *(DEAN and GAIL sit opposite each other. Knives scrape. They eat.)*

GAIL: How was your day?

> *(DEAN shrugs. He eats.)*

DEAN: It was good.

GAIL: Good.

DEAN: Pass the uh . . .
> *(He gestures toward a serving bowl. GAIL hands it to him.)*

GAIL: Mine, too.

DEAN: What?

GAIL: Good.

DEAN: Good.

GAIL: Quiet.

DEAN: Good.

GAIL: I had my cup of tea. Then I took my bath.

DEAN: Your bath.

GAIL: Yes.

DEAN: Your bath.

GAIL: Dean . . .

DEAN: Were you dirty?

GAIL: Dean, please . . .

DEAN: What?

GAIL: Please eat.

(*DEAN stares at her.*)
The food.

DEAN: Oh.

GAIL: It's getting cold.

(*DEAN eats. GAIL considers her meal. She pushes the food into a thick line down its center.*)

DEAN: Not hungry?

GAIL: No.

(*DEAN shrugs.*)

DEAN: More for the pigs.
(*He eats. She stares. Then, GAIL throws her head into the center of her plate and feeds from it as if it were a trough.*)

DEAN: That's better.

GAIL: Mmmm . . .

DEAN: 'S good, isn't it?

GAIL: Mmmhhhhhmmm . . .

DEAN: New recipe?

GAIL: Uhhhummh . . .

DEAN: What is it?

> *(Silence.)*

> *(GAIL takes her last bite. AH.)*

GAIL: Ham.

A courtroom.

LAWYER: Your Honor, as part of the divorce settlement, my client, the petitioner, is requesting custody of the couple's surviving pig. It is a, well your standard pig, pink, with a—a snout—uh, and it's seven years old, about 350 pounds. There used to be other pigs but they—well, my client requests custody of the pig. I am submitting into the record a recent photograph of the pig that my client took. Please excuse the obviously unimpressive photo processing, we had them do that one hour thing in about twenty minutes, the kid at the counter was very young—they are all so young these days—and I think he just . . . (*Pause.*) My client is very specific about the term 'custody,' she feels a significant bond with the animal and would to like to formally change its name to—to—Bruce. Bruce. Which was her father's—uh—she feels a kind of parental responsibility—a kind of . . . (*Pause.*) Your Honor, honestly, this has been a very difficult case. There are many additional—conflicting—factors. I am distinctly aware of a certain hostility at work here between the three—uh—members of this family, shall we say—In fact my client is unable to make this proceeding because of mobility issues that developed after . . . Early on, I tried to get her to leave the bastard, but she refused. She refused. And now—now . . .

> *(She looks down at her notes and cannot continue.)*
Your Honor, may I approach?

END OF PLAY

BURIED

by Audrey Webb

Buried was presented as part of the Samuel French Off-Off Broadway Short
Play Festival on Friday, August 24, 2018, directed by Nicky Maggio. The cast
was as follows:

CHLOE: Sophie Hearn
TYLER: Kevin Corkum

Audrey Webb holds an MFA in dramatic writing from Texas State University.
She was recently named the Grand Prize Winner in the LGBTQ Screenwriting Competition for her one-hour police procedural *Dead Name*. Audrey's
full-length play *Imagine That* was recognized for Distinguished Achievement
by the Harold and Mimi Steinberg National Playwriting Awards. She's the
2018 recipient of the Judith Barlow Prize for her one-act play *The Only Hills
We've Ever Had*. Her ten-minute play *Buried* was part of the Samuel French
Off-Off Broadway Short Play Festival in NYC in August 2018, and *Imagine
That* was a semi-finalist in the 2018 Eugene O'Neill National Playwrights
Conference and in the 2018 Austin Film Festival Playwriting Competition.
Her work is primarily in the absurdist tradition, pushing situations and characters to the extremities of reason. Audrey is fond of pit bulls (she is fearless); her spirit animal is Brock Lesnar (she is tough); she is an avid fan of a
hockey team that hasn't won the Stanley Cup since 1967 (she is optimistic
and patient); and she makes a mean gingersnap (she knows how to follow
instructions in a cookbook). Her plays have been produced by Shoestring
Radio Theatre (San Francisco), Articulate Theatre (New York), and

Mildred's Umbrella Theatre Company (Houston). Audrey is proud to be a member of the Dramatists Guild.

CHARACTERS

CHLOE, 17, in the final stages of cancer.
TYLER, 17, her twin brother.

SETTING

CHLOE's bedroom, late afternoon.

• • •

A girl's messy bedroom. A bed that looks like it's been occupied forever. Kleenex boxes. Books. Greeting cards. On a bedside table, there's a water glass with water in it, and a box, in which CHLOE keeps her stash of weed. On a dresser, there's a variety of dolls—this is the space of a girl who is somewhere in between childhood and adulthood. CHLOE, in bed, amuses herself with her smartphone. TYLER enters with a backpack and a bouquet of store-bought tulips, still in a plastic sleeve.

TYLER: Hey.

CHLOE: Hey.

TYLER: You awake?

CHLOE: Either that, or I'm having a really vivid dream.

TYLER: You Gonna Be A Smart Ass Your Whole Life?

CHLOE: I think I can keep it up that long.

TYLER: Fuck, I'm . . .

CHLOE: Yeah, I'm awake. Come on in.

(*TYLER comes in. He sits on the edge of her bed.*)

CHLOE: School out early?

TYLER: Yeah. Nah. Well, not for everyone.

CHLOE: Bro's making his own schedule.

TYLER: Screw the system.

CHLOE: What are those?

TYLER: Uhh, flowers.

CHLOE: I know they're flowers. Tulips. They grow by the garage.

TYLER: I bought these. Thought they might, you know . . .

 CHLOE: Thanks. Stick 'em in a glass for me, okay?
(He puts the flowers in a water glass on CHLOE's bedside table.)

CHLOE: Wait. You bought tulips? Once the snow melts, they're gonna be all over the place.

TYLER: Well, the snow ain't gonna melt for a while, so . . .

CHLOE: Three weeks, tops.

TYLER: Still a long time. Hey, where's Mom?

CHLOE: She can't sit here all day. She needs a break once in a while.

TYLER: She can't just take off.

CHLOE: She does whenever I'm about to smoke.
    (She opens a box, rolls a joint.)

It's so funny. Says she feels like a bad mother watching me do it.

TYLER: But what if . . .

CHLOE: Something happened while she was gone?

TYLER: Yeah, you could fall asleep, and your bed could, you know, catch fire and you could—

CHLOE: Die?

TYLER: Stop that.

CHLOE: Well, I'm gonna anyway, so what difference . . .

TYLER: That's not a given.

CHLOE: Tyler . . .

TYLER: It doesn't make sense. If you got it . . .

CHLOE: Cancer.

TYLER: I should get it too.

CHLOE: We're twins. Doesn't mean we share everything.

TYLER: Why were you the one to get it?

CHLOE: Cancer. Say the word. Cancer.
   (She takes a hit, offers him the joint.)

TYLER: If Mom comes back, she'll freak.

CHLOE: Mom already knows you smoke dope.

TYLER: No, she doesn't.

CHLOE: I told her.

TYLER: What?

CHLOE: She asked. So, I told her.

TYLER: Last time I tell you anything.

CHLOE: Probably . . . Didn't mean to rat you out. We were just talking. She's worried about you.

TYLER: Like she doesn't have enough to deal with right now?

CHLOE: She may get a little clingy for a while after. You're gonna be—well, you're gonna be everything.

   (TYLER takes a big hit, passes back the joint.)

TYLER: So today, in chemistry, Connor took a / test tube . . .

CHLOE: Tyler . . .

TYLER: . . . and he put a cork in the top / of it . . .

CHLOE: Look at me.

TYLER: . . . and then he had, I dunno, some water in it / I guess . . .

CHLOE: It's okay, you know.

TYLER: . . . and he put it over the Bunsen / burner . . .

CHLOE: I'm not scared anymore.

TYLER: . . . and the water boiled and then the cork blew out and hit Mr. Morrison right in the head and everyone in the room just—just fell apart—laughing . . .

CHLOE: Come here.

TYLER: I am here.

CHLOE: I mean *here* here.

(*TYLER gets up, sits beside her.*)

TYLER: This sucks, Chloe. I'm so . . .

CHLOE: I've been thinking. When I'm done with it, you should move into this room. It's bigger.

TYLER: Would you please just shut up?

CHLOE: I know you've always wanted butterfly wallpaper.

TYLER: Ha-ha, yeah. It absorbs, you know.

CHLOE: And you can keep the doll collection if you want.

TYLER: Yeah. No. They give me the creeps.

CHLOE: I can tell you where each and every one of these dolls came from.

TYLER: Don't. Just write it down or something. Write things down for me, okay?

CHLOE: You can have this room. And then at night, to get you in the mood to start jacking off—

TYLER: Oh my God, you're such a . . .

CHLOE: You can stare across the alley and see Christina get undressed.

TYLER: Are you shitting me?

CHLOE: She stands in front of the window, and all she has are these sheer curtains, and . . .

TYLER: Since when?

CHLOE: Since like forever.

TYLER: And you're telling me this just now?

CHLOE: Hey, you weren't always exactly talking to me, you know?

TYLER: Yeah. I know . . . I was a bit of a shit to you.

CHLOE: It's okay. It's what brothers are supposed to do.

TYLER: I promise you, I'm not gonna be a stereotype for the rest of my life, okay?

CHLOE: I'll make sure of it. I'll make something fly across the room or something. Something creepy. That way you'll know it's me . . . They're nice. The flowers. They smell like sunshine.

TYLER: Sunshine doesn't smell, dweeb. Oh, and I got you something else.
(He reaches into his backpack and pulls out a plastic bag. He hands it to his sister.)
Okay, so, a long time ago . . .

(CHLOE opens the bag, takes out a doll.)

TYLER: I took it.

CHLOE: Not it. Her.

TYLER: I was mad at you for something. I can't even remember what now.

CHLOE: Because I was spying on you and Jesse and Brendan when you guys were playing Spiderman in the basement.

TYLER: Yeah. Damn. That's right.

CHLOE: She's all dirty.

TYLER: I stuck her in a bag of Mom's potting soil. Remember the African violet phase? In the basement. Behind the furnace. A place I knew you were too scared to go.

CHLOE: Brat.

TYLER: I know. Sorry.

CHLOE: I knew you'd done something to her. I even asked you, and you looked at me, straight in the face, and lied to me!

TYLER: A stone-cold, baby-faced killer, yo.

CHLOE: I loved this doll so much.

TYLER: I know. I had one shot to get back at you. Made the most of it.

CHLOE: I'm surprised you even remembered where she was.

TYLER: I like checked up on her a lot.

CHLOE: You're a sicko, you know that?

TYLER: Yeah. I'm so sorry.

CHLOE: It's okay.

TYLER: About / everything.

CHLOE: Hey, get me a cloth, okay? A cloth and a bowl of warm water.

TYLER: What's wrong? You feel okay?

CHLOE: Not for me, numbnuts. For her. To wash off this mud.

>   *(TYLER takes one more hit of the joint.)*

TYLER: Whoo! That's strong shit. You know, you're pretty tough for a chick
with . . .
>   *(He hands the joint back to CHLOE, then rushes out of the room.
>   Offstage:)*

You want anything else while I'm up?

CHLOE: Yeah. I want you to say it.

TYLER: Say what?

CHLOE: Cancer. Cancer. Cancercancercancer.

TYLER: *(Offstage.)* Cancer. Now, shut up already! Just . . .
>   *(He enters with a bowl of water and a cloth.)*
. . . gimme it. Her.

>   *(CHLOE hands the doll to TYLER, who starts to wash the dirt off her.)*
She's gonna look just like she did the day I took her. Even better than how
you remember her.

CHLOE: Thanks, Tyler. *(To the doll.)* It's okay, Dolly. It's okay, girl. We've got
you now. Everything's going to be all right.

>   *(Lights fade to black.)*

END OF PLAY

DINNER DURING YEMEN

by Karen Malpede

An earlier version of the play was first read at The Commons, Brooklyn,
New York, November 18, 2017, by Kathleen Chalfant and Karen Malpede, as
part of an evening for the people of Yemen produced by Brooklyn for Peace.
The final version was staged as part of an evening of short works
Imagine:Yemen, at the Signature Theatre, New York City, June 25, 2018, pro-
duced by New York Rep.

Cast:
NITA: Kathleen Chalfant
RITA: Dee Pelletier
Screams courtesy of George Bartenieff
Directed by Markus Potter and Karen Malpede
Lighting by Tony Giovannetti

Karen Malpede is cofounder of Theater Three Collaborative. Writer/director
of nineteen plays. Ecodramatist. "These plays seek to bring us to our senses
intellectually, morally, and socially, and seek to do that, as all great theater
does, by deeply involving sensually as well," Marvin Carlson. "Brave and Pro-
vocative," *NY Times*, *Other Than We*, LaMama, Nov. 2019, published by Egret.
Dinner During Yemen, Signature Theater, June 2018, *Extreme Whether*,
LaMama 2018, ARTCOP Paris, 2015, Theater for the New City, 2014. Author,
Plays in Time: *The Beekeeper's Daughter, Prophecy, Another Life, Extreme
Whether. Other Than We*, summer 2018 workshop, LaMama. McKnight,
NYFA Fellowships.

CHARACTERS

NITA, a career diplomat, 60s.
RITA, a younger diplomat.

PLACE

Rita's home. She has prepared a fancy dinner for her boss.

TIME

2018.

• • •

NITA *and* RITA *meet for dinner at* RITA'*s house. They are friends from work, among the remaining career diplomats in the State Department.* NITA *is more knowledgeable in the ways of real politic than* RITA, *who works for, and looks up to, her. There is no need for realistic food or props. In the first performance, the actors stand with wineglasses in their hands. A terrible cry is heard.*

NITA: Is that an animal?

RITA: Or a child.

NITA Why ever for?

RITA: An animal, must be.

NITA: In a trap, perhaps.

RITA: Animal-like.

NITA: When they get that hungry, I suppose.

RITA: That's what I meant.

NITA: Civilization is but a veneer.

RITA: Why would anyone let their own child starve?

NITA: No one would, let, I suppose.

RITA: Not let, exactly.

NITA: It's complex.

RITA: Totally.

NITA: Allegiances, patronage, family.

RITA: Names difficult to pronounce.

NITA: One can't keep things straight in one's head.

RITA: Civil wars are the absolute worst.

NITA: So much suffering for what?

RITA: Would you like some oysters on the half-shell?

NITA: Moon Shoals and Kumamoto.

RITA: Afloat in their own juice.

NITA: So smooth sliding down the throat.

RITA: I don't think they cry like that.

NITA: Like what?

RITA: What we just heard.

NITA: A whimper, perhaps.

RITA: That's what I meant.

NITA: When they get weak.

RITA: Must have been an animal caught in a trap.

NITA: Unsettling, nevertheless.

RITA: They turn their heads; unclench their little fingers and toes.

NITA: That must be so terrible to watch.

RITA: Oh, my goodness. I could not watch that.

NITA: I turn the channel; that's what I do.

RITA: I meant if it were mine.

NITA: Yours?

RITA: Yes.

NITA: How could that be?

RITA: It couldn't, of course.

NITA: Well, that is a blessing, is it not?

RITA: How ever do such terrible things come to pass?

NITA: Much of the world's oil ships through the Bab al-Mandab strait.

RITA: Geography is destiny, do you agree?

NITA: Strategic link between the Indian Ocean and the Mediterranean Sea.

RITA: Gate of Tears, it's been called.

NITA: Strategic locations usually are. Troy was.

RITA: Please, try the baked bass.

NITA: Absolutely divine braised buttery sauce.

RITA: Times recipe. It's a proxy war.

NITA: The Saudis blockaded the ports.

RITA: It's not helpful to criticize the Saudis.

NITA: Quite right.

RITA: Saudi Arabia is our ally.

NITA: Delightful, this white Bordeaux.

RITA: We'll move to a red with the beef.

NITA: "Nobody makes what we make and now we're selling it all over the world."

RITA: Is that so?

NITA: I am quoting President Trump.

RITA: Whatever was he talking about?

NITA: Missile defense systems.

RITA: Such a comfort, they are.

NITA: The Houthis shot a missile at Saudi Arabia.

RITA: Iran gave it to them. That made everything worse.

NITA: Our missile defense system knocked their missile right out of the sky.

RITA: Well, of course, it did.

NITA: I'll take a piece of that roast beef.

RITA: Please.

NITA: Tender.

RITA: Grass-raised, organic.

NITA: If one is going to eat meat.

RITA: In moderation, our little sins.

NITA: No one in Saudi was hurt.

RITA: We can be thankful for that.

NITA: Please, I'll take another thin slice of the beef.

RITA: War with Iran.

NITA: Iran has had it coming quite some time.

RITA: Yemen imports most of its food.

NITA: They grow coffee, for export, and khat.

RITA: What is that?

NITA: Feel-good drug.

RITA: I'm glad they have some escape.

NITA: Frankincense and myrrh, they used to grow.

RITA: How biblical.

NITA: Medicinal, postpartum effects. Contract the womb. Clot the blood.

RITA: For Mary from the three Wise Men.

NITA: Khat, too, for Mary, do you suppose?

(*They laugh.*)

RITA: The Saudis won't stop.

NITA: I suppose they think they have no choice.

RITA: As long as the Houthis, of course.

NITA: The Shiite Houthi.

RITA: Are they?

NITA: Zaidi, yes.

RITA: And the Saudis are Sunni.

NITA: Wahhabi. Wahhabis. Salafi.

RITA: They don't like the Houthi.

NITA: The Houthi rebelled.

RITA: The Houthi promised the people reforms.

NITA: The Houthi want what they can't have.

RITA: Al-Qaeda, of course, is taking advantage.

NITA: We've had to put boots on the ground.

RITA: That's not so. Is that so?

NITA: I suppose so. Green Berets.

RITA: Air strikes, I know about.

NITA: We are simply refueling their jets.

RITA: Made by us. I'm full up.

NITA: Me too.

RITA: They might have been civilians.

NITA: I hardly think so.

RITA: Yes, in the market, fifty-two.

NITA: Precision instruments, first-rate intelligence.

RITA: A wedding party. More than one.

NITA: The area is thick with insurgents.

RITA: On the happiest day of one's life.

NITA: Was yours that?

RITA: No. Civilians in their beds.

NITA: They use civilians as human shields.

RITA: Barbarians.

NITA: He's a charmer, the Saudi prince, Mohamad Bin Salman.

RITA: He let women drive. Such piercing black eyes.

NITA: I could not survive without my car.

RITA: The sewage system in Sana'a has stopped working.

NITA: The Saudis are in charge of the reconstruction.

RITA: That's only fair; rebuild what you bomb.

NITA: Billions to be made in the private sector.

RITA: This is an aged white rind goat cheese, from Spain.

NITA: Weapons sales are essential to growth.

RITA: Take just a taste.

NITA: 2.3 billion promised to us by the prince.

RITA: It has the slightest peppery tang.

NITA: Follow-up with this salted dark chocolate. My small contribution.

RITA: There's cholera everywhere.

NITA: Chocolate is good for digestion.

RITA: The United Nations fears mass starvation.

NITA: Don't get me started.

RITA: Just a small piece. Not terribly caloric.

NITA: On the United Nations.

RITA: Oh, yes, nobody likes them.

NITA: We had such great hopes.

RITA: For world peace.

NITA: World peace, yes.

RITA: We can still wish.

NITA: We still do, of course.

RITA: What a marvelous meal.

(*A terrible cry is heard.*)

END OF PLAY

EVERYTHING IS FINE

by Lynn Rosen

Everything Is Fine (formerly *Take One for the Team*) was first presented as a public reading at The New Harmony Project in May 2017, featuring Nate DeCook as Josh and Mfoniso Udofia as Corkie, directed by Lori Wolter Hudson.

Lynn Rosen writes tragedies disguised as comedies which reveal her affection for the strivers and outsiders of the world. Recent plays include: *The Imperialists*, a farce for our times (Theatreworks New Works Festival, Silicon Valley, 2019); *Washed Up on the Potomac* (San Francisco Playhouse; The Pool, NYC); *Legerdemain*, a three-hander about magic, faith, and chain restaurants (New Georges Audrey Residency 2018); *The Firebirds Take The Field*, inspired by the story of the ticking girls of LeRoy, NY (EST/Sloan Commission; Rivendell Theatre, Chicago); *Bernhard: A Refugee Story* (UCSB Launch Pad commission and production). She's also worked with: Women's Project (*Apple Cove*), New Georges (*Goldor $ Mythyka: A Hero is Born*), Working Theater (*Back From the Front*); Playing On Air (*I Love You*), Studio Theatre D.C./Willow Cabin (*Nighthawks*); Theatreworks (*Man and Beast*), ATL, EST, Baltimore Centerstage, Barrington Stage, Fault Line, New Group, Geva, New Harmony Project, SPACE, The Lark. Recent commissions: a musical about Helen Gurley Brown and Betty Friedan, Theatreworks Silicon Valley; *The Overview Effect*, EST/Sloan commission; *The Claudias: A Revenge Play*, Red Bull Theatre inaugural new play commission. Lynn is currently developing a pilot with Milestone TV and Film; recently sold a pilot to Warner Brothers Horizon. Co-creator of the award-winning web series *Darwin*, directed by Carrie Preston. Also, proud cofounder of The Pool, a playwright-driven pop-up theater company. Lynn grew up in Gary, Indiana, has a B.A. in Theater Arts from Brandeis University, and resides in New York City. She is a Resident Playwright at New Dramatists.

CHARACTERS

CORKIE, 30, alpha female.
JOSH, 30, beta male.

PLACE

A trendy area in Washington, DC.

SETTING

The living room of CORKIE and JOSH's apartment.

• • •

CORKIE *and* JOSH *sit on their sofa. She's just told him shocking news. He simmers with rage. He can't even speak.* CORKIE *loves him, but it's clear she feels justified having done whatever horrible thing she just told* JOSH *about.*

CORKIE: I know you're shocked by this news, babe.

JOSH: Nnnn.

CORKIE: I hope you understand what I was trying to/ do.

JOSH: Nnnnn!

CORKIE: Right. Too soon to talk. You're upset. I'll wait.

(*He simmers. After a beat.*)

I just wanna say I know it's a lot.

JOSH: Mmm hmm!

CORKIE: But I had to be honest with you, Josh, because we swore in our vows to be honest with each other, and we are nothing if we are not honest with each other.

JOSH: Mmmm!

CORKIE: But like I said, this "event" between him and me meant nothing. It was totally unconnected to any sort of *connection* between him and me.

(He screams his pain. It's primordial and weird.)

JOSH: Aaaaaaaaeee!

CORKIE: Oh god, Josh.

JOSH: WRATH!

CORKIE: Yes! Get it out!

JOSH: ASHES!

CORKIE: Yes, yell things! Throw things! Atta boy!

(He grabs an oil lamp and goes to throw it.)

Wait! Maybe not the oil lamp we got on our honeymoon last year! We made so many wishes on that oil lamp.

JOSH: WISHES ARE DEAD! WISHES ARE FOR LITTLE GIRLS!

CORKIE: Not to quibble, Josh, but are you insinuating girls are merely dreamers and not doers, because I have a problem with that.

JOSH: You have a problem with that? YOU HAVE A PROBLEM WITH THAT?

CORKIE: I get it, but am I supposed to just, what? Abandon my principles?

JOSH: Haven't you already done that, Corkie?!

CORKIE: Ok. I hear you. *Or*, Josh, *or*—just to throw this out there, not married to it, but consider this—*or* by doing what I have done have I *fought* for my principles?

(He throws another thing at the wall.)

JOSH: RAGE!

CORKIE: I know this is a shock. But it's good to be shocked. These days we're overloaded by tragedy and inhumanity, we get numbed by it. Numb has become the new normal and—Oh wow. "Numb has become the new normal."
(She writes that down.)

JOSH: Are you writing that down?

CORKIE: Well, we *are* speech writers. I mean, I can't just suddenly *not* be what I am.

JOSH: My heart is an oil rig spewing pain, and you're honing your frickin' craft?!

CORKIE: Let's not curse, Josh. We love each other.

JOSH: Thou shalt not curse? How about thou shalt not FORNICATE WITH OTHERS!

CORKIE: I did *not* fornicate. And it wasn't plural. It was other, not other-s.

JOSH: Almost! You almost fornicated with *other!* Once is more than enough! It's plenty!

CORKIE: I told you why I almost fornicated, Josh. It wasn't lust or desire or anything emotional, so please don't construct some false narrative in your head that will . . .

JOSH: FAKE NEWS! YOU! FAKE NEWS!

CORKIE: That's sophomoric and also a cliché by now. Think outside the box, Josh.

JOSH: Corkie!

CORKIE: Sorry. I get wonkish when I'm nervous.

JOSH: GOD, YOUR NAME IS SO DUMB! CORKIE!

CORKIE: Well, I don't think name-calling about my name is very constructive.

JOSH: Corkie is a dog's name! It's a boat's name!

CORKIE: Fine. Get it out.

JOSH: It's a-a-a cork's name! You belong in a bottle of wine! Or a marina!

CORKIE: As you know, my immigrant parents wanted to name me something posh and they heard that name at the yacht club where they slaved away for years . . .

JOSH: Don't you DACA me! Don't you make me feel guilty! YOU guilty!

CORKIE: Shh! Our neighbors! The walls are so thin. What if Lacey is home next door playing with her dollies and she hears you? She's only eight, she thinks the world is awesome.
    (JOSH yells through the wall so Lacey might hear.)

JOSH: EXHAUST PIPE IN MY MOUTH, LACEY!

CORKIE: Stop it! (*Yells through the wall.*) Don't listen, Lacey! Dream your dreams!

JOSH: SANTA CLAUS IS YOUR PARENTS, LACEY!

CORKIE: Josh!

(*Turning on a dime, he starts to sob and mourn.*)

Oh no. Oh, sweetie pie.

JOSH: It's lasagna night tonight. I got parmesano-reggiano at that place that has Christmas lights year-round? I was going to surprise you. It's wrapped so perfectly in wax paper.

CORKIE: Oh, that is so sweet.

JOSH: (*Suddenly furious again.*) Sweet like a chump, like a fop, like a cuckold? Go to hell, Corkie! I HATE YOU!

(*CORKIE tries to hold in her tears—it turns into heaving. He softens.*)

Oh no. No, no, no. I hate when you cry, no, shhh. Your little seashell ears get hot. Your rashy neck. Come here, let me hold you. Shhhhhhh.

CORKIE: I love you, Josh. I love *us*. That is why I did this. I did it for us.

(*He pulls away.*)

JOSH: For us? You *almost* fornicated with *our boss*, Gerald Markum, the junior senator from the great state of woodchucks and syrup *for us*?

CORKIE: I also did it for democracy. I did it for America.

JOSH: *What?!*

CORKIE: The vote on the next Supreme Court justice is tomorrow and Markum is waffling on Espinosa. His vote could be the deciding vote. I had to steel his spine so he'd vote nay. I had to boost his manhood. It was an emergency! I thought you'd understand.

JOSH: I do not understand! Oh God, is it me? Did I get boring? In bed? At breakfast? Am I an old man? Is it these slippers? Should I never have talked about pooping in front of you?

CORKIE: Well, I do have a love-hate relationship with that. But you know we're best friends.

JOSH: We're newlyweds, Corkie. One year. It's the start. The top. The tip. The zenith of life.

CORKIE: Apex, apogee, crest.

JOSH AND CORKIE: Crown, cusp, peak.

JOSH: All our lovely words evaporated, vaporized, dissolved.

CORKIE: We still have our words. And we have many more to discover. Like Shakespeare with his "moonbeam" and his "all of a sudden." We have beautiful phrases yet to create.

JOSH: We were going to name our future baby Moonbeam.

CORKIE: We were? I didn't know that.

   (He's planned their whole life without telling her.)

JOSH: We were going to eat ice cream with our babies, all five of them, three girls, two boys—

CORKIE: Five?

JOSH: On a park bench and shake our heads at how fleeting life is, how ephemeral is joy.

CORKIE: We can still have that, Josh.

JOSH: The world is a jagged knife, Corkie. I can't raise five children on the edge of a knife!

CORKIE: What if Moonbeam were sitting here right now? She'd say, "Dada? Why you create alternative facts, Dada? You love Mama. Mama love you."

JOSH: Mama loves me?

CORKIE: I love you, Josh. I love you.

   (He turns on her again. In the voice of their baby.)

JOSH: Then why you sleep with your boss, Senator Markum, Mama?

CORKIE: I did not sleep with him. I told you! I only touched him in some places.

JOSH: (*Torturing her with this child voice.*) What kind of places you touch our boss, Mama?

CORKIE: Stop that!

JOSH: His thigh, Mama? Why touch thigh of Blue Dog namby-pamby Democrat, Mama?

CORKIE: I said stop it, Josh, stop it, stop being our baby!

   (*He drops the baby act.*)

JOSH: And where did he touch *you*, Cork? Huh? I keep seeing his pudgy hand with that stupid class ring clawing at you.

CORKIE: I don't remember. And it's not a class ring, it's a football ring. Like, for winning.

JOSH: Oh! For winning? Is *he* a winner, Corkie, and I'm not? He barely won his seat. He only won because our speeches made him sound smart! "Uh" is his bridge word, Corkie!

CORKIE: I didn't say he's a winner/ and you're not.

JOSH: And how do you know so much about his stupid foosball ring?

CORKIE: Football, not foosball. I don't know. It came up when he took the ring off, I guess.

JOSH: Oh, so he could touch you in your "places" without hurting you with his "winner" ring?

CORKIE: Yes.

JOSH: What? I was joking!

CORKIE: I'm being honest. You should be relieved.

JOSH: Relieved?!

CORKIE: Yes! My being honest proves that his touching meant nothing to me.

JOSH: (*Incredulous.*) Where am I? Am I on earth? Am I in a garbage can?

CORKIE: I don't care about him, Josh, so, yes, I'll tell you things like he took off his football ring before he touched me. I mean touched me *literally*, not *emotionally*, and that's a *good* thing.

JOSH: Monster! Electric bolts!

CORKIE: Oh, so a woman who is sexual is a monster? Let's think about that.

JOSH: This is not a frickin' TED talk, Corkie! This is us! Where's my angel I married?

CORKIE: Your angel died after the election.

(He gasps. She gets tougher.)
Wake up, Josh. Danger is imminent. Action must be taken. It had to be done.

JOSH: Those private places he touched are *my* private places!

CORKIE: No, they are *my* private places, Josh. My body is mine, not yours.

JOSH: You know what I mean! Like if your private places *had* to belong to someone *besides* you, they'd belong to me. Like if you died, the courts would rule for *me* to get your private places. You have no next of kin.

CORKIE: Josh, that is very disturbing.

JOSH: I'm just saying I'm all you've got in the whole world, Corkie. You're all I've got. We're all we've got, and now that's gone too.

CORKIE: I'm still here. But Josh, the world has changed. North is south, south is west. We can't be angels anymore.

JOSH: We were going to change the world. We were going to write the speeches that would fire up the nation.

CORKIE: Pretty words aren't enough. It's time to get dirty.

JOSH: Dirty?

CORKIE: I know I did wrong, but it was also very right. I . . . am a patriot, Josh.

JOSH: A patriot?

CORKIE: Do you think I wanted to touch Markum in his "places," Josh? It went against everything I believe about how women should navigate this misogynist world. But up is down now, Josh. Left is right. It's not about you or me anymore. *Supreme Court,* Josh. Drastic measures. Poor people, the middle class needs protecting—the people we come from. Hard-working people just trying to feed their kids and give them a good life. Immigrants—my parents. Civil rights. Gay rights. Women's rights. The environment. Health care. Democracy, the earth itself is at stake. Objective truth. Flint!

JOSH: You touched him in his places to fix the lead problem in Flint?

CORKIE: The Supreme Court pick meant more, Josh. I'm sorry, but it did.

JOSH: More than *me*?

CORKIE: Markum was starting to waffle. He was thinking of voting yea on Espinosa.

JOSH: But we wrote his nay speech. I have that great bit about bald eagles.

CORKIE: I know. And it's powerful. The thing with the beak and the cracking olive branch.

JOSH: I do like that part, thanks.

CORKIE: I tried using reason with Markum. Sports analogies, candy, nothing worked. And then I saw . . . he was looking at my boobs.

JOSH: They're *my* boobs.

CORKIE: No. They're *my* boobs.

JOSH: Ok. Yes.

CORKIE: He was shaking, Josh. At first, I was repulsed. But then I realized . . . he's lonely.

JOSH: He's a scum bag.

CORKIE: He is lonely, a widower, a workaholic. That was my way to change his mind—humanity.

JOSH: Humanity for him, heartache for me? Oh, that seems fair!

CORKIE: You're not hearing me. I want to slap you, Josh!

JOSH: Slap me? You would never . . .

(*She slaps him. He doesn't hate it.*)

Oh my god!

CORKIE: Wake up, Josh!

JOSH: 'Kay . . .

MARKIE: There is no more "fair," you hear me? There are only warriors! As I allowed Markum to fondle me, I could feel the fate of the country in my hands, Josh.

JOSH: How?

CORKIE: How? Well, if he votes for Espinosa to be on the Supreme Court . . .

JOSH: No. How did he fondle you? Did he grab at you or just, like, caress?

CORKIE: Both, I guess.

JOSH: Did it excite you?

CORKIE: (*Protesting too much.*) Of course not. No, no, no.

JOSH: Did you think of me while he did that?

CORKIE: It was too painful to think of you. I thought of Javier Bardem. Is that ok?

JOSH: Right. You've been pretty open about that with me.

CORKIE: Something about Javier. His face is like a sexy road map to his life.

JOSH: Please stop.

CORKIE: Right. Timing.

JOSH: Was Markum . . . tender with you?

CORKIE: Yes. It was awful.

JOSH: Wait, you don't like tender?

CORKIE: I hate tender. I mean, I like it sometimes, but not *all* the time. It's so soft.

JOSH: You do? Why didn't you say? I'm overly tender like every second of the day.

CORKIE: I didn't want to scare you.

JOSH: Scare me? Ok, look! I'm gonna hold you with lotsa force right now! Here I go!
  (*He hugs her hard.*)

CORKIE: Good! Way to bear hug! Great start! Yay, Joshy!

JOSH: Don't yay me. Yay is for soft, tender people, and that's not me anymore! I bet Markum was tender like a noodle, wasn't he?

CORKIE: Yes. I wanted to scream.

JOSH: So, scream.

CORKIE: (*An uptight scream.*) Aaah.

JOSH: Scream like you're in pain. I want us both in pain. Scream like our marriage is dying.
  (*A real scream full of agony because their marriage is dying.*)

CORKIE: Aaaaaah!

JOSH: Scream like we've lost our way.

  (*They both scream in agony. Then . . .*)

CORKIE: I didn't know you wanted five kids.

JOSH: I didn't know you hated soft and tender things.

CORKIE: What now?

JOSH: We find our way back.

CORKIE: How?

  (*A knock on the wall. It's Lacey, the little girl next door.*)

LACEY: (*Offstage.*) Everything ok? Josh? Corkie? Hello?

CORKIE: Yes, Lacey! Everything's fine!

JOSH: We're fine, Lacey! Nothing to worry about!

  (*They look at each other. They know things are not fine at all.*)

CORKIE: Nothing to worry about.

END OF PLAY

FISSSHHHH

by Jennifer Maisel

Fissshhhh was originally commissioned by Salt Lake Acting Company and was originally produced by the ArtsCenter at 10 by10 in the Triangle in 2009, directed by Joseph Megel.

Jennifer Maisel's *The Last Seder* premiered off-Broadway with Gaby Hoffmann and Greg Mullavey after productions around the country and abroad. Her Sundance-developed *Out of Orbit* was awarded an Ensemble Studio Theatre/Alfred P. Sloan rewrite commission for plays about science and technology, made the 2016 Kilroy List and won both the Stanley Award and the Woodward/Newman Award for Drama before premiering at Williamston Theatre and Bloomington Playwrights Project. Her Pen West Literary finalist, *There or Here*, had its London premiere in January 2018. Her *@thespeedofJake*, also a Pen West Literary finalist, premiered in LA with Playwrights' Arena. Jennifer has written movies for major networks and cable, as well as independent features; she recently sold a pilot to Super Deluxe with MomentumTV. Jennifer was one of five writers invited into the prestigious Humanitas 2018 PlayLA workshop, where she developed *Better*. Her *Eight Nights* premiered at Antaeus Theatre in 2019.

CHARACTERS

ANNE, shifts between 27, a bedraggled new mom; 32, in love with her daughter; and 44, trying to hold on.
RACHEL, shifts between 17, a careful study in teen construction; and 5, in love with the world . . . and her mom.

MARCUS, Anne's husband, Rachel's father. His age reflects Anne's.
LIZ, Rachel's best friend, 17.

SETTING

Areas should delineate Rachel's bedroom and Anne and Marcus's living room. No need for the kitchen sink. Areas of light, platforms, chairs are probably enough to define Rachel's bed and maybe a glider or a couch for Anne and Marcus.

TIME

Time shifts are delineated by a sound/music and light shift.

Note

The baby (baby doll) hopefully can "float" on a wire that is easily attachable and detachable. Some other device—puppetry or projection—is also a possibility.

• • •

(Music crashes. Lights up on ANNE, 44.)

ANNE: When you were in my belly, I became your ocean. I felt the roaring waves claim my uterus, the gentle swells lap. I was rich and full and salty—and salty and dewy and ripe. At night I dreamed my belly was clear, a snow globe where you floated in sparkle-infused waters, tapping on the clear pane, making giggly faces at me, eager to get out.

(A baby doll floats in the air—slowly illuminated.)

When you were in the belly, I couldn't help but be sucked into the rightness of it all. You were the extraordinary speck in my sea. And I got big—so big I could feel the sshlush sshlush sshlush of you sloshing around when I walked down the street. And I thought that sshlush sshlush sshlush . . . that's life . . . I'm almost all water . . . the world is two-thirds water . . . I am your world.

(Lights up on RACHEL [17] staring at her mother.)

RACHEL: Are you done? *(A beat.)*

ANNE: Yeah.

RACHEL: Good.

(She storms off to her bedroom, leaving ANNE staring after her.)

ANNE: And then you were born.

> *(Light and music shift. They split in place and time. LIZ is in RACHEL's room, MARCUS in the living room. ANNE (now 27) takes the floating baby doll and puts it her breast to nurse. BABY RACHEL. Their conversations overlap.)*

RACHEL (*To* LIZ.)/ANNE (*To* MARCUS.): Her goal may be to suck the life out of me. To take all the joy, all the life, right out and leave me a desiccated heap of cells.

LIZ: Oh please, your mom is really cool.

MARCUS: It may be.

ANNE: Fuck you, that's reassuring. Ow.

RACHEL: She has an ulterior motive. She thinks if she condones something, then I'm less likely to do it.

ANNE: (*Unable to get the baby off her breast.*) There's nothing left in there, bambino.

RACHEL: I've seen the parenting books she hides in the back of the night table and I think she's letting us do it because she's jealous.

LIZ: Rache! Ick!

RACHEL: She is.

ANNE: There's nothing left in there, bambino. Dried up.

LIZ: Your mom wants to sleep with Zak.

RACHEL: That's envious. And no.

LIZ: Because that would be beyond . . .

RACHEL: No.

LIZ: Beyond enmeshed.

ANNE: (*Sharply.*) There's nothing left in there, bambino!
> *(She pulls the baby off her breast. Piercing baby cry.)*

MARCUS: Anne.

ANNE: I'm tired.

MARCUS: I know.

ANNE: The no-sleep thing sucks the life out too.

MARCUS: You don't have to tell me.

(She gives him a look and he makes it up.)
I mean, if I'm this tired, I can't even imagine what you must be.

ANNE: That was good.

MARCUS: Wasn't it?

ANNE: God, it's in my bones. Stop crying stop crying stop crying stop crying. She hates me.

RACHEL: It's that she wants that time again. I mean, they don't have it. The newness, the excitement. How could they? They have been together for a million years. They have books in the back of both their night tables about recreating the newness and the excitement. You don't need books about things you already know how to do.

(MARCUS hands her a bottle of water.)

MARCUS: Hydrate.
(Hands her a beer bottle.)
Replenish. Think milk. Think waterfalls. Think rivers and floods and torrents and flow . . . (*Intones.*) Be the waterfall . . .

ANNE: Where the fuck did you hear that? You've been reading again.

MARCUS: Affirmations for a Nursing Mother.

LIZ: But to have permission for a real bed. She bought you condoms. She made you breakfast.

RACHEL: She baked fricking popovers. Overkill. She just wants me to like her again. She hates that she can't make me like her right now.

LIZ: Last week Craig and I had sex in the back of his dad's Yukon, which would have been fine, it seats nine, but he had gone fishing the weekend before and the smell . . .

RACHEL: Fish?

LIZ: You know how you associate things really strongly with smell?

RACHEL: Fish?

LIZ: Fish. So now whenever we do it, it won't get out of my head—or my nose . . .

(They crack up.)

RACHEL/LIZ: Fish fish fish fish fisssshhhh!

ANNE: *(Holding up the baby.)* What if she's not a Rachel?

MARCUS: What?

ANNE: What if that's not who she is?

MARCUS: It's after your mother.

ANNE: But what if that limits her somehow? What if she resents me for it? What if she's a Megan or a June or an Amber?

MARCUS: She's not an Amber.

ANNE: How am I supposed to know?

MARCUS: We know. You have to have faith.

ANNE: Faith? You want to name her Faith?

MARCUS: That it will come to us, what to do that deep in our core we know what to do with her, how to raise her, part historical genetics, part in our DNA, part because she is a mixture of our DNA.

ANNE: In between crying she is the most beautiful thing on the planet. God, the tears. That they're real tears. It kills me. Have you tasted them?

MARCUS: What?

ANNE: Her tears. Have you tasted them?

MARCUS: No.

ANNE: Taste them. I swear. They're sweet.
    (To the baby.)
Don't cry. Don't cry. Don't cry.

(Light and music shift. ANNE floats the baby doll back to its first position in their sky. RACHEL takes it as she moves to confront ANNE [44]. Class project.)

RACHEL: (*To Anne.*) It's this weird project for school. It pees, it poops, it cries. Will you babysit? I have plans with Zak.

ANNE: No.

RACHEL: Why not? You're not doing anything.

ANNE: It's your homework.

RACHEL: But as long as you're watching it, I'm covered.

ANNE: It? It pees, it poops, but it doesn't get a name?

RACHEL: Amber.

ANNE: Amber?

RACHEL: I didn't name her. It's printed on her ass. There's a schedule of things. You have to give her a bottle or she won't pee and you have to chart that. You feed her with this weird pasty crap you add water to and you give her a bath but you don't really give her a bath bath because she can't be fully immersed or it'll wreck the crying mechanism and then you just put her down and she'll sleep. It's easy.

ANNE: Easy.

RACHEL: Whatever. Come on.

ANNE: When you were little, we avoided giving you a bath as long as possible.

RACHEL: Ick.

ANNE: Yeah, well, we were scared. You were so little. So, we'd fill up the little tub and test the water and get out the towels and the diapers and your sleep sack but still we'd stop ourselves at your first little squeak. The water would be cool and you'd scream like you were being scalded—and I was stunned because when you were inside me you were *doing* water ballet, synchronized swimming, but now you were screaming nonstop water torture . . . and then one day, one day it just changed. You were a fish.

RACHEL: So, you'll babysit Amber?

ANNE: We used eggs.

RACHEL: What?

ANNE: Not so high tech, and most everyone's suffered some sort of brain damage by the end of the week. Your grandma hardboiled mine and packed it in my lunch bag by mistake. Little Alice.

RACHEL: So I have plans. With Zak.

ANNE: I'm sure the three of you will have a good time.

(Music and light shift. RACHEL floats the baby doll back to its place in their sky. ANNE [27] takes her down. BABY RACHEL.)

ANNE: (*To Marcus.*) Do you think I'm disappointing her?

MARCUS: What? She's six days old.

ANNE: So?

MARCUS: So, disappointment can't set in until you're aware there's something better out there in the world.

ANNE: But what if she knows that? Intrinsically? What if it's in her cells, in her old soul—you're the one that's been going on and on about how she's an old soul. What if she's longing for a mom who could do this better, a mom who could do anything better? What if from the get-go she's certain that somewhere out there, there is more, is better?

MARCUS: Then I'd say you've got a head start on adolescence.

ANNE: (*To baby.*) Be happy be happy be happy be happy be happy.

(Music and light shift. MARCUS takes BABY RACHEL from her and exits. RACHEL [5] leaps into ANNE's [32] arms.)

RACHEL: I got your nose.

ANNE: I got your nose.

RACHEL: Put it on your face.

(They put each other's noses on their own faces.)

I got your mouth.

ANNE: I got your mouth.

(They put each other's mouths on their own faces.)

RACHEL: I got your eyes.

ANNE: I got your eyes.

> *(They put each other's eyes on their own faces.)*

RACHEL: *(Dancing.)* I'm you I'm you I'm you I'm you I'm you.

> *(ANNE watches her, enthralled.)*

ANNE: Never grow up, baby. Please.

RACHEL: *(Dancing.)* I won't.

> *(Music and light shift. LIZ enters with the baby doll carelessly, sits on the bed. RACHEL [17].)*

LIZ: Mine won't pee or poop but she pukes. Does yours puke?
> *(She lies back on RACHEL's bed, then bolts back up.)*
You do change the sheets, right?

RACHEL: What?

LIZ: Fissshhhh.
> *(She shakes the baby doll.)*

RACHEL: Don't do that.

LIZ: Please . . .

RACHEL: Cut it out. Give me that.
> *(She grabs the baby doll. Puts it upright.)*

LIZ: It's a frigging doll.

RACHEL: I know, but . . .
> *(She holds the baby doll in her arms a moment, tender.)*
This is better. This is better.

> *(Music and light shift.)*

RACHEL: *(To Anne.)* You don't understand.

ANNE: I understand I can't do anything right for you. Ever.

RACHEL: I just need you to take the damn doll for an hour while I talk to Zak.

ANNE: I'm not doing your homework for you while you and Zak go . . . why the hell do you and Zak have to go anywhere? We gave you permission.

RACHEL: I didn't ask you for permission! Maybe I didn't want permission.

ANNE: We thought—I thought—it would be better than . . .

RACHEL: Isn't that your job? Aren't you supposed to be the one to make it impossible? I'm supposed to be the one desperate to make it possible. Those are the rules. That's the dynamic. Maybe I didn't want permission.

ANNE: What?

RACHEL: Mommy. Mommy.

ANNE: Baby—baby—what is it?

(RACHEL—crumbling—shrugs . . . she can't express it.)
Oh.

(ANNE takes the baby doll from her arms and puts it back to float in its place in the sky.)

ANNE: Oh.

(They look at the floating baby.)

RACHEL: Tell me about who I was when I was floating in your belly.

ANNE: You were a speck of love from Mommy and Daddy. You were a guppy tickling me from the inside. You made me a goldfish bowl you couldn't see into. You were a wiggly water creature breathing with my breath and taking me on, and I was the great body of water from which you evolved.

RACHEL: Fissshhhh.
(She comes into her mother's arms.)

ANNE: You took my nose. You took my eyes. You took my mouth. You took my heart. You'll always have my heart. You took it all, and you made it you. You took it all and became you.

(The baby doll hovers over them—illuminated as the lights fade on them, leaving the baby floating in the air before blackout.)

END OF PLAY

FROM ASHLEE TO ASHES AND DUST TO DUSTIN

by Rita Anderson

From Ashlee to Ashes and Dust to Dustin was produced in the 14/48 Festival at The Vortex Theatre. Austin, Texas, October 2016.

Director: Shannon Fox

DUSTIN: Sean Moran
ASHLEE: Emily Christine Smith

Rita Anderson has an MFA in Poetry and an MA in Playwriting. A published and award-winning playwright and poet, Rita was awarded a scholarship to The O'Neill Conference. Her play, *Frantic Is the Carousel*, was the National Partners American Theatre (NAPAT) nominee, and Rita won the Ken Ludwig Playwriting Award, the top national prize from The Kennedy Center for "Best Body of Work." Rita has had over one hundred publications and as many productions to include several each in London, Paris, and Dubai. *Final Conversations* and *Early Liberty*, internationally published (www.offthewall-plays.com), are on the "Best Selling Plays" list. Rita is the Dramatists Guild Regional Rep (Austin/San Antonio), and she's on the Social Media Team for International Center for Women Playwrights (ICWP), and the B. Iden Payne Arts Council (BIPAC). She is on the faculty at Interlochen Arts Academy (Co-Director Intermediate Theatre Ensemble and Acting Intensive), but the highlight of her emerging career was sitting on a panel with Christopher Durang. Recent publications include *Best Women's Monologues of*

2019 (Smith and Kraus), *Avalanche* in *30 New 10 Minute Plays 2019* (Applause Theatre and Cinema Books), and *Endlessly Rocking (An Anthology to Celebrate Walt Whitman's 200th Birthday)*. Rita is also Producing Artistic Director of Mélange Theatre Company. A member of Poets and Writers and The Academy of American Poets, Rita was poetry editor at University of New Orleans, and she has two volumes of poetry published: *The Entropy of Rocketman* (Finishing Line Press), and *Watched Pots (A Lovesong to Motherhood)*. Rita won the Houston Poetry Festival, the Gerreighty Prize, the Robert F. Gibbons Poetry Award, the Cheyney Award, and an award from the Academy of American Poets. She has over fifty poems published to include *Spoon River Poetry Review, EVENT Magazine, Blue Heron Review, Random Sample Review, Caesura, Ellipsis, The Longleaf Pine, Old Northwest Review, Cahoodaloodaling, The Blueshift Journal, Blotterature, Words Work, Transcendence, PHIction, Persona (50th Anniversary Edition), Di-Verse-City: An Austin Poetry Anthology, The Stardust Gazette*, and *Explorations* (University of Alaska Press). Currently, she is Senior Poetry Editor for Red Dashboard Publishing.

CHARACTERS

DUSTIN, Ashlee's husband, who died in WWI, plays 20s.
ASHLEE, former "Oldest Woman Alive." Actor may be any age. (Plays 119 but looks amazing and is quite mobile because of plastic surgery, technology.)

PLACE

A bare stage, since "place" is established with dialogue. Suggested joint burial plot.

TIME

Now, eternity.

• • •

(A sound wakes DUSTIN, in old military uniform. He's been "asleep" a long time in his half of a joint burial plot. He looks around, part wonder, part fear.)

DUSTIN: Huh?—Oh . . .

(ASHLEE, an "old" woman in church dress and sensible shoes, enters her half of the burial plot, thereby crossing over from life to death.)

(DUSTIN and ASHLEE glance at one another. He removes his hat, bows. She weakly nods back.)

ASHLEE: And *now* what?

DUSTIN: Now, we wait.

(ASHLEE laughs.)

ASHLEE: It is awfully dark down here!

DUSTIN: Your eyes will adjust. Give it a minute.

ASHLEE: Okay. (*Beat.*)

DUSTIN: Better?

(ASHLEE pauses before shaking her head "no.")

DUSTIN: Well, maybe you should try and relax.

ASHLEE: I *am* trying!

DUSTIN: Or we could try and take your mind off of it.

ASHLEE: Yes, okay. (*Beat.*) What should I do?

(DUSTIN wrings his hat.)

DUSTIN: We could uh . . . talk.

ASHLEE: *Talk*?! I'm not so sure that's a good idea. (*Beat.*) Alright, what the hell. Let's try that. Talking.

DUSTIN: Okay! . . . Uhm. (*Draws a blank.*) Guess I'm a little rusty in the conversation department. It has been quite a *while* for me.

ASHLEE: Yes, I imagine it has.

(Beat.)

DUSTIN: (*Saying her name nervously.*) Ashlee?

ASHLEE: Yes, Dustin?

DUSTIN: Ashlee . . . What. *Year*. Is this?

ASHLEE: Why, it's 2020 (*Change to current year.*)

DUSTIN: *2020*?! No!

ASHLEE: Yes! We're in the twenty-first century now!

DUSTIN: And humans aren't living on the moon yet?

ASHLEE: No. But we did send a rocket ship there!! Oh, you would've been proud!
(*Acts it out.*) "A small step for man, a leap for mankind." Or something . . .

DUSTIN: A *rocket ship*?! Wow. Is that how people travel now?

ASHLEE: (*Relaxing.*) Don't I wish! No, I still have to take the bus.
(*Laughs*) Or, I used to.
Maybe not so much anymore . . .

DUSTIN: So, you never did learn to drive?

(*ASHLEE shakes her head, "no." Silence returns. So does the awkwardness.*)

DUSTIN: I am . . . I am just so happy to see you again, Ashlee!

ASHLEE: You *are*?! (*Beat.*) I mean, are you?

DUSTIN: Of course, I am, Ashlee! Why wouldn't I be?

ASHLEE: Oooh, I don't want to talk about it, Dustin. It makes me uncomfortable. Just talk about something else.

DUSTIN: Alright then. Tell me this. If it's 2020, and I died right after the war . . .

ASHLEE: Oh! WWI, the Great War? That wasn't the *last* war.

DUSTIN: It wasn't?

ASHLEE: No! There have been *many* wars! World War II. The Korean War. Viet Nam. And *every* year in stores on Black Friday. (*Sighs.*) No, Dustin. I'm afraid we're still out there trying to blow each other up. Only our weapons got bigger. And badder!

DUSTIN: Worse than mustard gas?!

ASHLEE: Boy, howdee! Why, we have "germ warfare" now. And it's stuff so strong that it melts you from the inside out!

DUSTIN: They're using viruses now—as weapons?

ASHLEE: Oh, it's a different world now, Dustin, than when you and I were kids.

DUSTIN: I suppose it would have to be. And, let's see. If it's 2020, then that makes you how old?

ASHLEE: Dustin Cade, for golly's sakes! Where are your manners?!

DUSTIN: Oh, no, I'm just trying to catch up!

ASHLEE: Things *have* changed, Mr. Cade, but it is *still* rude to ask a woman her age.

DUSTIN: I meant nothing by it, Ashlee.

ASHLEE: But it still hurts my feelings, Dustin. Oh, just forget it. It all just burns me up!

DUSTIN: What does? (*Beat.*) Ashlee, honey. Talk to me.

ASHLEE: Why, there isn't *one* thing about this (*Points at their surroundings.*) whole situation that's *fair*!

DUSTIN: "Fair," how so?

ASHLEE: (*Points at him.*) First, my sweet husband is taken, and me, a child bride!

DUSTIN: I am sorry, Ashlee. But I had plans too, you know, and dying young wasn't one of them. I wanted to live by your side forever.

ASHLEE: What did we share as man and wife, Dustin? Two years?

DUSTIN: Two short years. But I loved every minute of it, Ashlee. Being your husband.

ASHLEE: And *now* look at me!

DUSTIN: Look at what?

ASHLEE: *What*?! Dustin, there you are—as handsome as ever! And I've become an old hag.

DUSTIN: No, Ashlee! How can you say that? You're my beautiful bride.
    (*He steps out of his spot to kneel before her, takes her hand, and kisses it.*)

And I see you *just as you were* the last time I saw you.

ASHLEE: Whoa. Really? Now, that's one good thing I must say about this *low* lighting!!

DUSTIN: And, darling. (*Beat.*) I am *not* handsome, anymore . . .

ASHLEE: But you are, Dustin! You're—why, you're the spitting image of your *perfect* self the last time I laid eyes on you. It's not fair!

DUSTIN: I'm grateful that you feel that way, sweetheart, because after *decades* in the grave, I'd be . . . Well. You know how it goes: "Ashes to ashes. Dust to dust."

   (*The reality of what he is saying dawns on her.*)

ASHLEE: Oh, my! You would be . . . different, yes.

DUSTIN: I'm afraid your Dustin has become dust. A skeleton, Ashlee. I'm nothing but a pile of bones.

   (*They gaze into each other's eyes.*)

But now that you're here, Ashlee. We finally get that eternity to spend together.

ASHLEE: Well, if we *are* going to start again, Dustin, then you must know.
   (*Standing taller.*)
I would've been 119. On Tuesday.

DUSTIN: *119*?! That's not even possible!

ASHLEE: One-hundred-and-nineteen-years-old AND made of plastic! Why, I got fake hips, fake knees. A glass eye and a pacemaker. I was the "Oldest Living Woman" in the world, Dustin—and your wife was quite famous!

DUSTIN: 119, wow. What was your secret?

ASHLEE: To longevity? I blame yogurt.

DUSTIN: What's "yogurt"?

ASHLEE: (*Laughing.*) So, yes, Dustin. I'm 119 years old—and made of pieces-parts!

DUSTIN: "Pieces-parts"?

ASHLEE: Yeah, all smashed together. Like a chicken nugget.

DUSTIN: What's a "chicken nugget"?

ASHLEE: You know, McDonald's? Yeah, okay. Never mind. But I'll tell you, Dustin.
I have been reduced to recycled pieces-parts. Now, do you *still* see me as . . . beautiful?

DUSTIN: As lovely as a bouquet of roses, fresh from the garden.

> *(ASHLEE, stunned, takes a moment to let it sink in.)*

ASHLEE: I knew that love was special. That it formed like this amazing bond between people, but . . .

> *(DUSTIN moves to take her in his arms.)*

DUSTIN: And I'm *still* under your spell, darling, and when it's *true* love, "No man can put asunder!"

> *(ASHLEE pulls away.)*

And your wedding ring, Ashlee! It means so much to me that you're *still* wearing it.

> *(ASHLEE removes the ring and pockets it.)*

ASHLEE: About the ring, Dustin . . . It isn't yours.

DUSTIN: The ring's not mine?

ASHLEE: That is to say, the ring's not . . . *ours* . . .

DUSTIN: But it was on your finger! You were buried with it, means it meant something to you.

ASHLEE: No, it means my son—or my great-grandson—put it there.

DUSTIN: Your . . . *son*?!

> *(ASHLEE nods.)*

Oh, Ashlee! We had a child?!

ASHLEE: No, *we* didn't.

DUSTIN: *So?*

(This section is rapid-fire. Make it build.)

ASHLEE: So! His name is Vladimir and . . .

DUSTIN: "*Vladimir*?!"

ASHLEE: Yes, Vladimir. And I met his father, Igor, when I was living in the commune.

DUSTIN: The "commune"?

ASHLEE: Yes, in Iceland.

DUSTIN: Iceland! *(Beat.)* Wait. What's a *commune*?

ASHLEE: What can I say, Dustin? It was the '60s! Tie-dye. Macramé.
LeChow in a can!
Oh, we were *all* about, "Make Love, not War."

DUSTIN: But in the 1960s you would've been almost sixty yourself . . .

ASHLEE: *(Confessing.)* Vladimir *was* a miracle baby. But I had *lots* of "free love," Dustin, alright! And it's a looong story!

DUSTIN: *(Laughs and gestures.)* Well, look around, my mysterious lady. We just may be in the perfect place for a *long* story.

ASHLEE: Oh, I got lots of those! Watergate. Teflon! Pet rocks. Donald Trump's hairdo—more like a "hair-don't"!

(DUSTIN holds her hand and laughs.)

DUSTIN: And I want to hear about them all, Ashlee. Every single one.

(Beat.)

ASHLEE: So then, you're not mad? About Vladimir, Igor, Iceland—or the commune?

DUSTIN: Why should I be? You're not with Igor.

ASHLEE: Well, umm, Igor wasn't my only, ahem, *other* husband. *(Beat.)* I had three of them.

DUSTIN: You've had three husbands?!

ASHLEE: Yes, more like "three strikes, you're out." I'm afraid I was a bit of a "free agent," so to speak.

DUSTIN: But you're not with them, my long-lost angel, are you? No. You're here. With me.

ASHLEE: It *was* my dying wish, Dustin. To be buried with you. You were my one "great love."
 (She kisses him.)

 (Lights swell, if possible.)

DUSTIN: And I've waited a looong time to hear that—and I don't want to miss a thing.
So, tell me *everything*, love. And start from the top!!!

END OF PLAY

FUCKING CUPCAKES

by Judith Leora

Originally produced by New York Madness as part of Urban Legend Madness on November 18, 2012, at Shetler Studios, New York City. The cast was as follows:

EMMA: Jody Christopherson
NATALIE: Diana Oh
MIA: Rivka Borek
SOFIA: Lilli Stein
TODD: Will Arbery

Directed by Ilana Becker

Judith Leora began her career writing sketch, animation, television pilots, and screenplays. She is a Founding Member and Managing Director of New York Madness. She is a Robert Askins Fellow with the Lone Star Theatre. Productions: *Showpony* (Victory Theatre, Burbank, CA, September 2018), *Elijah* (Bristol Valley Theatre, 2017), *Gideon* (Ego Actus/Paradise Theatre, New York City, 2016), *The Cookie Fight* (Bristol Valley Theatre, 2016), *Weird About the Baby/Icon Plays* (Ego Actus Productions/New York City). Recent readings: *Showpony* (LRS, The Blank Theatre; Next Stage Festival, Capital Rep; Lone Star Theatre), *The X and the Y* (Bristol Valley Theatre Reading Series), *The Cookie Fight* (Last Frontier Theatre Conference), *Heart-Shaped Uterus* (MadLab Readings, New York Madness), *Elijah* (Semi-finalist, O'Neill). Webseries #GoingHomeless currently in post-production. Many, many short plays with New York

Madness, Sticky, One Minute Play Festival (6x), Pussyfest, and Brain Melt Consortium.

CHARACTERS

EMMA, 30s, creative type.
NATALIE, possibly non-white, not sure what she wants to do.
MIA, possibly non-white, kinda grumpy.
SOFIE, young.
YVONNE, older, non-white.
TODD, young guy.

Scene

An office break room.

• • •

EMMA *drinks coffee.* NATALIE *enters.*

NATALIE: Did you hear anything?

EMMA: What? Oh. Not yet.

> *(NATALIE exits. SOFIE enters. She circles around the room. She exits. EMMA watches her go. MIA enters with coffee. She sits.)*

EMMA: Hey.

MIA: Hey.

EMMA: Monday.

MIA: Yup.

EMMA: Do anything fun this weekend?

MIA: I ironed this shirt.

EMMA: Wow. I feel okay now.

> *(Beat.)*

MIA: What'd you do?

EMMA: Random birthday party. Lots of 20-somethings. Like puppies. Hopping around and pawing at each other.

MIA: Why are you at a party with 20-somethings?

EMMA: I'm friends with everyone.

MIA: Ew.

>   *(EMMA shrugs. SOFIE enters. She circles the room again. She is about to exit.)*

EMMA: You can sit.

SOFIE: Oh. I wasn't sure.
>   *(She sits.)*
So, this is the break room? It's very nice.

>   *(It's not. They sip coffee.)*

I'm Sofie. I'm the new temp.

EMMA: Hi.

MIA: We know.

>   *(NATALIE enters.)*

NATALIE: My stupid phone. The stupid pages won't load. Come on, come on . . .

EMMA: You're looking for the code?

NATALIE: I'm so hung over. I need something to eat.

MIA: You guys are obsessed with that place.

EMMA: We're not obsessed. It's just free.

NATALIE: Come on, you fucking bastards. It's 11:15. It's always up by 11:15.

EMMA: Actually, I think I hate that place. Fucking Sprinkles. They're destroying my life.

NATALIE: Fucking Sprinkles.

SOFIE: Oh, I saw that there's a Sprinkles in the bottom of this building.

NATALIE: That's what we're talking about. They tweet a code every day . . .

EMMA: Twice a day.

NATALIE: Twice a day, and the first one hundred people who go down and whisper the code get a free cupcake.

MIA: The whispering is weird.

> (*YVONNE enters with her coffee cup. She sits at the table.*)

SOFIE: Oh my God. That's awesome. Free cupcakes. This is the best job ever.

YVONNE: You got the code?

EMMA: Not yet.

YVONNE: You tell . . .

EMMA: I'll tell you the code. (*To* MIA.) One of the cupcakes last week was like seven hundred calories. That's obscene.

MIA: Then just don't get a cupcake.

EMMA: I try, but once I know the code, I'm screwed.

NATALIE: I need to buy a new phone. This one's fucked. I'm so hungry.
> (*Beat. Sits. Continues to play with phone. To EMMA:*)
Did you see that girl on Facebook who posted a picture of herself in her underwear and it got reposted on Facebook and then there were like thousands of comments?

MIA: She was on the *Today* show this morning.

SOFIE: I don't have a TV.

EMMA: I saw it. She looked beautiful. Good for her.

MIA: Good for her?

NATALIE: Some of the comments were nasty.

SOFIE: What's wrong with her?

EMMA: She's a size 14 or something.

SOFIE: That's a bad idea. You don't want your future husband to see you online like that. My aunt says that men don't like fat girls.

YVONNE: (*Mouthed to* EMMA.) Who is this?

EMMA: Temp.

MIA: She was a sixteen. At least.

EMMA: Okay, first of all, she's not that fat. Second of all, it's her life. If it makes her feel good about herself, leave her alone.

MIA: So, we're all supposed to applaud her lack of self-control?

NATALIE: I think she has some kind of disorder where she can't lose weight.

SOFIE: My aunt has a disorder.

EMMA: It's her body.

MIA: And she put it on the freakin' internet.

EMMA: If you don't like it, don't look.

MIA: I'm not!

SOFIE: My aunt says that men are very visual.

NATALIE: I'm really hungry.
   (She fiddles with her phone.)

YVONNE: If you get . . .

NATALIE: I'll give you the code.

MIA: She put herself out there. She deserves what she gets.

EMMA: I think she's brave.

MIA: I didn't make the rules. But this is the way the world is. She's not brave, she's just stupid.

EMMA: Don't project your crap onto her.

NATALIE: My mom keeps forwarding me ads for Christian Mingle. What do you think that's about?

SOFIE: What is that?

MIA: Don't analyze me. This is just reality.

NATALIE: It's like Match.com for Christians. (*To* EMMA.) You've done Match, haven't you?

EMMA: Stop trying to change the subject.

NATALIE: You're both giving me a headache.

MIA: She's just fat. She's not beautiful.

EMMA: Why do you care either way?

MIA: When we try to tell men that fat is just as beautiful as skinny, we sound like morons.

EMMA: She's a student at NYU. She's more than her body.

NATALIE: I don't think I've eaten since lunch yesterday.

SOFIE: My aunt says that the more education a woman has, the less likely she is to get married.

NATALIE: (*Shaking her phone.*) I just came in here for the fucking cupcakes code.

YVONNE: Language, Natalie.

MIA: Shut up about the code. I have the code.

EMMA: You have the code?

NATALIE: Oh my God, the code.

YVONNE: What's the code?

SOFIE: What is it?

MIA: Find it yourselves.

YVONNE: My niece wants a cupcake. Give me the code.

NATALIE: I'm starving. You have to give me the code.

MIA: No. Afterward you both just whine about how you shouldn't have eaten the cupcake. I'm not a part of this anymore.

YVONNE: I'm not a part of any of this. Give me the code.

SOFIE: I won't whine.

NATALIE: Give me the code.

EMMA: You're just pissed 'cause we don't agree with you.

MIA: This is New York. You may not like it, but how you look matters.

NATALIE: Give me the code.

YVONNE: You better not make me miss that cupcake.

SOFIE: My aunt says that a single woman over the age of thirty in New York has more of a chance of getting hit by a bus than getting married.

EMMA: Shut up about your aunt. I hate your fucking aunt.

NATALIE: I feel light-headed.

EMMA: Give her the code.

MIA: Get your own code. You don't need any more cupcakes.

EMMA: Excuse me? Did you just call me fat?

YVONNE: I think this break should be over.

MIA: I thought you don't care what anyone thinks about your body.

EMMA: Are you worried you're going to have to look at our fat, disgusting bodies? Is that what you're afraid of?

NATALIE: Come on, just give me the code.

MIA: No.

EMMA: Give her the code.
　　(She starts to take off her top.)

YVONNE: Emma.

MIA: What are you doing?

SOFIE: What's going on?

EMMA: Give her the code. Or you're going to get some reality.
　　(She continues to disrobe.)

EMMA: Look, it's so disgusting. My not-perfect body. Can you handle it?

MIA: Stop it.

NATALIE: Emma, you don't have to do this.

EMMA: You can't always sit on the fence, Natalie. What's your opinion?

NATALIE: I don't know.

MIA: You're not the only one who can act like a freak.
   (She starts to take off her clothes.)

YVONNE: You both have problems.

EMMA: Bring it on!! (*To* NATALIE.) Come on, Nat. Do you think you have the right to decide whether you can eat a cupcake? (*To* MIA.) Give her the code.

MIA: No.

EMMA: Yes.

MIA: No.

EMMA: Yes. Natalie! Do you want the code?

NATALIE: I want the code, I want the code.
   (She starts to take off her clothes. SOFIE panics and starts also.)

MIA: No.

EMMA: Yes.

MIA: No.

EMMA: Yes.

YVONNE: What is wrong with you girls?

(MIA and EMMA circle each other like gladiators. TODD wanders into the break room. They all freeze. He does not notice them and gets a cup of coffee. He turns around. He looks at them. They look at him. He dumps his coffee and runs from the room. They all stare at each other.)

EMMA: What the fuck are we doing?

YVONNE: Who was that?

(They all start to get dressed.)

EMMA: (*To* SOFIE.) Why the hell did you take off your clothes?

SOFIE: (*Near tears.*) I don't know.

(MIA is dressed first and starts to leave.)

EMMA: Mia . . .

MIA: It's mocha, okay? Go whisper "I love mocha."
   (She exits.)

YVONNE: Excellent.
   (She exits. NATALIE is still undressed.)

EMMA: Get dressed!

NATALIE: I do love mocha.

   (Blackout.)

END OF PLAY

GET MOM

by C.S. Hanson

Get Mom was presented by Naked Angels at Theatre 80 in New York City, on December 17, 2019, as part of the Tuesdays@9 "Twistmas" special. The Artistic Director of Naked Angels is Jean Marie McKee. Creative Directors for the show were Michael C. O'Day and Arya Kashyap. The cast was as follows:

ANGEL: Theresa Rose
DUNCAN: Frankie Provenzano
DAD: Erik Svendsen
DENNIS: Matt W. Cody

C.S. Hanson is a playwright with Off-Broadway and regional credits. Her work has been seen in two International Fringe Festivals: Montreal and New York. Her ten-minute play *Stalk Me, Baby* is a favorite on college campuses and high schools. *Prick Perfect*, commissioned and produced by Theater for the New City, won an EstroGenius Festival Choice Award. Hanson's work has been developed thanks to The Lark, Lake George Theater Lab, EST, LaMaMa, Abingdon Theatre, Naked Angels, and New Jersey Rep. Her plays have been anthologized by Applause Theatre and Cinema Books and by Smith and Kraus. She is a four-time finalist for the prestigious Heideman Award. She began 2020 as a resident artist at The Cell Theatre in NY, where her play *I Could Never Live Here* had a reading directed by Kira Simring. She is a proud member of the Dramatists Guild of America.

CHARACTERS

ANGEL, 30s, female.
DUNCAN, 13, male.
DAD, 40s, male, Duncan's father, also known as DAVE.
DENNIS, 40s, male, uncle to Duncan and brother-in-law to Dave.

SETTING

Duncan's bedroom on the eve of Christmas.

TIME

Present day.

• • •

DUNCAN *opens a jewelry box, pulls out a shiny gold necklace, puts it on, looks in the mirror. A golden light appears and out pops* ANGEL, *a vision of angelic loveliness except she is dressed for a round of golf and carries a golf club.*

ANGEL: Who's that for?

DUNCAN: Who are you?
    (He scrambles to take off the necklace and put it in the box.)

ANGEL: That for me?

DUNCAN: It's for my mom.

ANGEL: A pwevent for yo mom?

DUNCAN: I can say my Rs.

ANGEL: Aw, you learned how to say your Rs?

DUNCAN: (*Calling out.*) Mom! Mom!

ANGEL: She can't hear you.

DUNCAN: I'm thirteen. I say my Rs. I don't think you should be here.

ANGEL: You're not getting any presents this year.

DUNCAN: Yes, I am.

ANGEL: You've been a very bad boy, Duncan.

DUNCAN: I have not. I'm a good boy. I'm a very good boy.

ANGEL: Well, I'm an angel, and I know things.

DUNCAN: You don't look like an angel. You look like it's summertime. And I know I'm getting presents.

ANGEL: I am an angel. And yes, you're probably getting presents, but not the ones you really want.

DUNCAN: Why not?

ANGEL: Because you're not living authentically.

DUNCAN: What's that mean?

(ANGEL reveals a party dress, jewelry, and a bag of cosmetics.)

ANGEL: What if I were to give you this pretty little party dress and these long, dangly beads, and this lip gloss and . . .

DUNCAN: Wow. I mean, no. I'll wrap it for my mom.

ANGEL: No? You say no to . . .

DUNCAN: It's girl stuff.

ANGEL: Why didn't you ask Santa for this for Christmas? You really want another flannel shirt and a Minnesota Timberwolves jersey?

DUNCAN: Mom! Mom!

ANGEL: She can't hear you.

DUNCAN: Mom!

ANGEL: This is what we call suspension of disbelief.

DUNCAN: Mom! Help!

ANGEL: I'm in your head.

DUNCAN: Get out of my head.

ANGEL: What do you want for *Quistmas*?

DUNCAN: It's Christmas, not *Quistmas*. I can pronounce my Rs. Stop making fun of me. I want you to leave.

ANGEL: Why don't you put that necklace back on?

DUNCAN: It's a pwesent—PRESENT—for my mom. I have to go eat. Everyone's eating. And I'm starving.

ANGEL: Duncan, this is a truthful exchange. If you speak untruthfully, you will die a slow, excruciatingly painful death.

DUNCAN: Okay, I'm not starving.

ANGEL: Truth, Duncan. Avoid pain by telling the . . .

DUNCAN: Okay, okay. I ate ten cookies and half, er, the whole bag of chocolate kisses, some lime Jell-O, frozen waffles, and I stole my sister's Red Bull and . . .

ANGEL: That's enough. Thank you for the truth.

DUNCAN: But I didn't eat the lutefisk. Because I hate lutefisk.

ANGEL: It's disgusting. That's the truth.

DUNCAN: I always tell the . . .

ANGEL: Do you like your name?

DUNCAN: Yes. I mean no.

ANGEL: I'm giving you a new name. I'm giving you the name PINKY.

DUNCAN: Is that a name?

ANGEL: Now it is. And if you don't take this name, which is kindly granted, you will suffer a slow and excruciatingly . . .

DUNCAN: I'll take it. I'll take it. I hate my name. I want a new name.

ANGEL: Good, Pinky! Now, put on your new outfit. Go on, just put it on over your shirt and jeans.

(*DUNCAN puts on the party dress and necklace.*)

DUNCAN: Wow. How do I look?

ANGEL: You look like Pinky. And you're about to make your entrance.

DUNCAN: I can't go out there like this.

(*Suddenly, DAD enters.*)

DAD: Hey buddy, what are you doing? . . . Duncan? Why are you . . . ?

DUNCAN: Um, I think my name's Pinky.

DAD: Why are you in your Halloween costume? Take it off. We're about to unwrap the presents.

DUNCAN: It's not a costume, Dad. I'm living authentically.

DAD: Duncan, take that off. Uncle Dennis and Caroline are waiting. They came all the way from Brainerd just to see you open your . . .

DUNCAN: What? A baseball glove? Dad, I hate baseball. How about some lip gloss and glitter eye shadow? That's what I want. Why doesn't anyone see me for my authentic self?

DAD: Margaret? Get in here, please.

ANGEL: She can't hear you.

DAD: Where did you . . . ? Duncan, leave calmly. Tell your mom there's an intruder.

DUNCAN: Dad, she's an angel. She really is.

ANGEL: It's okay, Pinky. He knows me.

DAD: Wait, do you play golf at the Century Country Club?

ANGEL: I did. I used to. A lot.

DAD: You were the top female—oh, oh, but you're . . . you had that . . .

ANGEL: Yeah, that accident on I-29 when the semi jackknifed off the exit on Christmas Eve a year ago.

DAD: That was terrible. We all felt . . .

ANGEL: And now I'm the angel of . . .

DAD: You're an angel? Duncan, run. Run.

ANGEL: I am the Angel of Authenticity and Truth. Is there anything you want to tell me? (*Beat.*) Oh, c'mon. This is my job now. I have to get people to—you know, tell their . . .

DAD: This is a fake, a hoax, a . . . Duncan, get out of those ridiculous clothes.

DUNCAN: My name is Pinky.

DAD: It's time to open the presents. Now!

ANGEL: And what's the most important present this year? Think, Dave, think.

DAD: Obviously, health. Good health.

ANGEL: You are not going anywhere with that attitude.

DAD: It's Christmas Eve. My wife, and my brother-in-law and his wife, and her parents are waiting.

ANGEL: Well, I'm on the job. If I can get three people in one house in the Midwest on Christmas Eve to tell the truth, I'll finally get a chance to go to the great golf course in the sky . . . and you know how much I love to play golf.

(DUNCAN puts on lipstick.)

DUNCAN: Dad, maybe the greatest gift is a day at the spa for me and Mom.

DAD: Wipe that off your lips. Margaret, call the police!

ANGEL: The door's locked. This room is soundproofed. And your son needs a role model. What's in your pocket there, Dave?

DAD: What the cockamamy . . .

(ANGEL swoops in and pulls a gift box out of the pocket of DAD's sport coat. She opens it.)

ANGEL: Nice!

DAD: Give me that!

DUNCAN: Wow.

DAD: That's none of your . . .

ANGEL: A Rolex. Now, who could that be for?

(DENNIS enters, wearing a blue sweater covered with tinsel.)

DENNIS: Hey, Dave, Margaret wants you to get out the elderflower glogg.

DUNCAN: Hi, Uncle Dennis!

DENNIS: Ooh, did I inter . . .

DUNCAN: I love the tinsel on your sweater. That color really brings out your beautiful blue eyes.

DENNIS: (*To* DAVE.) Why's he's wearing a dress? (*Looking at* ANGEL.) And who's this?

DUNCAN: This is the Angel of Authenticity and Truth.

ANGEL: (*To* DAD.) These are crucial moments, Dave. What kind of example will you set for your son?

(*DAD grabs the box out of ANGEL's hands and gives it to DENNIS.*)

DAD: Dennis, this is for you.

DENNIS: Wha . . . wha . . . going . . .?

DAD: I know you love watches, so I . . .

DENNIS: You're out of your mind. I don't want that. We don't give each other watches or cologne or silk robes.

ANGEL: Dennis, it's time.

DENNIS: I have to get back to my wife. We may never have another Christmas Eve—

ANGEL: She's going to live a very long life. That ovarian cancer scare? It's a scare. After the hysterectomy, the biopsy will be negative. Clean bill of health. You won't be administering morphine in her last days.

DENNIS: How dare you talk about my . . . She's not going to die?

ANGEL: It's not her time.

DAD: (*To* DENNIS.) That's great, right? Caroline's going to be okay.

DENNIS: Great? Yes, great. (*Looking at* ANGEL *now.*) But how do you know . . . ? Wait, you look like the . . .

DAD: The golf pro. At the Century. It's her.

DENNIS: You had that terrible . . .

DAD: She's trying to get her truth wings or something. I don't know. I don't really understand.

DUNCAN: It's a suspension of disbelief, Uncle Dennis. Look at me. I'm happy she's here.

ANGEL: I lived in the body of a woman, feeling like I belonged in the body of a man, my whole life. When that semi-trailer jackknifed, it was a relief. No more pretending that I was just a girl jock. I see the truth in everything and everyone. Starting with me. I was too scared to go pro, too scared to do anything that felt real.

DENNIS: I fell in love with you, Dave, the minute my sister brought you home and introduced you as the guy she was going to marry. I love my wife, but not the way I love you.

DAD: I love you, too, and I don't want to hide anymore.

DENNIS: But now? On Christmas Eve? The timing's not . . .

DAD: The timing's never going to be right. And to wait until we're widowers? . . . Dennis, what do you say?

DENNIS: Oh gosh, well, I don't want to lie about the watch. It's gorgeous. And I got you a little something, too.

DAD: Save it for later, darling. C'mon. Let's do this now.

DUNCAN: What's Mom gonna say?

(ANGEL takes on wings and is raised high above the stage.)

ANGEL: Mom will handle it. She's been handling everything for a long time. She might not be all that surprised. Just make sure she feels special and loved. Merry Christmas, Pinky. Merry Christmas, Dave and Dennis. Oh, there it is, the great golf course in the sky. I'm free.
(She vanishes.)

(Lights fade.)

END OF PLAY

GETTING IN TOUCH WITH YOUR DARK SIDE

by Laura Rohrman

First produced:
July 18–July 23, 2006
Part of "The Women In Boats" Series
The Producers Club
358 West 44th Street
New York, NY 10034

Produced by Kathy Towson and Le Wilhelm, RCL Writer's Workshop
Directed by Ian Streicher

The cast was as follows:
JULES: Pernell Walker
MARY-ANN: Miranda Jonte
SUSAN: Gail Herendeen

Laura Rohrman is a New York City playwright, actor, choreographer, and teacher who grew up in Northern California (Penngrove, CA). Her full-length plays include: *Reporter Girl*, about the life of her grandmother, Dale Messick, creator of the comic strip *Brenda Starr Reporter* in 1940 (O'Neill Semi-Finalist, Wessiberger Award Nominee, Princess Grace Finalist, AFF Second Rounder). Other plays include: *My Life as You* (Finalist Playwrights First Award) and *Hoboken* (Hollywood Fringe Festival). Laura's one-act plays include: *Below 14th*, *Without*, and *He Says His Name Is John*, all finalists for the Samuel

French Short Play Festival. Laura is published in anthologies by Smith and Kraus and Applause. MFA: The Actors Studio Drama School/New School for Drama.

CHARACTERS

MARY-ANN, 32, broke up with her now-famous comedian boyfriend two
    years ago. Is obsessed with their old relationship and him. Will use any
    excuse to talk about him.
SARAH, 35, obsessed with her job as an executive at a fashion house
JULES, 40, very calm. Into healing medicines.

SETTING

A canoe on a river.

• • •

*Three women paddle down a river in their canoe. At random moments, two of
the women sip on a raspberry-colored drink in a water bottle. This is a weekend away from their busy lives in New York City.*

MARY-ANN: This was a good idea, Jules. Feel that sun? Oh yes. Too bad Maria couldn't come. Everything okay with the two of you?

JULES: It's fine, uh . . . she's fine, she's fine.

MARY-ANN: Okay. Don't worry, I believe you. You two have a fight or something?

SARAH: Yeah, where's she been? I haven't heard a peep out of her in like a week. I called her to tell her about . . .

JULES: (*Stronger.*) I said she's fine. She sends her regards, Mary-Ann.

MARY-ANN: Well, she usually calls me back when I . . .

SARAH: Mary-Ann, now be quiet, remember what we talked about?

MARY-ANN: Right. Got it. Well. She's missing out. Jules, you are awesome. Where'd you hear about this place?

JULES: My group.

SARAH: Oh yeah.

MARY-ANN: Group. Group? That's where you do all that stuff.

JULES: Inner work?

MARY-ANN: Yeah, that.

SARAH: You know, stuff that we go to our therapists in New York for . . .

MARY-ANN: Oh yeah. Right. Which reminds me . . . this week at my therapy there was a photo on the wall . . . I didn't think anything about it. It was of an owl. But it caught my eye, you know. And then I realized—it symbolized Dan. That's what my therapist said.

SARAH: An owl symbolized Dan? Your therapist said that?

MARY-ANN: Well, I gave her my interpretation. That Dan has deep, unfinished issues with our relationship and that he watches over me. You know, like the time I ran into him on the street after I was almost holding hands with that guy . . .

SARAH: You were broken up for a year already. It's okay if you . . . oh, never mind. My boss is like an old owl, no, she's a crow, a black dark bitch of a crow.

(MARY-ANN laughs, then SARAH laughs. They laugh together like old times for a moment.)

JULES: The owl isn't always dark.

SARAH: Anyway . . . did I tell the two of you what my bitch boss did this week? I was putting this presentation together, right, and of course, it was brilliant, like all my presentations are, right? And . . . well, it was a meeting, right? And I wanted to have all my ideas in order, so I made a handout . . .

JULES: Was it color-coded?

SARAH: Of course. Anyway, she told me *not* to bring my handout. You know why? Well, it was because she didn't have one. She didn't want me to look better than her.

JULES: Sarah, you just need to relax. At a company, you need to play the game, you know. It's not a race.

SARAH: Yes, it is.

MARY-ANN: You guys ever race?

SARAH: What do you mean, of course we race. I was on the track team in high school. I ran the New York Marathon last year, you know this. You were there cheering me on.

JULES: I always took dance classes . . .

MARY-ANN: Dan ran mini-marathons. Every weekend.

SARAH: We know, we know . . .

MARY ANN: But did I tell you one time I ran one with him? And halfway through, I just had to stop, you know. And I was panting and so was he. And he sort of jogged in place and turned to me. He was all perspiring . . . and he told me he loved me.
   (Suddenly, she becomes angry.)
Can you believe that he said that?
   (She just ponders this for a moment.)
Well? After everything he did, can you *believe* that he said he loved me? He doesn't know what love is.

SARAH: Today is a really beautiful day. Jules, what time is dinner?

JULES: The cabin is serving us a special dinner at six.

MARY-ANN: Hey, I'm talking to you guys . . .

JULES: I know.

SARAH: Yes, we know, Mary-Ann.

MARY-ANN: Well, after he cheated on me, I just can't believe that he could have ever said that he loved me. He wasn't even good in bed. Do you know that he used to always beg for me to suck his dick, but he'd never do the same favor for me . . . I mean, what an asshole. I'm so pissed about all the times I . . . you know . . . and then he said that I was stalking *him*. And he told my friends. THAT FUCKING ASSHOLE.

JULES: Why don't you yell it, Mary-Ann?

SARAH: NO. Jules . . .

JULES: No, Mary-Ann . . . yell it at this river.

   (The ladies stop paddling and look out at the river.)
It's called getting in touch with your dark side.

MARY-ANN: That's just a bunch of bullshit.

JULES: My meetings really work. Everyone has a dark side. Yell it, Mary-Ann. Tell these trees how much you hate Dan.

SARAH: You know this is some crazy shit, but I bet you can't just yell at your therapist's office.

JULES: Do it.

SARAH: Do it, Mary-Ann.

MARY-ANN: You guys are crazy. When's the appointment for the facial?

JULES: Are you chicken?

MARY-ANN: No.

SARAH: I don't know why you don't just do it.

JULES: Get in touch with your dark side.

>   *(The ladies start paddling . . . well, SARAH and JULES do. MARY-ANN just reacts to them as if she doesn't know what to do.)*

SARAH: Wow! You are a chicken.

MARY-ANN: I . . . just. Look how I feel about Dan. I don't even care about him, okay? He can go fuck his whore, what do I care.

SARAH: It's just that you can't stop talking about him.

MARY-ANN: That's not true. Jules . . . tell her that's not true. You and I had lunch the other day and I hardly brought him . . .

JULES: Only eight times.

MARY-ANN: You were counting?

JULES: Have you noticed that people don't return your calls?

MARY-ANN: What?

SARAH: That people try to avoid you?

MARY-ANN: No . . .

SARAH: Broken lunch dates? Calls and texts not returned?

MARY-ANN: What are you trying to say?

SARAH: This was a rescue mission, Mary-Ann.

MARY-ANN: A rescue mission?

SARAH: Yes. If you don't get in touch with your goddamn dark side or whatever and yell at these trees . . . we won't be friends with you anymore.

MARY-ANN: What do I care? With friends like you . . . I don't need friends like you. Turn this boat around.

(*SARAH and JULES laugh.*)
I said, turn this boat around!

SARAH: Or what? What are you going to do, kick my ass?

MARY-ANN: I have plenty of friends.

SARAH: Sure you do.

MARY-ANN: Why are you doing this to me?

JULES: We are trying to save you. This is the best therapy for you. It's been two years . . . you need to give him up.

(*MARY-ANN sits quietly, venting.*)
Think about everything he did to you. So, you dated for a few months. He cheated on you and then he called you a stalker. He's no friend of yours. You'll get over him someday, you will . . . I promise. But you need to deal with your hate. It's deep, this pain you feel, but you need to recognize who hurt you.

SARAH: Yeah!

JULES: This is the deepest pain you will feel for this relationship. It's over, and you need to reach into your dark side and fight.

(*All of a sudden, MARY-ANN lets out a dying animal cry, then triumphantly she sounds like a lion roaring.*)

MARY-ANN: I hate you, Dan George . . .

SARAH: He even has a dumb name.

JULES: Louder!

SARAH: Let it rip, bitch . . .

MARY-ANN: I hate your small dick!

SARAH: He had a small dick?

JULES: Sarah . . .

SARAH: Well, she never said that . . .

MARY-ANN: I HATE YOUR SMALL DICK, DAN!

JULES: Feel better?

MARY-ANN: YOU MOTHERFUCKER. YOU ARE GOING TO DIE. I'LL KILL YOU WITH MY BARE HANDS AND EAT YOU.

JULES: There you go!

MARY-ANN: Ah!!!!!!!!!!!!!!!!!!!! ASSHOLE!!!!!!!!!!!!!! DAN!!!!!!!!!!!!!!!!!!! DIE, MOTHERFUCKER, DIE.

SARAH: Is it supposed to be so dark? I mean, does she have to say she's gonna off the guy?

(MARY-ANN continues to scream, but it comes in yelps. JULES and SARAH talk within breaks of MARY-ANN's screams.)

JULES: (*To* SARAH.) She's getting in touch with her dark side. (*To* MARY-ANN.) Good girl. Get it out.

(MARY-ANN is getting stronger and more passionate.)

MARY-ANN: I'm gonna kill you, asshole!

SARAH: Okay, okay, I get it. But this is just mean. You already said he had a small dick.

MARY-ANN: That's not the half of it. I'M GOING TO CUT YOUR HEART OUT OF YOUR CHEST WITH MY TOOTHBRUSH . . .

SARAH: Toothbrush? At least use a knife.

JULES: This is good. Keep going!

(MARY-ANN is now standing on the edge of the boat, reaching her arms out. SARAH is looking rather disgusted.)

MARY-ANN: Yeah, yeah, yeah . . . OHHHHHH!!!!!

(She starts to have an orgasm standing up. It will go something like this.)
Uh, uh . . . uh . . . yes, YES, YES . . . oh yeah . . . not you . . . this is . . . uh, uh
AHHHHHHHHHHHHHHHHHHHHHH.
YAHHHHHHHHHHHHHHHHHHHHHHHHHHHHH.

(She collapses in JULES's arms. They all react to the boat rocking. There is a long beat. MARY-ANN comes to.)

JULES: It's okay, it's okay.

(Beat. SARAH goes to take a sip of her drink, then thinks about it and puts it aside.)

SARAH: So, you do this often?

JULES: Just once a month.

SARAH: Just like this?

JULES: Oh no, it's boats and boats of us . . .

(SARAH reacts to seeing something in the distance.)
What is it? You seeing something, honey?

SARAH: Nothing. It's getting dark. I'm . . . chilly. We should head back. I'll row. You . . . hold on to her.
(SARAH rows like a type-A person.)

JULES: Hey, hey . . . what's your hurry, girlfriend?

SARAH: NO . . . hurry. Just trying to get a workout.

(A very loosened-up MARY-ANN speaks.)

MARY-ANN: Yeah, what's your hurry? Relax, girl.

SARAH: Oh, God.

MARY-ANN: What?

SARAH: (*Very sarcastic.*) How was your orgasm?

MARY-ANN: Oh . . . chill, sister, you should do it! You need to get out all your aggression about your boss. You hate her, right?

SARAH: What's that light? I see a light over there. Is that a flashlight or a . . .

MARY-ANN: Coming from where? Are you seeing things, Sarah?

SARAH: Nowhere. Never mind.

JULES: Maybe it's the dark spirits . . .

SARAH: Oh, shut the fuck up. What did you put in my drink, Jules? Did you do this?

MARY-ANN: Ohhh . . .

SARAH: I'm getting the hell out of here. Mary-Ann, pick up your goddamn paddle and help me. Jules is obviously into witchcraft or something. This really isn't helping the situation, Jules.

JULES: Just relax, Sarah.

SARAH: What did you put in my drink? I have allergies! Why are you such a weirdo? Huh? You know I put up with a lot from you, but this is . . .

JULES: Sarah, this is what this weekend is all about.

MARY-ANN: (*Very relaxed.*) This weekend is a call to action.

JULES: It's a rescue mission for you too.

MARY-ANN: (*Like a drunk.*) That's right!

SARAH: Shut up, Mary-Ann. I don't know what she did to you, but . . . Jules, what kind of drugs did you give Mary-Ann?
    (*She rubs her eyes, seeing things off in the distance.*)
It's getting closer. Oh, Jules. Help me. Who is coming? Why are there . . . are those . . . Lights. Cloaks. What is this?
    (*She starts to hyperventilate.*)

MARY-ANN: Jules is so smart. You know that she told me this was a rescue mission to save you. We planned all of this to release you from your anxiety over your job.

SARAH: Me? (*Breathing a quick little yoga breath.*) I don't have any anxiety issues whatsoever. And if I did have them, I would vent at my therapist's office and ahhhh (*She screams.*) take drugs like normal people . . . Are these people wearing dark cloaks holding candles your friends? ARE WE HERE TO BE SACRIFICED?

MARY-ANN: Oh, calm down. You are the one who is such an overachiever. Why do you always have to be so perfect, Sarah? Ever since high school, perfect grades, perfect hair, perfect boyfriends . . .

SARAH: Don't forget the perfect college—Princeton. And perfect skin and teeth.

JULES: Yes, everything is perfect. Except your job. You hate your boss, don't you?

SARAH: NO, I love my job. Can I go home now? Please?

JULES: She gets under your skin.

MARY-ANN: She does. She wouldn't even let you present your color-coded presentation. And we know what happened.

SARAH: What?

JULES: Why don't you give up, Sarah?
    (She takes the oar and rows slowly. MARY-ANN now starts to row.)
What are you doing?

MARY-ANN: I called you last week.

SARAH: So?

MARY-ANN: At work.

SARAH: So, I was . . . hey . . . where are we going? Why are you rowing so quickly?

JULES: What if she was here, tied up, and you could torture her?

SARAH: I don't want to . . . do that.
    (She sees something frightening.)
What's going on? Who are those people?

MARY-ANN: Just go with it. Tell the bitch boss how you feel. We know she fired you.

SARAH: She didn't. I've been . . .

JULES: You got fired two weeks ago, and you've been pretending to get up and go to work.

MARY-ANN: How long did you think you could hide it from us?

(JULES turns and is suddenly holding the oar in a frightening position over SARAH's head.)

JULES: It's okay, it's okay. This is just going to take a minute.

SARAH: (*Crying.*) So this weekend is about more than waxing and facials?

JULES: Oh, it's about much more.

MARY-ANN: I think it's great.

MARY-ANN: Why would you hide being fired, Sarah?

JULES: From us—your best friends.

SARAH: Who are those people?

MARY-ANN: I don't know what you're talking about. I don't see anybody.

(JULES hands SARAH the oar.)

JULES: It's your mind, Sarah. Tell them, tell us why you want to hide everything and pretend your life is so perfect.

MARY-ANN: Yes, tell us.

(SARAH grabs the oar and swings out at the trees.)

SARAH: Because . . . everyone wants to be perfect . . . don't they?
(Looking out, wanting her problems to be solved, she gets angrier and swings again and again as she screams.)
What's wrong with wanting something and talking about it until it becomes a reality? What's wrong with desiring a little perfection? How come you are so quiet, Jules? Don't you have any problems? Haven't you ever had some monumental failure that you've wanted to hide?

MARY-ANN: But failing is okay. I do it all the time.

JULES: Are the lights gone now? Are the people gone? Do you feel safe?

SARAH: They are gone, yes. But . . .

(There is the sound of police sirens and a male voice on a loudspeaker.)

POLICEMAN: (*Offstage.*) Julia Jones. We have you surrounded. Row the boat in safely.

SARAH: Oh my God.

POLICEMAN: (*Offstage.*) The other two women with you, Sarah Mills and Mary-Ann Bailey, please row the boat in. Julia Jones, keep your hands up, way up.

MARY-ANN: Oh my God. What have you done?

SARAH: Jules, what have you done?

(*JULES raises her hands way up as the other women row quickly.*)

(*Blackout. We hear screams from all three women and gunshots. Lights up on SARAH and MARY-ANN rowing alone, wearing different outfits. It's years later.*)

SARAH: So here we are.

MARY-ANN: It's been such a long time.
(*She takes a deep breath.*)
Remember those people you thought were in the trees?

(*SARAH takes another breath in and thinks before she speaks.*)

SARAH: Let's just enjoy the day, shall we? We made a promise.

MARY-ANN: Jules would be proud of us, for making it back here . . . after everything . . .

SARAH: She would, she'd be really proud.
(*She takes another long inhale.*)

MARY-ANN: If only she were alive.

SARAH: I know, I know. But let's not talk about it.
(*Beat.*)

MARY-ANN: It's just that . . .

SARAH: Mary-Ann . . .

MARY-ANN: But we didn't know that she had killed Maria.

SARAH: Well . . . she paid the ultimate price.

MARY-ANN: It was so awful. Executed.

SARAH: You know, Jules just wanted us to cleanse ourselves.

MARY-ANN: So we wouldn't do anything irrational, like she did, I know. She was a good woman, Jules.

SARAH: The best.

(They reflect on this for a moment.)

MARY-ANN: Somehow it reminds me of Dan.

SARAH: Why's that?

MARY-ANN: Oh . . . 'cause I wanted to kill him.

SARAH: But you didn't, and you wouldn't, right?

MARY-ANN: No, of course not. But it's good to talk about those dark feelings.

SARAH: And obsess . . .

MARY-ANN: If we need to.

SARAH: Right.

MARY-ANN: How's your boss these days?

SARAH: I am the boss.

MARY-ANN: It's okay to be perfect, Sarah.

SARAH: I know, but people will always hate you for it. And you have to find it in your heart to forgive. I have underlings . . . who drive me mad. They can't do a thing right. Fashion is a tough business.

MARY-ANN: That reminds me of Billy. He's so fashionable.

SARAH: I thought you and Billy broke up last month.

MARY-ANN: We did, we did. But did I ever tell you about the first time we met?

SARAH: Many times.

MARY-ANN: Would you like to hear it again?

SARAH: Absolutely.

MARY-ANN: Well . . . he was wearing one of his sexy suits, right . . . and I was just standing on 34th and 7th trying to hail a cab and he asked to share a cab with me?

(Lights begin to lower as the women row and MARY-ANN continues to blab on and on.)

I said okay, he said where are you going? We were going to the same place—it was like fate or something.

(Blackout.)

END OF PLAY

I KNOW

by Jacquelyn Reingold

I Know was first produced at Ensemble Studio Theatre in their Marathon of One-Act Plays, June 2011. It was directed by Dan Bonell, and acted by Beth Dixon and Jack Davidson.

Jacquelyn Reingold writes for theater and television. Her plays, which include *String Fever, Touch Me Somewhere Else, I Know, They Float Up, Girl Gone, A Very Very Short Play, 2B (or not 2B)*, and *Acapulco*, have been seen in New York at Ensemble Studio Theatre, Naked Angels and MCC Theatre; at Actors Theatre of Louisville, Portland Center Stage in Oregon, PlayLabs in Minneapolis; and in London, Dublin, Berlin, Belgrade, and Hong Kong. Honors and awards include: New York Foundation of the Arts playwriting grant, two Sloan Foundation commissions, and the Kennedy Center Fund for New American Plays. She was a finalist for the Susan Smith Blackburn prize and received MacDowell Colony and Hermitage Artist Retreat Fellowships. She has been published in two *Women Playwrights: The Best Plays* anthologies (Smith and Kraus), in several *Best American Short Plays* (Applause Theatre and Cinema Books), and by Samuel French, Vintage Books, Dramatists Play Service (*Things Between U*, a collection of her one-act plays). Several of her short plays have been recorded for radio/podcast by Playing-on-Air. In television, Jacquelyn is a Writer/Co-Executive Producer for *The Good Fight*. She wrote for Netflix's *Grace and Frankie,* and all the Mia episodes for HBO's Emmy-nominated *In Treatment*, starring Gabriel Byrne and Hope Davis. She is a playwright member of Ensemble Studio Theater, an alumna of New Dramatists, and a proud founding member of Honor Roll.

CHARACTERS

LILA ZWICKER: 70s, an actress.
DANIEL RASKIN: 70s, an actor.

PLACE

A Manhattan apartment.

TIME

Now.

• • •

Living room in a prewar New York City apartment. The furniture is worn, comfortable, holding up. Lots of bookcases and books. A good rug. Real art on the walls, and maybe some theater posters. A couple of photos of Daniel in his favorite roles. One photo of LILA when she was young and perfectly, almost painfully, beautiful. LILA is on the couch. In her 70s, she is beautiful, perhaps more than ever. She is waiting for DANIEL, maybe with a cup of tea. It is evening. DANIEL enters, like a storm, with bags of groceries.

DANIEL: (*With pace and drive.*) Hello, darling—happy to see you—I missed you—you look beautiful as always—no, *more* beautiful, though how that is even possible I cannot imagine.

    (*He kisses her.*)

How are you? (*No response.*) Well, I had a helluvan actor's nightmare of a day, so to make things a little worse, I went shopping at Fairway. Remember when it was just a store with good produce, and all you had to fear were the crazy ladies with their carts? Now it has its own zip code, and every time I go, everything's been moved, so it makes even less sense than the no sense it used to make. You hungry? I thought I'd make a special "Daniel Raskin" dinner. With back rub for dessert. (*No response.*) How 'bout a drink? I know I could use one.

    (*He heads for the kitchen, keeps talking.*)

You wouldn't believe the audition I had: some godawful movie about Libyan terrorists living in an air pocket below the Hudson, who, when discovered by outer space aliens, mate to create Mutant Terrorists poised to take over the world, and *I*, if cast, would have the memorable pleasure of playing a night watchman who utters the very important words "What are you doing here?" then gets killed by the Aliens' plutonium shooting third arm—for scale.

(He enters with glasses, bottle, pours drinks.)

So, I went to my agent's office to suggest I not be submitted for such garbage, and, between phone calls, he told me that all the casting directors who say I'm a pain in the ass are wrong, which, of course, was his way of telling me what he really thinks of me, without actually saying it. He did, however, mention five or six times, that if *you* were interested in changing your theatrical representation, since everyone loves *you,* he'd be thrilled to take you on and steal your ten percent.

(He gives them each a drink.)

So, my dearest and amazing woman, here's to you, because above all else, no matter what happens, and how awful it is or might be, I adore you. As I enter the lobby, slip past our sleeping doorman, I'm filled with anticipatory delight, and when I step into the elevator, it's not the only thing that albeit, slowly, starts going up. How are you? What did you do today? Tell me everything. *(No answer.)* What's going on? Is it monologue night?

LILA: I think you should go.

DANIEL: Go where?

LILA: Just, leave. It would be best.

DANIEL: I'm not fully understanding, my love. Maybe you could fill me in a little.

LILA: It's over. Ok? It's done. So . . .

DANIEL: What do you mean?

LILA: I don't want to fight or have a big drama, so if we can do this quietly . . .

DANIEL: What's going on?

LILA: I'm asking you to leave.

DANIEL: What—you don't want to me cook? We'll go out. Or I'll order in . . .

LILA: I'm not joking.

DANIEL: How about sushi?

LILA: Stop it. All the charm, the chat, the-the scudding cloudage.

(He, finally, stops everything. Looks at her.)

I know.

DANIEL: Ok. What do you know?

LILA: I know you have been free to do what you wish.

DANIEL: I think by now it's pretty clear for whom I wish.

LILA: You lied. And cheated.

DANIEL: How exactly did I do that?

LILA: Dorothy Englewood.

DANIEL: Dottie Englewood? She's been dead twenty years.

LILA: I know.

DANIEL: The tap dancer with no rhythm?

LILA: Maybe she had some with her shoes off.

DANIEL: That's funny.

LILA: It's good we're not married; it makes this easier.

DANIEL: Lila, many things happened between us, over many years.

LILA: Don't change the subject. You're very good at that, you know you are: you avoid, you distract.

DANIEL: Why are you bringing this up now?

LILA: See, you did it again.

DANIEL: Whether I did or did not sleep with Dorothy Englewood more than two decades ago, does not strike me as grounds for kicking me out of here today.

LILA: Don't make this complicated.

DANIEL: It's you and me, Lila, everything is complicated.

LILA: This is simple.

DANIEL: Did she send a letter from the grave, and it arrived today, "I fucked Daniel Raskin. Yours truly, Dorothy"?

LILA: Did you?

DANIEL: Does it matter?

LILA: Of course it matters.

DANIEL: Why?

LILA: Because everything matters, ok?

DANIEL: My love, we are not exactly conventional people. We are brimming with passion. Since when is—uh—retroactive monogamy your greatest concern? (*No response.*) Don't shut me out, Lie, you put up that wall and there's no way to get through.

LILA: This isn't open to debate. This is something if one of us says, the other one doesn't get to argue. If you had said it first, and I always feared you would, I would have had to accept it, no matter what I felt.

DANIEL: Why would you have that fear? What have I ever done . . . ?

LILA: Oh, Danny, don't even try! Point is: two people together, married or not, when one says it's over, the other doesn't get to insist it isn't.

DANIEL: Bullshit! I insist. I don't care about whatever you just said. This is not happening.

LILA: You're mistaken.

DANIEL: No. I have made a million mistakes in my life: Mondale, Dukakis, Castro—maybe. Jill Stein—definitely. And, ok, telling Jerry Zaks, Daniel Sullivan, Doug Hughes, Andre Bishop, and Bernie Gersten that they were egomaniacal fascists, those were mistakes. Not to mention: Sidney Pollack and Marty Scorcese.

LILA: Joe Papp.

DANIEL: I never said that to Joe. (*Beat.*) Ok, I said something like that. But at that moment it was true. Point is, or was: I admit it. I make mistakes. Big ones. But this, being here, is not one of them. This is the thing I did right.

LILA: I packed your things.

DANIEL: *What?*

LILA: You can go to Abigail's. I already called her.

DANIEL: You called my daughter? You don't even like her.

LILA: That is not true—I may not feel—a lot of warmth for her, because she is, well, a borderline borderline, but I do, in my way, like her.

DANIEL: Did you pack all my things?

LILA: Most of them.

DANIEL: My Drama Desk?

(She nods.)

My Obie?

(She nods.)

My Chekhov?

(She shakes her head no.)

Well, I'm not going.

LILA: You don't have a choice.

DANIEL: I do own the apartment.

LILA: So, you'd rather *I* leave?

DANIEL: This is crazy. At our age? I'm seventy-five, who cares what happened . . .

LILA: I know, Daniel. You think I didn't know? I knew. Every lie. For forty years. Every late-night rehearsal, every ball game, every time you 'didn't hear the phone ring,' every time I came home and my things had been removed then replaced. You think I didn't notice? I noticed. Every meal that was cooked for you, every gift you got, every excuse, every explanation, every woman's smell you brought into our bed. You think I don't know your type? I can't spot her at each opening or closing night party? You know what it's like, to feel that? To wonder—always. Who is he with? How much younger is she, how round are her hips, how smooth is her face? Does he kiss her like he used to kiss me?

DANIEL: Oh, Lila, that is so not—*I* kiss you. I would like to kiss you. Right now. I . . .

LILA: Don't.

DANIEL: Let me. You're upset, all right. I want to hold you.

LILA: Don't. I don't want that.

DANIEL: Ok, then tell me what you want, I'll do whatever you say.

LILA: I want the truth. Tell me the truth. About her.

(*Beat.*)

DANIEL: I slept with Dorothy Englewood, thirty years ago. She was gorgeous. The sex was exquisite. I craved her like you can't believe. For years. But I ended it after that one time. Because of you. That's the truth.

LILA: Thank you. Now go.

DANIEL: Lila.

LILA: I don't respect you. As a partner. As a man.

(*He doesn't move.*)

I don't want you in my life. You have to give me this. *GO.*

(*DANIEL, at a loss, exits, but takes nothing. The 'wall' crumbles, as LILA falls in on herself. Maybe she manages to get up. Looks through the peephole: no DANIEL. Maybe she looks out the window. DANIEL enters quietly, he sees her in her true state, before she sees him.*)

DANIEL: Lila . . .

LILA: (*Overlaps.*) Get out, I told you—to get out!

DANIEL: (*Overlaps.*) Listen . . .

LILA: (*Overlaps.*) You left, so you cannot come back . . .

DANIEL: Sweetheart, please . . .

LILA: Once you go—you're gone . . .

DANIEL: Ok, but I didn't even . . .

(*LILA maybe tries to push him out.*)

LILA: Stop it, just stop it. Do as you're told.

DANIEL: That's what I'm trying . . .

LILA: This is your chance, Danny.

DANIEL: Ok, calm down . . .

LILA: You are impossible, sneaking in, spying on me. I will not have it.

DANIEL: Ok, wait . . .

LILA: I am kicking you out.
       (She throws something at him.)
Out! Out!

DANIEL: I know.

LILA: You always have an answer and it always sounds right, but it's usually wrong.

DANIEL: I know.

LILA: You're like a Chihuahua, you won't shut up and you won't go away!

DANIEL: Lila, I know. He called me. Aberwacky, Athernacky, whatever his name is.

       (LILA freezes.)

LILA: Abernathy.

DANIEL: Yes. He called me. Today. After you left his office.

LILA: He shouldn't have done that.

DANIEL: Well, he did.

LILA: He isn't allowed. You're not my . . .

DANIEL: Well, maybe to him, I am.
       (He approaches her.)
Why didn't you tell me? I didn't even know there was a problem. You've been fine, for what, eleven years?

       (She nods.)

I would have gone with you. I want to go with you. We'll get another opinion.

LILA: No. This is what I want.

DANIEL: How 'bout what I want?

LILA: Look at me, Dan. What's left of me? I . . . I won't be able to work. Me—not working?

DANIEL: Well, if we lived in a sane country with sane values, there would be a theater built for you, playwrights would be paid to write for you, and directors would have to audition—for you.

LILA: Ok, Danny, that's not what I'm saying . . .

DANIEL: We give our lives to the theater, and, no, it doesn't exactly give back, that's not why we do it, but when you're not respected, it can turn you into a Chihuahua like me, but *you*, what is left of *you*? You are luminous. Your exquisite humanity abounds: on stage and off. I adore you more than I know how to say. I mean, *I* am a pain in the ass. *You* are a national treasure.

LILA: Danny, I already can't walk across the park, my knees don't want to hold my torso, which is in worse shape than my legs. My breasts, I cannot even talk about. My face is falling, no—fallen. When we sleep, I lie like a plank, because if I try to curve, against you, even a little, it hurts. And all of that is just aging, normal, crappy aging, but *now* . . .

DANIEL: Ok . . .

LILA: No. Listen. There are no other opinions. There is no ambiguity. I am not going to get better. I am not even going to get slowly worse. It is going to end. *We* are going to end. This may be the best moment I will have. And it sucks. This moment truly sucks. So, please. I am doing this for you.

DANIEL: You're not.

LILA: I am being selfless. Generous.

DANIEL: If you were being generous, you would not deny me the privilege of being with you. And if God or fate, or whatever it is, is cruel or indifferent or fucked up enough to take you first, then I am goddamn going to walk with you every step of the way. There is no ambiguity.

LILA: Ok, then I'm being selfish. And doing it for me. Because I don't want you here. I don't want you to see me. I can't. Do you understand? It is hard enough, every day, at my age, to let you see me like this. Ok?

DANIEL: But . . .

LILA: And don't tell me you don't like young, sexy women. I know you.

DANIEL: Ok, I like women; it's true. I love to look at them, their bodies, their faces, but so do you. I am not the only one who is drawn to others, you know that. But what we have, it's not comparable to a pair of breasts, and I love breasts, I do. But this . . .
    (He indicates them.)
has meaning. Us. Our life. I would never . . .

LILA: I know how you'll look at me. I don't want to see that look. I can't bear it. And I don't have to. We're not married.

DANIEL: Why is that, anyway?

LILA: Because you never asked.

DANIEL: You never insisted.

LILA: Why would I insist, Danny? Why would I have had to insist? People used to tell me that all the time: the only way to make a man propose is to give him an ultimatum. No thanks. That's not how I wanted it.

DANIEL: How did you want it?

LILA: Forget it. It doesn't matter now.

DANIEL: Maybe it does.

LILA: No, it is utterly irrelevant. Now.

DANIEL: But at one time, you would have liked it.

LILA: At one time, yes. I wanted a big party. I wanted my mother to be there. Our friends. Your family. I wanted you to stand up and say it, in front of everyone. But whenever I brought it up, you went on a tirade, accused me of all kinds of things, or you took a mental vacation, twice, I swear, you fell asleep while I was talking, so, well, I dropped it . . .

    (DANIEL, with some difficulty, gets down and kneels on one knee.)

What are you doing?

DANIEL: I should have done this decades ago.

LILA: Stop.

DANIEL: Truth is, I thought I needed to leave the door open—just a little. Dumb.

LILA: Get up.

DANIEL: Once I'm down, I don't think I can get up. I, uh, I didn't buy this, 'cause you know how I feel about the gold mining industry, but. Here.
(He pulls a ring out.)
It was my mother's.

LILA: Where did you get that?

DANIEL: Abigail had it.

LILA: You went to Abigail's today?

(He nods.)

After the doctor called?
(He nods. She takes this in.)

So, when you came in, you were . . .

DANIEL: Yes.

LILA: But you left, when I said I didn't respect you, you left.

DANIEL: No. I walked to the elevator, and came back. I did not leave. I made a false exit. I didn't know what else to do. Nothing could ever make me leave. Ok?

(She is overcome. This is what she wanted to hear. She tries to contain it. He touches her.)

LILA: Ok. But we're not getting married. It would be foolish. You *do* own the apartment. And. You understand what could happen—the amount of money you could owe, if we're married? The medical debt you'd end up with. Let's be practical. The answer is no.

DANIEL: Yes, of course, you're right. As usual. (*A beat.*) But to be blunt, I don't give a shit about being practical, since when are we people who care more about money than love? So. Though I'm sure I don't deserve you, I am humbly asking anyway, because I have to, I want to, I need to: Lila Zwicker, will you marry me?
(Beat.)

LILA: The reason I never insisted—and I thought about it maybe every day—for decades. But I was afraid. I didn't want to be without you. Because. I so. Enjoyed. You. Every day. All of you.

DANIEL: Please put your hand out, my legs are killing me.

(She puts out her hand. He puts the ring on her finger.)

With this ring, I thee wed, and with all I am and all I have I honor you. You were my yesterday . . .

LILA: You are my today . . .

LILA and DANIEL: You will be my tomorrow.

LILA: Look, it's too big.

DANIEL: My mother had fat fingers. Kiss me.

(They kiss. He tries to get up, but can't. She helps him.)

Doctors can be wrong, you know.

LILA: I know.

DANIEL: Are you hungry?

LILA: Starving.

DANIEL: Me, too.

LILA: That wasn't it, was it? I mean, you actually *do* want to get married. For real.

DANIEL: I do.

LILA: *(She nods.)* Let's make dinner.

DANIEL: Yes. But first.
    (He kisses or touches her.)
I want you. Again, and again.

(She kisses or touches him.)

Then we'll make dinner.

(They embrace passionately.)

END OF PLAY

INAUGURATION

by Jenny Lyn Bader

Inauguration was performed by La Jolla Theatre Ensemble on January 26–27, 2020, as part of their presentation of Jenny Lyn Bader's short play cycle *The Age of Trump* in La Jolla, California. It was directed by John Carroll Tessmer. The cast was as follows:

ALEXANDER: Cris O'Bryon
PAULETTE: Joy Yvonne Jones
DINA: Julie Alexandria

Jenny Lyn Bader's recent productions include *Mrs. Stern Wanders the Prussian State Library* (Luna Stage) and *Equally Divine* (Theater at the 14th St. Y). Other plays include *In Flight* (Turn to Flesh Productions), *Manhattan Casanova* (Hudson Stage), and *None of the Above* (New Georges). One-acts include *Worldness* (Humana Festival of New American Plays), *Miss America* (NY International l Fringe Festival/Best of Fringe selection), and *Beta Testing* (Symphony Space). Jenny Lyn co-founded Theatre 167, for when she co-wrote *The Jackson Heights Trilogy* and *The Church of Why Not*. For This Is Not a Theatre Company, she wrote the audio play *The International Local* (Subway Plays app) and co-authored *Café Play* (Cornelia St. Café) and the immersive audio spa *Play in Your Bathtub*. A Harvard graduate, she has received the 2019 Best Documentary One-Woman Show Award (United Solo Festival); 2019 Athena Fellowship; Lark Fellowship; and the O'Neill Center's Edith Oliver Award for a playwright who has, in the spirit of the late *New Yorker* critic, "a caustic wit that deflates the ego but does not unduly damage the human spirit." Her work has been published by Applause

Theatre and Cinema Books, Dramatists Play Service, Smith and Kraus, Vintage, W.W. Norton, and the *New York Times,* where she served as a frequent contributor to the "Week in Review." She belongs to the Dramatists Guild. For more, see www.jennylynbader.com.

CHARACTERS

ALEXANDER, a reporter, 30s–40s.
PAULETTE, a museum curator, 30s–40s.
DINA, a reporter, 30s–40s.

TIME

January 2017. Evening.

PLACE

A restaurant.

• • •

January 2017. A bistro in Washington, DC. ALEXANDER *("ALEX") and* PAULETTE *are on a date and it's going well.*

ALEX: So, tell me more about the exhibit!

PAULETTE: It's going to be very exciting because the whole Vernay collection will be in one place.

ALEX: And how often does that happen? Give or take?

PAULETTE: You don't follow art at all, do you?

ALEX: No, but I love it. I want to learn.

PAULETTE: Never. It happens never. Has never happened. It's a historic first!

ALEX: Wow!

PAULETTE: I'm sorry I said that about you not following art, that was rude. I was just surprised you didn't know, 'cause there's been so much hype.

ALEX: I'm sure there has. In the . . . (*Dismissively.*) . . . arts section.

PAULETTE: You don't read the arts section?

ALEX: Oh, I do, of course, a lot of the time! But, during the election this fall, I guess I started reading it less and less . . . because I got so obsessed, you know, with some of the other sections.

PAULETTE: I know, everyone did. It was probably the most important election in our lifetime.

ALEX: Our lifetime? In American history.

PAULETTE: You think?

ALEX: When's the last time the American people suddenly spitefully elected someone so utterly obnoxious? . . . I guess Andrew Jackson. But still, it felt so unprecedented, so surprising . . .

PAULETTE: I was surprised. But were you? Even with . . .

ALEX: Yeah, you would think, with my job, I would have seen this coming, right? Nope. No clue. Wait, how did we get onto this?

PAULETTE: It's impossible to avoid right now. And you were saying you had stopped reading the arts section . . .

ALEX: Oh yeah. There was all that obsessive news reading around the election. And then, the holidays. When I need to relax and read fewer sections. You know what I mean?

PAULETTE: Please. I get it. Now, I've met people who've *never* read the arts section. And *that* would be . . . unthinkable.

ALEX: Of course, it would! So. Tell me more. About the exhibit.

PAULETTE: Really?

ALEX: Yes. I want to hear it.

PAULETTE: Okay. What I love most about the work of Vernay is the subtlety of the . . . Alex? Are you okay? Why are you looking over there?

ALEX: Congressional sighting. Three o'clock.

PAULETTE: I'm sorry, which one?

ALEX: In the green power tie . . . Rick Crawford. Montana.

PAULETTE: Wow. Interesting. What's he into?

ALEX: Oh, who knows? . . . Okay, I know. Livestock subsidies.

PAULETTE: Can you recognize any member of Congress?

ALEX: Pretty much.

PAULETTE: I learn so much from you.

ALEX: And I from you.

PAULETTE: Really? Because we met so recently, but sometimes, I feel . . .

ALEX: Insecure?

PAULETTE: Is that what I feel?

ALEX: It's what we all feel.

PAULETTE: I guess. So, what I mean about Vernay . . . Alex? You seem distracted.

ALEX: One sec.

PAULETTE: Who are you waving at? Is this another congressional sighting?

ALEX: Nuh-uh.

PAULETTE: Senate?

ALEX: No, no . . . It's someone I . . .
   (Calls out.)
Hey, Kenigsberg!

   (DINA approaches.)

DINA: Fitz! Oh my god!

ALEX: I thought you were back in the Chicago bureau! What are you doing here?

DINA: They gave me a new beat.

ALEX: Oh yeah? What is it?

DINA: The Court.

ALEX: Get out! The Court? That's incredible. You always wanted that.

DINA: I know.

ALEX: This calls for a drink.

DINA: Oh, I don't want to interrupt your . . .

ALEX: Please, it's no interruption. We're just sharing a beautiful bottle of wine. We have extra glasses because they're for water, but water is not as fun as wine. (*Pouring wine.*) And Paulette won't mind, right, Paulette? It's not like it's our first date. It's . . . (*Mentally counts for a moment.*) our fifth!

PAULETTE: Fourth. Don't rush me.

ALEX: Right. Fourth. Paulette, this is Dina. She's a fellow journalist.

PAULETTE: Mm. You guys have worked together?

ALEX: Not exactly together, but together. Aaah, let's not talk about all that. Dina's got a great new job now that she's wanted since she was . . . seventeen?

DINA: Fourteen.

ALEX: I knew it was some precocious age.

DINA: Oh, it was a tender, tender age. You hear Ellie got posted to London?

ALEX: No! Now, that's an assignment she'd like.

DINA: She does. Certainly a lot more than . . .

ALEX: (*Changing the subject quickly.*) How about this wine?

DINA: (*Sipping.*) Mmm. Can you believe the inauguration is coming up? Hey, Congressman Crawford. Three o'clock.

ALEX: I saw!

DINA: He's eating steak.

ALEX: Appropriate.

DINA: And there's an about-to-be former cabinet member at the bar.

ALEX: No! Which?

DINA: You're slipping! Transportation.

ALEX: Well-spotted! It's good to see you, Dina.

DINA: And you. (*To* PAULETTE.) And to meet you. Thanks for letting me join your fifth-fourth date.

PAULETTE: The fifth-fourth is the charm.

DINA: You work on the Hill?

PAULETTE: No. By the Hill. Near the Hill . . . At the Smithsonian. The art museum. I'm an archivist.

DINA: And is that fun?

PAULETTE: It's incredible because it's all new. I've never done this exact job before.

DINA: Just like our president-elect.

PAULETTE: (*A little offended.*) But I've worked in the field!

DINA: Oh, that's different then . . . It's amazing what's happening over there. At your museum. With the entire Vernay collection coming over? It's a whole festival of subtlety.

ALEX: Why, you little show-off.

DINA: What? It was all over the arts section. (*To* PAULETTE.) Alex doesn't really read that.

PAULETTE: How do you know which sections he reads?

DINA: Oh, because we were . . .

ALEX: Long story.

PAULETTE: Did you two date?

DINA and ALEX: (*Simultaneously.*) No!

DINA: So, Paulette, how did you and Alex meet?

PAULETTE: We met cute. I was walking my dog. Pissarro. And Pissarro just runs up to Alex.

DINA: Really?

ALEX: I had beef jerky in my pocket.

DINA: Why?

ALEX: Uh, I was on assignment at a hotel and the restaurant had closed and I had to get food at the gift shop so it was cheese and crackers, Tic Tacs, or beef jerky. I got all three, and then remembered I don't like beef jerky, so it was just in my jacket pocket for a while.

DINA: Bizarre. Okay. So, the dog comes up to you.

ALEX: And at first, I have no idea why. But then I realize, and soon enough I offer the beef jerky to Pissarro and myself to Paulette.

PAULETTE: We just started talking. I mean, I had to, my dog was trying to fix us up!

DINA: It was fate! Or . . . jerky.

ALEX: Some combination thereof.

DINA: What kind of dog is Pissarro?

PAULETTE: Cavalier King Charles.

DINA: The sweetest and happiest of dogs.

PAULETTE: Yes!

ALEX: He did cheer me up.

PAULETTE: Alex was having some kind of post-traumatic stress reaction after the election.

DINA: Yeah, we all were.

PAULETTE: All Americans?

DINA: That too. (*To* ALEX.) Why won't you just tell her how we met? She's probably imagining something terrible by now.

ALEX: I'm just concerned that . . . Uch, you're right. I'll tell her. (*Confessing to* PAULETTE.) Dina was one of the reporters with me on the campaign bus.

PAULETTE: Oh! Wow. What was that like? Alex said he's not as troubling in person as on TV?

DINA: Mmm, usually in small groups he cohered more. And on the phone, he really kept it together on the phone, if you were calling on behalf of a major news outlet. Of course, there were times he cohered less, like when he yelled at all the reporters as a group and instead of saying our names, called us "The Media." Who knows? No one has any idea what he's gonna do next. We need to keep an eye on this one.

ALEX: Absolutely! Too bad we don't have a front-row seat anymore.

DINA: So, what's the big deal? Why didn't you want to tell her I was on the campaign bus with you?

ALEX: I don't know, it's not anything, I just . . .

PAULETTE: I think I know why. On our first date, Alex said you all got so close to the people on that bus, riding around for months, it was more intimate than having an affair with them. So, he just didn't want me to feel all . . .

DINA: Oh! Yeah, that's true. It's sort of a cross between an affair and group therapy. You get to know the other reporters' craziest fears and fantasies . . .

PAULETTE: Like what?

DINA: Okay, this one woman could not bear to be near mushrooms. Fungophobia. It became a bit of a problem on the campaign trail, both around farming communities and big banquets, so it really crossed boundaries, just like the campaign was trying to do. You just never knew when it was gonna . . . mushroom outta control!

PAULETTE: Oh no!

DINA: Then this one guy was a sleepwalker and would repeat the names of different supermodels during his walks. And just . . . late at night people would tell you stuff. I'll never forget the time one of the guys told me he had been obsessed with the inaugural parade since he was a small child and a political junkie growing up in DC, and when we got back, he was going to try to date a woman whose windows overlooked the inaugural parade. Just anyone who lived on the parade route! Of course, that was back when we all thought the election was gonna turn out differently . . . I wonder if he's still that jazzed about the inauguration.

PAULETTE: (*It hits her; she reacts coldly.*) Oh, I think he is. Once a political junkie, always a political junkie. (*A beat.*) I'm assuming that last one was Alex?

DINA: Yeah, it was. Are you saying you live . . . ?

PAULETTE: On Pennsylvania Avenue. (*To* ALEX.) So, you . . . You were just . . . using me for my windows!

ALEX: In my defense: in all these years living here, I have never seen the parade! And after all those months on that godforsaken bus covering that guy . . . and never knowing what he'd do next . . . and here we sort of know, right? It's a ceremony with such weight, such an extraordinary history. It's still that. Isn't it? Should we give up already, before it's even started? Here's possibly a chance to see him try. To try to behave with a little dignity. To try to be his best self. Maybe it's never too late to be your best self. Paulette: I know I'd like to try, if you let me! (*A pause as he waits for* PAULETTE *to react.*) And I . . . so enjoy hearing you talk about art.

PAULETTE: You've never read the arts section, have you?

ALEX: Is that a trick question?

PAULETTE: It's over. Just go.

ALEX: Good night.
   (*He starts to go.*)

DINA: I'll be right back, Paulette.
   (*Follows ALEX.*)
Alex, hey! Sorry about that. I didn't mean . . .

ALEX: Not your fault. Thought it was worth a shot. Just a little dream of mine. It's good to see you, inauguration or no inauguration. (*Beat.*) You think she's okay?

DINA: You go. I'll make sure she's okay.

ALEX: Women are so thoughtful. We should get together now that you're in town.

DINA: Definitely.

   (*ALEX exits. DINA returns to the table.*)

I just want to assure you, not all journalists are that ruthless.

PAULETTE: Just you two?

DINA: Sorry?

PAULETTE: You figured it out right away, didn't you?

DINA: Pretty much. The timeframe checked out. The lack of common interests. The mysteriously convenient beef jerky.

PAULETTE: "Fate . . . or jerky!" You called it. More wine?

(*They clink glasses.*)

DINA: To Alex, who, when I told him I was coming back here, said, "Women are so thoughtful!"

PAULETTE: (*Laughing.*) And did you explain?

DINA: What was I supposed to say? Paulette and I just made friends in the same few moments while she was realizing she shouldn't date you?

PAULETTE: More or less. Thank you so much. I had a feeling he was up to something. You want to order?

DINA: Yeah, I'm starving. What's good here?

PAULETTE: Anything involving red meat or kale. Are you gonna date him?

DINA: I don't know! On the bus it was like we were all on one big date, so it felt unnecessary.

PAULETTE: Right.

DINA: But now, I'm not sure. He's got that manipulative side . . . I know people who had already booked their airline tickets, train tickets, thinking we'd be having a historic inauguration of the first woman president . . . and now they're rerouting their plans to go anywhere else. It's amazing he's still so fixated.

PAULETTE: Mmm. Not as many people have been asking me about coming over to watch this year.

DINA: Really?

PAULETTE: I think you're right.

DINA: About what?

PAULETTE: It won't be quite as well-attended. As it has been.

DINA: Did I say that?

PAULETTE: You basically did. But he's right too.

DINA: About what?

PAULETTE: No matter who's elected, it's never boring to watch the procession from my place.

DINA: So, tell me about these windows of yours.

PAULETTE: Twenty feet high. You'll have to come watch the inaugural parade with me.

DINA: I thought you'd never ask.

END OF PLAY

IS IT COLD IN HERE?

by Julie Weinberg

Original Production: Bridge Initiative: Women in Theater Bechdel Test Fest 2.0, Tempe, AZ, April 26–28, 2019.

Julie Weinberg has been the recipient of the Kennedy Center Mark Twain Prize for Comic Playwriting for *Bad Daughter,* Arizona's Bechdel 2.0 Short Play Prize for *Is It Cold in Here?* and a three-time finalist for KCCTF one-acts and short play divisions. *You're Not the Type*, commissioned by the Edna Ferber Estate, was included in Five by Ferber produced by NJ Rep in 2018 and published by Smith and Kraus. Other plays include *Face It,* featured in the Actors Studio New Works Festival, *Starring America* and *Pet Peeves,* an evening of seven plays that includes *Is It Cold in Here?* Her work has been produced and/or developed by NYC's Workshop Theatre, The Actors Studio, ATHE, The Warner Theater Festival, Ramapo College Emerging Play-wrights, Brooklyn's Gallery Players, Short and Sweet, Spokane's KYRS Radio among other venues. She is a proud member of the Dramatists Guild and Actors Equity and a graduate of Lesley University's MFA Program in Writing for Stage and Screen.

CHARACTERS

ESSIE, 70s, opinionated and strong and sarcastically funny.
JACKIE, Early 40s, Essie's baby, single and close to Mom.
CASSANDRA, Mid-forties, Essie's older daughter, married and mother of two, devoted to her daughters.

SIMON, 25–75, Supervising Cryonaut, earnest and happy. He loves his cause.

SETTING

A posh living room in Old Westbury, Long Island.

TIME

The present.

• • •

The sound of a cat yowling loudly and then lights come up on a posh living room in Old Westbury, Long Island. ESSIE lies on a bed in the middle of the room. JACKIE and CASSANDRA are sitting on two chairs they've pulled close to her, intent on her every word.

CASSANDRA: (*Shocked.*) What?

JACKIE: Mom—what did you just say?

CASSANDRA: Mother—this must be a joke. I don't understand.

ESSIE: What don't you understand?

CASSANDRA: We're talking frozen—like a steak?

JACKIE: They're going to freeze you?

ESSIE: That's right.

JACKIE: When? When is this happening?

ESSIE: When it's (*Beat.*) time.

CASSANDRA: You told me Mom's chemo was working.

JACKIE: (*Upset.*) That's what she told me.

ESSIE: Look at me, girls—you think the chemo's working?

JACKIE: Oh, Ma—you can't give up.

ESSIE: I'm not. I'm counting on the future. (*Slowly.*) In the future lies salvation.

CASSANDRA: What is all this? Who are you quoting?
(*She looks suspiciously at JACKIE.*)

JACKIE: Don't look at me. I know nothing.

CASSANDRA: Really? You're here morning, noon, and night.

JACKIE: Oh, so now that's a crime?

CASSANDRA: You told Mom to take Yoga. It almost killed her.

JACKIE: I didn't tell her to get herself frozen.

ESSIE: Please don't fight.

JACKIE: Ma—was this on PBS?

ESSIE: What's the difference?

CASSANDRA: (*Condescendingly.*) Jackie and I just want to understand.

ESSIE: Do not take that tone with me. It's called cryogenics. They freeze you when you die and wake you up later when they've cured your disease. I'll be back before you know it.

CASSANDRA: What if they're wrong? Who are these freezing people? Are they doctors? What does the oncologist say?

ESSIE: He's devastated. He thought if I stayed on chemo long enough, it would pay for his new kitchen in the Hamptons.

JACKIE: Ma—please. Just tell me why.

ESSIE: Look at me. I'm off antidepressants—finally. I'm not afraid to die. I will live again. I'll see my girls again. Maybe I'll wake up and you'll both be happy and fulfilled and . . . (*To* JACKIE.)

Maybe I'll have more grandchildren. (*More calmly.*) Girls—I want to live. What's so strange?

JACKIE: I want you to live. I don't want a frozen mother.

CASSANDRA: No one lives forever.

ESSIE: (*Sarcastically.*) Oh, thank you. I didn't know that.

JACKIE: Have you talked to anyone who's done this?

(Looking at JACKIE, CASSANDRA and ESSIE pause to consider this absurd question.)

CASSANDRA: One question. Are these people Nigerian?

JACKIE: Wait—wait. They have to cure cancer before they defrost you?

CASSANDRA: My God—do you have any idea how long that might take?

ESSIE: So much negativity in this family.

CASSANDRA: Jews don't do this.

JACKIE: Who cares about that?

CASSANDRA: I care. Our mother is sick.

JACKIE: Oh—I had no idea you knew.

CASSANDRA: I have a husband. I have kids. You try it, and then tell me what a terrible daughter I am.

JACKIE: Ma—why didn't you tell me?

ESSIE: I knew what you'd say.

JACKIE: What if I'm dead by the time they defrost you?

ESSIE: You'll be in your fifties. You'll still be young.

CASSANDRA: What am I going to tell my rabbi?

JACKIE: Your problem isn't Mom dying—or being frozen. Your problem is what to tell your rabbi?

CASSANDRA: You may no longer care that you're Jewish, but I do. (*To* ESSIE.) We can't even sit Shiva for you.
    (*Beat.*)

JACKIE: (*Beat.*) Mom, I will respect your wishes—whatever they are.

CASSANDRA: I respect her wishes. I respect your wishes, Mom. I'm just upset.

JACKIE: (*Starting to sniffle.*) I'm beyond upset.

ESSIE: I'm sorry, girls—but it had to be talked about.

CASSANDRA: (*Thinks.*) Ma—doesn't this cost money?

ESSIE: Of course it costs money.

CASSANDRA: Just how much money are we talking about?

ESSIE: You can't put a price on immortality.

CASSANDRA: Try.

ESSIE: Don't interrogate me.

CASSANDRA: Have you signed something? Don't sign anything before I read it.

ESSIE: Don't worry—they're good people. They were so sweet about Kenny.

JACKIE: Kenny? What about Kenny?

ESSIE: Kenny's coming with me. He's been so sick—hides under the bed all day. (*Calls cat.*)

Kenny? Ken-Ken? (*To them.*) They're coming for Kenny today.

CASSANDRA: Have you lost your mind? You've been hoaxed.

ESSIE: How could I abandon him? He's my best friend.

JACKIE: You're choosing the cat over me?

ESSIE: Honey—I thought you worked on that in therapy. I can't afford to freeze the whole family.

JACKIE: This is a nightmare. Somebody, wake me up.

CASSANDRA: (*To* JACKIE.) She's choosing the cat over her grandchildren. That's what's appalling.

ESSIE: Don't be absurd. They don't freeze children.
        (*Pauses, then laughs.*)

CASSANDRA: Mother—I believe the cancer drugs could be affecting your mind.

ESSIE: Cassandra—I don't need your opinion or your permission.

JACKIE: She's right—it's her money.

CASSANDRA: Not if we get her declared incompetent.

ESSIE: Over my dead body.

CASSANDRA: If necessary.

JACKIE: What are you saying? She's not crazy.

CASSANDRA: Let's just see. Mother—what day is this? Who's the president?

ESSIE: It's Sunday, May 19th, 2019. (*Painful.*) Do not make me say his name.

JACKIE: See?

CASSANDRA: Ma—what's his name?

ESSIE: I can't . . . Okay, Donald Trump. You happy now?
    (*Looks at them both earnestly.*)
Girls, it's simple. Do you want me or my money?

JACKIE: Ma—what a question.

CASSANDRA: Mom, this scam is going to hurt us all. Don't you see that?

ESSIE: All I see is the future. I like having a future.
    (*Beat.*)

CASSANDRA: Mom, we're broke. (*Pause.*) Bob lost everything with Madoff, you remember? We still haven't made it back.

JACKIE: (*Suspicious.*) Wait a minute. Is that true?

CASSANDRA: Don't you want the girls at Vassar? We can't do it without you, Mom.

    (*ESSIE takes a moment.*)

ESSIE: I suppose I could just freeze my head.

CASSANDRA: What? What do you mean?

ESSIE: There's a head-only option. They freeze your head but dispose of the rest of you. Many people do that.

JACKIE: Oh my God—that's horrible.

ESSIE: It's a lot less expensive. The girls could go to Vassar.

JACKIE: Absolutely not—they can get loans. Cass—tell her.

CASSANDRA: (*Thinks.*) Tell me a little more about this head-only thing.

ESSIE: By the time they defrost me, I might be able to choose a new body. Doesn't that sound like fun?

JACKIE: Not another word. I can't allow this.

ESSIE: You two seem to think you have some control here. This is my body, my life—my death. And I am in charge.

(*The doorbell rings.*)

I told you—they've come for Kenny. Somebody, please get the door.

(*CASSANDRA and JACKIE move to get up and eye each other warily.*)

CASSANDRA: You're younger—you go.

JACKIE: No, I don't think so. You're coming with me.

(*A man in a doctor's white coat, with a clipboard, enters.*)

SIMON: Sorry. Your front door was open. Esmerelda?

(*She nods yes.*)

Dif-tor smusma, Esmerelda.

CASSANDRA: What does that mean?

SIMON: It means—"May you live forever."

JACKIE: (*Sarcastically.*) No—it means, "Hi—I'm here to decapitate you."

ESSIE: Please, girls. This gentleman, Mr. . . . ?

SIMON: Please call me Simon.

ESSIE: Thank you. Simon is here to help us.

SIMON: Is Kenneth Abramowitz available? I need to take a look.

ESSIE: Of course. (*Calling.*) Kenny—Kenny, where's my pussycat?

JACKIE: He's hiding under the bed.
(*She reaches below the bed and brings up a stiff-looking yellow cat.*)
Oh, Mom, I'm sorry—I think he's dead.

ESSIE: (*Crying.*) Simon—is it too late?

(*SIMON extends clipboard.*)

SIMON: If you'll just sign these, I'd be happy to take a look.

CASSANDRA: I'm afraid not.
(*She blocks the bed.*)

JACKIE: Cass—what are you doing?

CASSANDRA: Enough already. We have to stop them.
(*She grabs the clipboard.*)

ESSIE: Cassandra, stop it this instant.

CASSANDRA: I'm sorry—my mother's head and her cat in a freezer in exchange for my children's' future? No way!
(*She pulls the papers off the clipboard.*)

JACKIE: Cass—no!
(*She knocks the papers out of CASSANDRA's hand, and they scatter all over the bed.*)

ESSIE: Stop it, girls. Stop it!

CASSANDRA: Grow up, Jackie. Mom's sick—she's desperate. It's a racket.

ESSIE: (*Coughing, hand to heart.*) Girls—stop!

JACKIE: You don't give a shit about Mom. You'd do anything for those kids. You're a cold, heartless liar!

CASSANDRA: Me, a liar?! Ma—remember Tootie, your parakeet? Jackie left the window open. Jackie killed that bird—not me—it was Jackie. I covered for her!!

JACKIE: Ma—she was shopping when Daddy died. Shopping! I covered for you! She was at Saks!

ESSIE: (*Clutching chest.*) Oh—oh—aaahhhhh!

(*SIMON puts a stethoscope to ESSIE's chest. She looks happily up into his eyes.*)

SIMON: No problem, Essie. We have your paperwork on file. No worries—thank God we were already here for the cat.

(He puts ESSIE and KENNY on a gurney and rolls it out the door. A stunned moment—then CASSANDRA runs after SIMON, shouting.)

CASSANDRA: Sir—excuse me—Simon. She changed her mind. She wants the head-only option. Sir—Sir!

JACKIE: Sir—don't listen to her—sir!!!
(She runs to catch up.)

(Blackout.)

END OF PLAY

I THINK I WOULD REMEMBER IF I HAD SEX WITH DENZEL WASHINGTON

by Yvette Heyliger

I Think I Would Remember If I Had Sex with Denzel Washington was presented in the Ken Davenport Ten-Minute Play Contest on June 28, 2012, and won the 2012 Finalist Award. The play was produced in association with Twinbiz and was directed by Mario Giacalone. The cast was as follows:

BERNADINE: Yvonne Farrow
BERNADETTE: Yvette Heyliger

Yvette Heyliger is a playwright, producing artist, educator, and activist. She is the recipient of the AUDELCO Recognition Award for Excellence in Black Theatre's August Wilson Playwright Award and her play *What Would Jesus Do?* won Dramatic Production of the Year. She received a Best Playwright nomination from NAACP's Annual Theatre Awards. Author of *What a Piece of Work Is Man! Full-Length Plays for Leading Women* and *Autobiography of a Homegirl*, she has also contributed to various anthologies, including *She Persisted: Monologues from Plays by Women Over 40*, *Performer Stuff*, *The Monologue Project*, *Short Plays on Reproductive Freedom*, *Later Chapters: The Best Scenes and Monologues for Actors over Fifty*, *WE ARE THEATRE*, *24 Gun Control Plays*, *The Best Women's Stage Monologues 2003*, and *The Best Stage Scenes 2003*. Upcoming academic publication: *Performing #MeToo: How Not to Look Away*. Other writings include various articles for *The Native Society:*

Personalizing Thought Leadership, The Dramatist, Continuum: The Journal of African Diaspora Drama, Theatre and Performance, Black Masks: Spotlight on Black Art, and *HowlRound*. After many years in front of the footlights, Heyliger returned to the stage as a solo artist in her one-woman show, *Bridge to Baraka*, which she performed in the United Solo Theatre Festival and the National Black Theatre Festival, among others. Memberships: Dramatist Guild, AEA, SDC, AFTRA-SAG; League of Professional Theatre Women, Honor Roll, Harlem Arts Alliance, and Theatre Resources Unlimited. A partner in Twinbiz, she is co-recipient of the first National Black Theatre Festival Emerging Producer Award. She has a BA and an MA from New York University; an MFA in Playwriting from Queens College; and a Master of Theatre Education from Hunter College. She was an Obama Fellow during President Obama's reelection campaign and was a founding member and longtime volunteer with Organizing for Action. As a citizen-artist, she has worked on many issues including: gun violence prevention, equal opportunity and pay for women artists, and most recently, the #MeToo movement. Yvette is a Dramatist Guild NYC Ambassador and lives in Harlem, USA.

CHARACTERS

BERNADINE, in her early to mid-50s and formerly a dancer, she is an
    attractive African American woman who is the twin sister of
    BERNADETTE.
BERNADETTE, in her early to mid-50s, she is an attractive African
    American actress who is the twin sister of BERNADINE.

Note on Casting

The author appreciates that finding "identical" twins (twins developed from one fertilized egg which splits and forms two embryos) may pose a challenge to casting (although it should be noted that identical twins may not look exactly alike in later years due to environmental factors and life experiences after being born). An alternative choice would be to cast actors who would be "non-identical" or "fraternal" twins (twins who develop from a separate egg, with each egg having been fertilized by its own sperm cell) or casting actors who look similar but would be considered "Irish" twins (siblings who look similar but are born less than a year apart).

SETTING

Stage Door of the Cort Theatre, 138 West 48th Street, New York City.

TIME

June 2010.

· · ·

Nighttime. Street noises. BERNADINE *and* BERNADETTE *have just seen* Fences *by August Wilson on Broadway. They are each armed with a Playbill from the show and a Sharpie.*

BERNADINE: (*To departing befriended* Fences *audience members.*) Goodbye. Nice to meet you. (*Beat.*) No, we're going to wait.

BERNADETTE: Bye, now. Have a good rest of your evening. (*To her sister.*) Come on, let's go too.

BERNADINE: You've been saying, "Let's go" for the past twenty minutes.

BERNADETTE: I don't want to see him.

BERNADINE: You said you did.

BERNADETTE: I changed my mind.

BERNADINE: Look, I left my husband at home, put on a girdle, my best padded bra, high heels . . .

BERNADETTE: I told you we shouldn't have dressed up. No one goes to the theatre dressed up anymore. We look like a couple of tourists.

BERNADINE: Yea, tourists who coughed up a lot of money for an aisle seat in the orchestra.

BERNADETTE: That was your idea. My wallet and I would have been happy with a seat in the mezzanine.

BERNADINE: I told you, if you buy an aisle seat, they make you buy the seat next to it. I needed that aisle seat to stretch out my right leg. Besides, I'd think you'd be happy we were so close to the stage. You're the one who refuses to wear glasses. Who in their right mind uses binoculars in the orchestra?

BERNADETTE: Well, you're the one who refuses to use a cane. Who in their right mind wears high heels after knee surgery?

BERNADINE: I told you, I don't need a cane. People get up and walk after these surgeries now, like Lazarus.

BERNADETTE: Not in heels, they don't. (*Beat.*) Come on, put your hand on my shoulder and let's go.

BERNADINE: We're not leaving here until I get my money's worth, Bernadette—some face time with the star and an autograph I can sell on Ebay.

BERNADETTE: You got your money's worth, Bernadine. Both Denzel and Viola gave Tony Award–winning performances.
    (*Putting away her Playbill and Sharpie.*)
Now, come on. Let's go.

    (*BERNADINE doesn't move.*)
Look, I'm starting to have second thoughts about him seeing me, OK?

BERNADINE: Why?

BERNADETTE: I'm older.

BERNADINE: He's older.

BERNADETTE: I'm heavier.

BERNADINE: He's heavier.

BERNADETTE: I'm about to be a grandmother.

BERNADINE: Well, you got me there. I don't know about grandkids, but I heard his youngest just entered college.

BERNADETTE: What if he brings it up?

BERNADINE: Brings what up?

BERNADETTE: The thing.

BERNADINE: Which thing?

BERNADETTE: The soup thing.

BERNADINE: (*Loudly.*) So you gave Denzel Washington diarrhea. So what? It was before he was "Denzel Washington."

BERNADETTE: For heaven's sake, be quiet! What if someone hears you?

BERNADINE: Who cares? It's ancient history.

BERNADETTE: He was a rising star, destined for fame and fortune, and I gave him diarrhea.

BERNADINE: I told you not to put in so much garlic. What, was it like ten or twelve cloves?

BERNADETTE: Are you sure it was the black beans? Maybe it was . . .

BERNADINE: That's what Pickens told me.

BERNADETTE: *Pickens?!* What did he say exactly?

BERNADINE: Well, Pickens told me, that Denzel told him, that "dem twins" gave him diarrhea. Mind you, I had nothing to do with it. You're the one who cooked.

BERNADETTE: Black beans, brown rice, salad, and corny bread.

BERNADINE: The man came. The man ate. The man sat on our couch and put his feet up. We had him all to ourselves, and you send him home . . .

BERNADETTE: I had an audition the next morning.

BERNADINE: All the way to Mt. Vernon.

BERNADETTE: Well, that's where he lived.

BERNADINE: I'm sure he would have appreciated spending the night. (*Beat.*) Bernadette, the man is fine.

BERNADETTE: Yea, so?

BERNADINE: So . . . were you married?

BERNADETTE: No.

BERNADINE: Was he married?

BERNADETTE: No.

BERNADINE: Was I married? No. You see where I'm going with this?

BERNADETTE: No. (*Changing the subject.*) Where is he? The show let out almost forty minutes ago.

BERNADINE: Maybe he has diarrhea. (*Beat.*) Look, I thought you said Denzel stands outside after the show giving autographs?

BERNADETTE: That's what he did during the run of *Julius Caesar;* every single night until the last Playbill was signed.

BERNADINE: Well, why didn't you get his autograph for me then?

BERNADETTE: I didn't see *Julius Caesar.* I can't sit through Shakespeare's tragedies—not even for Denzel Washington. Why can't they do more *new* plays on Broadway? I swear, if I sit through one more show by a dead white man . . .

BERNADINE: Or a living one.

BERNADETTE: Or a British one. And what about all these revivals? I loved *Fences,* but August Wilson is not the *only* black playwright out there, OK?

BERNADINE: Don't you start in on August Wilson. He's our black Shakespeare.

BERNADETTE: See! Why does he have to be our "black Shakespeare"? Why can't he just be our black August Wilson?

BERNADINE: Oh, Lord, here we go!

BERNADETTE: Do you think white folks go around saying, "He's our white August Wilson" or "She's our white Lorraine Hansberry"? No! And Lorraine Hansberry is *not* the "first" black woman playwright! As if no black women were writing plays before her . . . or after her, for that matter. (*Beat.*) Are you listening to me?

BERNADINE: All of Broadway is listening to you! I wonder what is keeping Denzel? He must have lots of guests in his dressing room. Either that or he's waiting for the crowd to thin out.

BERNADETTE: The crowd has thinned out!

BERNADINE: Maybe he left through another exit.

BERNADETTE: What other exit? We're at the Stage Door.

BERNADINE: With all these Hollywood stars doing Broadway shows this season—Scarlett Johansson, Catherine Zeta-Jones—you know there has to be an alternate escape route.

BERNADETTE: (*Pulling flat shoes or sneakers out of her tote.*) Come on, let's go have a McFlurry and talk about the show. My feet hurt.

BERNADINE: Don't you dare change your shoes! He might come out any minute.

BERNADETTE: He's married to a black woman. I'm sure he'll understand.

BERNADINE: Well, you do have a point there.

(BERNADINE and BERNADETTE both change their shoes.)

Look, Bernadette, we waited all this time; we may as well wait a little longer. I want to ask Denzel a question.

BERNADETTE: *A question?* What question, Bernadine?

BERNADINE: (*Reciting Troy's son Cory's line in* Fences.) "How come you ain't never liked me?"

BERNADETTE: "How come . . ." See, August is turning over in his grave right now, you stealing a line from *Fences*.

BERNADINE: Well, I want to know "how come." I mean, I was cuter than you back then—not to mention more muscular, flexible, athletic . . . But Denzel liked *you*.

BERNADETTE: Go on! (*Beat.*) You think so?

BERNADINE: Well, I don't understand it myself; but yes, I think so. Of course, you blew it, Bernadette; you and your naiveté. The man was in our home for dinner . . . *and* dessert.

BERNADETTE: Wait. There was no dessert.

BERNADINE: *We were dessert*, Bernadette—us two cream-filled Twinkies. It was *Training Day* with a *Man on Fire* looking to have a *Déjà Vu* as the *Inside Man* in our Denzel twin-Twinkie sandwich.

BERNADETTE: Like I'd have sex with anyone with *you* in the bed!

BERNADINE: Having a *ménage a trois* with "dem twins" was the fantasy of a lot of men we knew back then.

BERNADETTE: It was not!

BERNADINE: It was. And what about that rumor about you and Denzel sleeping together? (*Beat.*) Well?

BERNADETTE: Well, what?

BERNADINE: Did you?

BERNADETTE: I don't kiss and tell.

BERNADINE: To me, you do! I am your sister and closest confidante.

BERNADETTE: Well, maybe, just maybe, I want to keep something to myself for once, Bernadine. A memory, a secret, something that's mine alone, just for me—

BERNADINE: And sleeping with Denzel is the one thing you pick? (*Beat.*) You mean to tell me you had sex with Denzel and kept it from me for over thirty years?!

BERNADETTE: Just because we are twins doesn't mean we have to share everything!

BERNADINE: Of course we do! *Who are you?* I don't even know who you are.

BERNADETTE: Oh my God! Relax. I didn't have sex with the man. Happy now?

BERNADINE: I knew it was a lame excuse, you sending me to the store for what, *toilet paper?!*

BERNADETTE: We ran out.

BERNADINE: And now we know why!

BERNADETTE: Seriously? I see I'm never going to live that down.

BERNADINE: Glad to know where I stand, *sister.*

BERNADETTE: This is ridiculous. I think I would remember if I had sex with Denzel Washington! Come on!

BERNADINE: I've done things I don't remember. Like that time . . .

BERNADETTE: Can we not make this about you again, please? (*Beat.*) I did not sleep with Denzel.

BERNADINE: Yea, but people *think* you did. How about that producer you told me about; the one who was trying to feel you out to see if it was true?

BERNADETTE: Don't remind me.

BERNADINE: Why didn't you just tell him you didn't? Put an end to the matter right then and there?

BERNADETTE: Because *it's nobody's business who I have sex with,* that's why. Just like whom I vote for, how old I am, or how much money I make. It's nobody's business!

BERNADINE: Amen, sister! Besides, he wasn't even "Denzel" yet. (*Beat.*) But, you know, men talk . . . their buddies assume . . . no one confirms or denies . . . rumors start . . . and bam! Belt's got a notch—real or imagined.

BERNADETTE: Are you saying that you think Denzel may have given someone the impression that we slept together?

BERNADINE: I'm saying you're the victim here, Bernadine; the victim of a salacious, unsubstantiated rumor; fodder for the gossip mill. Any other woman would have tried to parlay that rumor into something more; try to milk it to her advantage; use it as leverage to further her own lot.

BERNADETTE: Someone like you?

BERNADINE: I'm going to pretend I didn't hear that. Look, there are a lot worse things people could be thinking than that you slept with one of the finest, most talented black men to ever hit the silver screen. I'm just saying!

BERNADINE: (*Looking off stage.*) Look. There. A limo just pulled up. Do you think it's for Denzel?

> (*BERNADETTE rummages through her purse. She finds her binoculars and looks.*)

BERNADETTE: Oh, my God! The driver's making a call. I bet you he's calling Denzel! How do I look?

BERNADINE: Mature.

BERNADETTE: What does that mean?

BERNADINE: It means we're not twenty-two anymore.
> (*She gets her compact, reapplies her lipstick, and then hands them to BERNADETTE.*)
Here, better freshen up.

BERNADETTE: Thanks. How can you see anything in this light?

BERNADINE: Well, if you don't know where your own lips are at this age, then I don't know what to tell you.

BERNADETTE: (*Nervous excitement.*) My God, it's been over thirty years since I've seen him! What if he doesn't remember me?

BERNADINE: He may not remember *you*, but everybody remembers "dem twins." Turn that mirror around.

(*BERNADETTE does so. BERNADINE fixes her hair.*)

Look, Bernadette, bottom line? If he didn't become "Denzel Washington," Hollywood hunk and mega-star of stage and screen, no one would care if you slept with him or not.

BERNADETTE: I care. It's my reputation on the line here. I was in college back then, and working as an usher at the Negro Ensemble Company. Denzel was playing Private Peterson in *A Soldier's Play*.

BERNADINE: I remember. Pickens was in that too.

BERNADETTE: Yes, James Pickens, Samuel L. Jackson, Adolf Caesar, Larry Riley, Charlie Brown, Eugene Lee . . . It was a dream cast. Sometimes Denzel and I would go have a couple beers between shows and watch basketball at a sports bar over on Ninth Avenue. Denzel watched with such focus, you know? He's the kind of guy that, whatever he focuses on, receives his full attention, on stage and off. When he did talk to me—on the commercials— he was like, waaaaay over my head.

BERNADINE: What do you mean, "Way over your head"?

BERNADETTE: I mean, he was talking, but I couldn't understand him. I didn't "get" him. He was deep. Intense. Brilliant. I remember thinking that the woman who would be right for Denzel would have to be really special, you know; to know how to listen to him; how to talk to him; how to *be* with him.

BERNADINE: Did you ever stop to think that maybe he didn't know how to "be" with you? Maybe he was quiet, eyes glued to the TV, because he didn't know what to say to *you*?

BERNADETTE: Look, I'm not going to pretend there was some hot and heavy, unrequited romance going on. There wasn't. We were just friends. We hung out sometimes. That's it.

BERNADINE: OK, but obviously he felt comfortable enough with you to take the A train all the way to Brooklyn to have your cooking. When a man wants to eat your food, it means something. (*Beat.*) Wish I'd had a crack at him. I would have known what to do with "Private Peterson." You can believe I'd have been polishing that big black boot all night long.

BERNADETTE: So, the truth comes out after all these years! You wanted Denzel all for yourself, didn't you!

BERNADINE: Well, let's just say an experienced chef would have put dessert on the menu!

BERNADETTE: Why do you always have to do that—make it seem like you're more experienced than me?

BERNADINE: Because *I am* more experienced than you.

BERNADETTE: Just because you started having sex before me . . .

BERNADINE: Way before you, and in many different ways before you. Being a dancer had its advantages.

BERNADETTE: Alright, Ms. Pay-Up-The-Wazoo-For-An-Aisle-Seat; bet you can't wrap that leg around anyone's neck now.

BERNADINE: You take that back!

BERNADETTE: Just because you were born first you think you have to be first at everything— News flash: I was *supposed* to be born first!

BERNADINE: You'd better talk to Mother Nature about that.

BERNADETTE: Mother Nature?! You kicked me out of the way!

BERNADINE: Because I wanted it more.

BERNADETTE: Wanted what more?

BERNADINE: (*Dramatically.*) *To be born!*

BERNADETTE: Oh my God. Look, you weren't even supposed to be there. I told you he was coming over for dinner. You crashed my date with Denzel Washington!

BERNADINE: I did not crash your date! We were roommates! Where was I supposed to go?

BERNADETTE: Anywhere! Same as I did for you—many times!

(*A man in a hat and overcoat darts out of the stage door and into the limo that is waiting off stage.*)

BERNADINE: Oh my God, is that . . . was that him?!

(*Sound of car door closing.*)

BERNADETTE: Where? Where? (*Looking through her binoculars.*) It is! Denzel!!!

BERNADINE: Denzel!!!

BERNADETTE: Denzel!!!

(*Their eyes follow the limo as if it is making a right turn onto the street downstage; it stops center.*)

BERNADINE: Denzel, it's us!

BERNADINE and BERNADETTE: "DEM TWINS!"

BERNADETTE: Quick! He's rolling down the window!

(*They rush down stage center to the car, BERNADETTE with her binoculars and BERNADINE leaning on her sister's shoulder, hobbling a bit. Bending down, they talk to Denzel Washington through the limousine's window.*)

BERNADINE: Denzel, it's me, Bernadine. Loved *Fences*! You were fabulous as Troy!

BERNADETTE: Denzel, it's me, Bernadette! Hey, way to stick it! Good luck at the Tonys!

(*Voice-over from the movie* Remember the Titans *is heard.*)

DENZEL WASHINGTON: "I'm a winner. I'm going to win."

BERNADETTE: (*Also quoting from the movie.*) "Leave no doubt!" (*For her sister's benefit.*)
And Denzel . . . the sex was great!
   (*She winks at him. BERNADINE's jaw drops.*)

(*Blackout.*)

END OF PLAY

A LATE SUMMER

by Liz Amberly

A Late Summer was produced originally at Edmonds Driftwood Players in Edmonds, Washington, in July 2015. The director was Ted Jaquith, and the producer was Carissa Meisner Smit. The cast was as follows:

THE WOMAN: Diane Jamieson
THE MAN: Dennis Moore
THE GIRL: Emily Fortuna
THE BOY: Woody Lotts

Liz Amberly's plays include *Blueberry Waltz* (published by Samuel French), *The 11:05* (published by Smith and Kraus), *Embers* (2019 semi-finalist in the O'Neill National Playwright Conference), *Whisper Down the Lane* (winner, Full-Length Play Contest at Asylum Theater), *Double Whammy* (also a screenplay, winner of Reel 13 Short Film Contest, aired on WNET-Channel 13), *Beyond the Cabin* (commissioned work), and others. Her plays have been presented at New World Stages, Workshop Theater, Neighborhood Playhouse, Barrow Group, American Globe Theater, London's Unrestricted View Theater, and others. She is co-owner of Kindle Productions, and she writes reading tips for Dolly Parton Imagination Library (published by Penguin-Random) www.lizamberly.com.

CHARACTERS

THE WOMAN, 60s–70s.
THE BOY, 18.

THE GIRL, 18.
THE MAN, 60s–70s.

SETTING

A beach.

TIME

The present and years ago.

• • •

A beach. THE WOMAN, *wearing a nice beach coverup and sunglasses, in a beach chair. She rises, picks up a few shells on the ground, and puts them in a small basket.* THE BOY *enters. He is filled with nervous energy. He fingers a set of keys and looks around for someone.*

THE BOY: (*To himself.*) Where is she?

> (*He tosses the keys in the air, then catches them.* THE GIRL *appears. She wears a dress and carries a large bag. She approaches* THE BOY *and pours water down his back.*)

THE GIRL: Whoohoo!!! Gotcha, Johhny!

THE BOY: Damn it, Bren, you scared the shit outta me!

THE GIRL: (*Pulling a towel off the back of the chair.*) Here's a towel. Don't be mad.

THE BOY: (*Drying off with the towel.*) Thought you'd be here half an hour ago.

THE GIRL: If I refuse to wait on customers, I'll be out of a job.

THE BOY: Donna should handle the register for you when you've got a lunch plan.

THE GIRL: Like you stand up to your boss?

THE BOY: At least a job by the water's got perks. Now we don't have much time.

THE GIRL: Why you so tense? I'll get lunch ready.
> (*She spreads out a blanket for them to sit on.*)

(THE MAN appears, wearing sunglasses and summer attire. He sits in the lounge chair, drops his keys on the table. THE WOMAN walks back over to her chair.)

THE WOMAN: Excuse me . . . My chair. You're sitting on my chair.

THE MAN: No, ma'am, you weren't anywhere near it. Sorry.

THE WOMAN: My towel was on it. What happened to the towel?

THE MAN: Guess maid service took it.
(Holding out a folded-up white towel.)
I brought one; you can have it.

(THE GIRL does a little spin, showing off her dress.)

THE GIRL: Did my toenails . . . see? Feeling good this morning, Johnny . . .

THE WOMAN: *(Registering who THE MAN is.)* Hey . . .

THE MAN: Oh my God. You're Brenda Wilks.

THE WOMAN: I can't believe it.

THE MAN: I didn't recognize you behind those glasses.

THE WOMAN: *(Taking off her sunglasses.)* Johnny.

THE MAN: *(Taking off his sunglasses.)* John.

THE GIRL: Johnny?

THE BOY: Just watching you. That a crime?

THE GIRL: Not as long as you like what you see.

THE WOMAN: It's been a million years. You look different.

THE MAN: Tell me about it.

THE WOMAN: No, you look good.

THE BOY: You do look good, Bren . . . You . . .

THE MAN: . . . look wonderful, Brenda.

(The two couples continue in their own worlds.)

THE GIRL: I didn't tell Donna. Did you tell anybody?

THE BOY: I told you I wouldn't.

THE MAN: (*Suddenly realizes he is still sitting.*) Oh, here, I'm sorry. Take your seat back.

THE GIRL: Sure. I brought drinks. Want a Coke?

THE MAN: I'll freshen up your drink.

THE BOY: A Coke? Sure.

THE WOMAN: Thanks. Rum and Coke . . . I didn't mean to throw you out of your seat.

THE MAN: Sure you did.

(*They smile.*)

I'll be right back.

(*He exits, taking her drink with him. She sits on the chair.*)

THE GIRL: I made baloney and cheese.

THE BOY: I wish I could've offered to take you to the Waterside Inn.

THE GIRL: Someday. Come sit.
(*She pulls out sandwiches and bottles of Coke.*)

THE BOY: I'm just . . . don't wanna sit yet.

THE GIRL: Made some cookies, too. Toll House. Got up early this morning. So here I am, baking before work, and my mom comes into the kitchen barely awake and thinks I'm crazy. (*Laughs.*) But I just wanted fresh cookies to bring today, you know? Wasn't just gonna only bring baloney!

(*THE MAN reenters from the bar with a fresh drink and one for himself. He brings it over to THE WOMAN. They sip.*)

(*In their area, THE BOY looks at THE GIRL.*)

THE GIRL: Why do you keep staring at me like that?

THE BOY: Just . . . You look pretty, Bren. Different today.

THE MAN: You look pretty, Brenda. Just the same.

THE WOMAN AND THE GIRL: (*Simultaneously.*) Pretty enough for the . . .

ALL: . . . best lifeguard at the shore.

(They laugh. THE BOY joins THE GIRL on the blanket.)

THE GIRL: It's kinda cold.

THE MAN: Are you cold? You look like you're cold.

THE BOY: You always get cold by the water.

THE WOMAN: Maybe a little.

THE MAN: Here.
(He opens the towel and puts it around her shoulders.)

(THE BOY puts a towel around THE GIRL at the same time, paralleling them. THE BOY keeps his arms around THE GIRL as they begin to eat.)

THE WOMAN: I often wondered if you ever got married.

THE MAN: Almost did a couple of times. But . . . no.

THE GIRL: Donna's getting married. She waves her ring in everybody's face when they walk in the store. (*She holds up her ringless hand, mimicking Donna.*)

(THE WOMAN holds up her hand, points to ringless finger.)

THE WOMAN: I got married, but not for long.

THE MAN: Sorry to hear it.

THE WOMAN: With a beautiful daughter and wonderful grandson, I count myself lucky.

(THE BOY moves away.)

THE GIRL: Your mind is turning. I am not hinting for a ring. Did you think I was hinting?

THE BOY: No, no. Just . . . so, you getting warmer now?

THE GIRL: Almost warm enough to take a dip. Should we go skinny dipping?

THE BOY: No. Bren . . .

THE GIRL: See what you've done to me . . . I'm a wild girl now.

THE BOY: Stop.

THE GIRL: Really, what is up with you?

THE MAN: So what's up with you nowadays?

THE BOY: I kinda have to tell you something . . .

THE GIRL: What?

THE BOY: It's a good thing.

THE WOMAN: Some good things, some not so good. Isn't that how life is?

THE GIRL: What's a good thing?

THE BOY: Kinda good . . . I mean, in the big picture of things.

   (Long pause. An awkward silence.)

THE MAN: Listen, I feel bad I didn't ever contact you again.

THE WOMAN: We all moved on.

THE GIRL: Just say it.

THE BOY: Well, you know how I was gonna turn down that cruise line job?

THE GIRL: Yeah.

THE BOY: Changed my mind. I'm taking it.

THE GIRL: Oh.

THE BOY: It's . . . a big opportunity. (*Silence.*) And it's only one year. (*Silence.*) But I'll be back, absolutely for sure. And we'll still do everything we said.

THE MAN: I didn't realize I wouldn't come back.

THE GIRL: You suddenly decide that you're moving away? Today?

THE WOMAN: You wanted to get away, and you did.

THE GIRL: Because I slept with you last night?

THE BOY: No! . . . No.

THE GIRL: I knew I shouldn't have believed what you said.

THE MAN: I thought it would be a good job.

THE WOMAN: I scared you away.

THE BOY: This is good for both of us.

THE GIRL: No wonder you were so insistent about going all the way
. . . You said beautiful words before, but afterward, dead air.

THE BOY: I just . . . I didn't know what to say when you started crying.

THE GIRL: But now you sure do.

THE BOY: No, it's . . .

THE GIRL: Don't talk to me.
    (She packs up the food.)

THE MAN: I figured it was a good opportunity.

THE BOY: Brenda . . .

THE MAN: And I was going to come back for you.

THE WOMAN: I'm sure you never looked back.

THE BOY: We gotta look forward. You want to always eat baloney
sandwiches? Live in our parents' houses? Have nothing?

THE GIRL: You call what we have nothing?

THE MAN: I thought I could make something happen.

THE WOMAN: You were off getting rich.

THE MAN: No.

THE WOMAN: No.

THE MAN: Got fired within days.

THE WOMAN: But your parents said . . .

THE MAN: I lied to my folks. To everybody. I was afraid to come home
broke, so I stayed away and tried to get another job.

THE WOMAN: How did that go?

THE MAN: Let's just say . . . poorly.

THE WOMAN: I bet you did okay.

THE MAN: No. Disastrously. Really, for a while.

THE BOY: Don't you want to have a chance at something better?

   (THE GIRL grabs his keys.)

What are you doing?

THE GIRL: Throwing these into the water.

THE BOY: Come on, you really think losing the keys to the umbrella shack is gonna matter? I'm quitting my job, so I don't need them anyway.

THE GIRL: How many other girls have you taken in there with you?

THE BOY: You're mad 'cause I got a decent job.

THE GIRL: How many?

THE BOY: The time is gonna seem like nothing.

THE GIRL: How many!!

   (Silence. She throws the keys at him, and he catches them.)

THE BOY: Brenda, this is for both of us. I'll be back next summer.

THE GIRL: We'll see.

THE BOY: I'm really coming back.

THE WOMAN: I wasn't surprised you never came. Sad, but not surprised.

THE GIRL: So, had you decided this before last night?

THE BOY: Not yet.

THE GIRL: So, I am the reason you want to run away from here.

THE BOY: You're not the reason.

THE GIRL: I'm not anything, am I?

   (She exits. THE BOY follows her off.)

THE MAN: You were the reason. But not because I wanted to get away. Because you deserved more.

THE WOMAN: I would have followed you anywhere, whether you had more of everything, or nothing. And now here you are . . . at the same beach.

THE MAN: With the prettiest girl.

THE WOMAN: (*Picking up his keys.*) If I were smart, I'd throw your keys out in the surf for never coming back. And these are not umbrella shack keys this time. Hmmm . . . Mercedes. Got other keys to your car?

THE MAN: You wouldn't dare.

THE WOMAN: (*Handing the keys back to him.*) No, I wouldn't. Not now. At this point, I just wish you well.

THE MAN: Could I at least offer you lunch at the Waterside Inn?

THE WOMAN: We could finally see the inside of that place.

THE MAN: I bet their menu doesn't taste as good as your baloney sandwiches.

THE WOMAN: I'm sure not.

THE MAN: I'll go see if they have any reservations available. Be back momentarily.

(*He exits. THE WOMAN looks out to the water.*)

(*THE BOY, with a different shirt, renters and looks out as well. THE WOMAN turns to him.*)

THE WOMAN: Johnny.

THE BOY: You gotta stop saying that.

THE WOMAN: . . . Johnny . . .

THE BOY: Gram, I'm not him.

THE WOMAN: I just . . .

THE BOY: (*Gently.*) Do you understand? . . . I'm not the doctor, I'm not your brother, I'm not my mom's new boyfriend, and I'm definitely not some jerk who pissed you off a lifetime ago. Take a look . . . just take a minute and see . . . do you know me?

(*They look at each other.*)

THE WOMAN: I do.

THE BOY: Jeremy.

THE WOMAN: Yes, I see you, Jeremy . . . You know, I have a feeling you'll break some girl's heart at the beach. Maybe you already have.

THE BOY: I'm sorry the guy left you.

THE WOMAN: But today he came back. It took a long time, but he came back.

THE BOY: Gram. He never came back.

THE WOMAN: He was here.

THE BOY: We haven't seen anybody since we got out of the car.

THE WOMAN: He said I still was the prettiest girl. And he's taking me to lunch over at the Waterside Inn.

THE BOY: Do you want to have lunch at the Waterside Inn? With me?

THE WOMAN: I've always wanted to eat there.

THE BOY: Okay. I'll see if they have reservations.
    (He exits in the direction of the restaurant.)

    (THE WOMAN picks up her basket and looks through her shells, lost in thought, perhaps sheds a tear. THE MAN returns.)

THE MAN: Made a reservation for two.

THE WOMAN: Perfect . . . and . . . Johnny . . . ?

    (Beat.)

THE MAN: . . . Yes?

THE WOMAN: When you said you were coming back . . .

THE MAN: I really did intend on keeping my word.

    (Beat.)

THE WOMAN: And so you have.

    (She takes his arm. They walk off toward the restaurant together.)

END OF PLAY

LIGHTNING BUGS

by Royal Shirée

Lightning Bugs premiered at The Spot's Original Works Festival, in Arroyo Grande, California, September 21–30, 2013. It was directed by Wendy-Marie Martin. The cast was as follows:

MAN: Mark Plater
WOMAN: Charly Schaad

A playwright/solo performer, Royal Shirée has been produced by Lynchburg College, Randolph College, Waterworks Players Theatre, Leading Ladies NY, Downtown Urban Theater Festival NY, Live Arts Charlottesville, and a professional reading by Virginia Playwrights and Screenwriters Initiative. Her solo show, *Clippings*, has been performed throughout Virginia and in New York. MOJOAA Performing Arts Company performed her piece *Victory* in "Reclamation, Female Voices of Color." Her ten-minute plays have been produced from coast to coast. Shirée completed the collaboration of the historical play *Sisters* with Joanne Hudson, funded by the Cultural Alliance of Western CT, through a grant given by the State of Connecticut and the National Endowment of the Arts. She was nominated for the James River Council Arts and Humanities', Celebrate Diversity: Black Artists in Lynchburg. Shirée is a former board member and producer/director for Riverviews Artspace, where she created "Perspective Presents," training non-professional and novice storytellers to perform true stories interpreted from themes, and she is currently a board member at Hamner Theatre in Crozet, Virginia. Shirée earned a hybrid English MA in Scholarship and Creative Writing from Lynchburg College in 2012 an an MFA in Playwriting from

Hollins University in 2013. She is a Fellow at the Virginia Center for the Creative Arts and a Dramatists Guild member.

CHARACTERS

MAN, a gentle septuagenarian. He is her husband.
WOMAN, a gentle septuagenarian. She is his wife.

SETTING

A field in the country. It is nighttime. The moon lights the stage. There is a hay bale.

TIME

The present.

Playwright's Note

The jar of lightning bugs can be artificial Easter grass or real grass. The lightning bugs can be sparkles sprinkled throughout the grass. The glass can be a mason jar. All director's choice. This is a simple and frugal prop. Although it would be ideal to have mature actors, younger actors may fit the role with wigs and baby powder on the hair, or whatever the director and/or actors come up with. They simply should look chronologically appropriate.

• • •

An older couple sits on a bale of hay in the country. It is night. The stage is aglow with the light of the moon.

MAN: Remember this, honey?

WOMAN: What, coming here?

MAN: No, look around.

WOMAN: I am.

MAN: Remember?

WOMAN: What am I supposed to remember?

MAN: Look.

WOMAN: I am!

MAN: Now do you remember?

WOMAN: All right. I give.

MAN: I just want you to remember. It was here, right here.

WOMAN: Yes, we've been here, silly. We grew up here. A lot happened here. (*A little flirty.*) You should remember that.

MAN: How could I forget? It's all grown over now. Is that all you remember?

WOMAN: What kind of question is that?

MAN: Three miles for an eight-year-old is saying something.

WOMAN: It's saying you were a silly boy. I would have rode Nellie the Cow. Silly boy.

MAN: Silly boy, is it?

WOMAN: Well?

MAN: Well, nothing. Just goes to show.

WOMAN: Show what?

MAN: Tha-a-at girls aren't always as smart as boys.

WOMAN: Oh, really?

MAN: Yes, really. Because we're going to be your hero one day. Don't know what day, but one day.

WOMAN: And that one day can take years, I suppose.

MAN: Or days. For years. Even sixty years.

WOMAN: Okay. So, we were saying . . .

MAN: I was saying, I remember. Today's the anniversary. Sixty years. And I still haven't said a word. Not even to you.

WOMAN: You haven't?

MAN: Silly girl. It was our secret. And my promise.

WOMAN: For a silly boy, you were sweet.

MAN: I still am! I knew if I kept the secret—It was a heavy hand. We can talk now.

WOMAN: That was no secret. Everyone knew that.

MAN: He was a heavy drinker.

WOMAN: On a plow. At night.

MAN: No one questioned it. Some said he had it coming.

WOMAN: I remember. A lot.

MAN: Okay. So, look around. Remember?

WOMAN: What is it that you're getting at?

MAN: Remember the lights?

WOMAN: Lights? What lights. You're too old for that. Have you been smoking?

MAN: No! But the lights? Look around.

WOMAN: We're in a country field. At night. There ain't no light here. Can't even get cell phone out here, silly boy.

MAN: But the light.

WOMAN: You mean the lightning bug lights?

MAN: It was my first gift to you.

WOMAN: Yeah. A necklace of lightning bug butts. With grass. How'd you do that, anyway? I couldn't quit smelling them all night.

MAN: And I gave you a jar.

WOMAN: A jar with more lightning bugs flashing their butts in grass and stinking up everything through the holes you put in the lid to keep them alive. I can still smell it.

MAN: But you wore the necklace. And took the jar.

WOMAN: I had to. You were blackmailing me. And they still died.

MAN: That's not true. (*Beat.*) Well, they did die. (*Beat.*) I found the spot.

WOMAN: Yes, they did. (*Beat.*) What spot? (*Beat.*) You did?

MAN: The fence post and fence and house and everything's gone now. Except the crow stand.

WOMAN: Where?

MAN: (*Pointing.*) You can barely see it now, but look at the top of my finger, where it's pointing. See it?

WOMAN: No. Where?

MAN: It looks like a black stick sticking up, pointing to the sky under the moon. Over tall grass. Over-r-r there. See it now?

WOMAN: Is that where it is?

MAN: Right there. Where the crow stand is.

WOMAN: Isn't it odd that that's the only thing standing?

MAN: Maybe the scarecrow got scared and leapt off the pole. The pole was stuck, held by a heavy hand, I guess.

WOMAN: I bet that's what it is.

MAN: And we came back to this very spot and sat on a bale of hay. Just like this. I was here. With you. We were.

WOMAN: You were the only friend I had.

MAN: That's because nobody else around here was our age.

WOMAN: Don't diminish it.

MAN: I'm not. I'm reinforcing it. Who else was here?

WOMAN: I know. Just us. I kept dreaming about hands. All these little hands running around like five-legged crab spiders.

MAN: But it was over.

WOMAN: And then I wasn't scared anymore. He was.

MAN: You didn't hear my crow-call.

WOMAN: I didn't hear anything except what was stuck in my head.

MAN: He never . . .

WOMAN: He never did that. He did the ribs and the arms and the back and my mind instead.

MAN: I knew when you didn't hear the crow . . .

WOMAN: It was the final round. The white lightnin' round.

MAN: And I didn't hear nothing.

WOMAN: He'd be drunk. He'd preach. And I waited 'til he passed out. It always wore him out.

MAN: I was a little scared, too.

WOMAN: And I don't know where it came from. In my hand. Mama was gone.

MAN: So I was quiet, trying to walk on that creaky porch.

WOMAN: Each strike. And if. Thy right hand. Offend thee, cut it off, and cast it. From thee.

MAN: And I crowed real low.

WOMAN: That's all I heard.

MAN: But you didn't hear me.

WOMAN: I don't remember.

MAN: And I opened the door, slow.

WOMAN: It was like two hands shaking.

MAN: And you were still.

WOMAN: I was all red.

MAN: You were mad.

WOMAN: He woke up.

MAN: He was drunk.

WOMAN: You took his hand. Put it down. Put him on the tractor. Mama was gone.

MAN: Nobody believed him.

WOMAN: He never said anything. To me.

MAN: He was a drunk.

WOMAN: On a plow.

MAN: Not the first time.

WOMAN: For the last time.

MAN: Pa said he had it coming. He was a doctor.

WOMAN: An animal doctor.

MAN: Like I said.

WOMAN: No one ever found his hand.

MAN: Pa patched him up.

WOMAN: He knew. He took me in.

MAN: Ma and Pa.

WOMAN: Took kindly to me.

MAN: They took the secret to their grave.

WOMAN: No one would believe him. Not even Mama. He took her with him.

MAN: Holding her from behind. Happy anniversary.

WOMAN: He was drunk. On her back.

MAN: He burned with the house.

WOMAN: With Mama. Tryin' to run. Fireplace, fiery timbers, and an old rug.

MAN: Fanned the flames. Sixty years.

WOMAN: And here we are.

MAN: (*He gets up.*) May I have this dance?

WOMAN: There's music?

MAN: As a matter of fact, there is.

> *(They dance. He sings a '40s-style ballad.)*

> *(Singing.) The moon was high, in the dark night sky, your vision was the only light. Starry nights twinkle, before the morning dew, Lightning Bug, I . . . love . . . you.*
> *(He kisses her, gently.)*
Now do you remember?

WOMAN: I remember a lot.

MAN: It was here, right here. Sixty years ago tonight, we had our first dance. I was yours forever. Everything. Remember?

WOMAN: I'm not that old. Why do you keep asking? Oh, you mean the lightning bug lights?

MAN: We're not that old. I want us to share the same memory. It was my first gift to you.

WOMAN: Yeah, a necklace of lightning bug butts with grass. I couldn't quit smelling them all night.

MAN: And I gave you a jar.

WOMAN: A jar of lightning bugs flashing their butts and stinking up everything through the holes you put in the lid.

MAN: Exactly. White lightnin' and yellow lightning bugs are two different lights. They may die, but not their light.
> *(He reaches behind, retrieves a jar with lightning bugs and grass, and gives it to her.)*
The crow pole has a heavy hand holding it up. Happy anniversary.

> *(Lights dim low.)*

END OF PLAY

MAKE NO MISTAKE (A FANTASIA)

by Betty Shamieh

Make No Mistake (*A Fantasia*) had its world premiere at the Golden Thread Theatre's ReOrient Festival in November 2017, directed by Susannah Martin.

The cast was as follows:
AMAL: Atosa Babaoff
AMY: Jessica Risco

Betty Shamieh is an Arab-American playwright and the author of fifteen plays. She is currently a Mellon National Fellow and Playwright-in-Residence at the Classical Theatre of Harlem. Her New York premieres include *The Black Eyed* (New York Theatre Workshop), *Fit for a Queen* (Classical Theatre of Harlem), *The Machine* (Naked Angels), and *Roar* (The New Group). *Roar* is the first play about a Palestinian-American family to premiere off-Broadway and is widely taught at universities across the United States. Her major European productions in translation include *Again and Against* (Playhouse Theater, Sweden), *The Black Eyed* (Fournos Theatre, Greece), and *Territories* (European Union Capital of Culture Festival). She was an NEA/TCG Playwright in Residence at the Magic Theatre in 2009. Shamieh was awarded a 2016–2017 Guggenheim Fellowship for the Creative Arts and named a UNESCO Young Artist for Intercultural Dialogue. She is a two-time recipient of the New York Foundation for the Arts Playwriting Fellowship and was selected as a winner of The Playwrights' Center's McKnight National Commission. Her works have been translated into seven languages. www.bettyshamieh.com.

CHARACTERS

AMY, an American woman in her twenties.
AMAL, a Yemeni woman in her twenties.

SETTING

This play could take place in an abstract setting. It can also be staged in the two different bedrooms of these two women.

TIME

The present.

• • •

Lights up. Both women address the audience.

AMAL and AMY: Make no mistake about it.

AMY: I had other options.

AMAL: I had a choice.

AMY: I was smart in school. Driven. Ambitious to get out of my Midwestern town, and I did. No one can ever say that I never made it out of that town.

AMAL: I could have said, "No, I can't do it. I can't marry him."

AMY: I didn't have to become what I became. I had other ways to get ahead in life, it's true. I didn't have to rely on my ability to . . .

AMAL and AMY: . . . inspire desire . . .

AMY: . . . in a man more powerful than I would ever be . . .

AMAL: . . . more powerful than everyone I knew would ever be.

AMAL and AMY: To tell the truth.

AMY: I was always interested in power. Why some people had all of it and why I always felt like I had none. But I guess that's all relative, isn't it? I mean, it's not like I was born in Saudi Arabia or anything.

AMAL: I was called a gift, but everyone knew I was more than a gift.

AMY: I was introduced to him at a fund-raiser for his campaign.

AMAL: He was being strategic by marrying me.

AMY: It was one of *those* introductions. You know the kind, where one man says to another, "Mr. President, have you met Amy?" But I'm not actually being introduced. No one's talking to me, the men are smiling at each other, communicating with each other. "Have you met Amy?" isn't a question. It's a statement. It means "Here. Check this one out. She's game." The thing is, it was true. I was game.

AMAL: Osama wanted to align himself with my family's tribe. He thought he might have to move to Yemen, that it was only a matter of time before all his friends in Afghanistan and Pakistan would turn on him. If you marry into my tribe, you become one of us. The men of my tribe are known to be noble. Loyal. Brave. Osama's men scouted around for a proper girl, interviewed a few of my cousins along with me. They were looking for a girl who was grounded, who wouldn't buckle under pressure, but a girl who did what she was told. I was clever enough to hide my cleverness, to present myself as humble. Pliant. Devout. I wanted to be picked. They were clear with my father that it was likely that I would spend the rest of my life on the run. My father took me aside and said, "Amal, you don't have to do this. I can tell them you don't have the stomach for that kind of life."

AMY: My parents did the best they could for me. I come from a very decent family. That's the word I would use to describe my family. Decent. My father was a mailman and a volunteer firefighter. I think I was selected to be a mistress to the president by his handlers because I have a shyness about me. I wasn't the type of person who would go telling my tale to the press. Make no mistake—I felt I was selected and presented to him in that way and for that purpose by his handlers because every good handler knows how a man more powerful than him likes being handled. I'm a private person. Most people can sense that about me. Once upon a time, I was truly interested in a career in politics. Thought I could go pretty far. Maybe even go back home and run for state senator. But I was ready to be stripped of my illusions of grandeur when I met the man who would become my lover and my president.

AMAL: I had skipped two grades in school and was training to be a teacher. At a girls' school, of course, but I could have stayed in Yemen and married a boy from my village—had a quiet, safe life. I knew it would be dangerous to be the wife of such a man. That's all I knew when I agreed to marry this stranger that not even my parents had met.

AMY: You see, I am a woman with a past, the kind of past that would always haunt my future. I wasn't wild, but I acted wildly. Does that make sense? I did stupid things—things uncharacteristic of me—because I was trying to change my character, to shake off my natural reticence—overcompensate for it, eradicate it. So, yes, there are pictures of me topless floating around. Yes, I'm sure they would float to the surface if I ever tried to do anything of note, like try to make money by telling the press I was being pursued by the president. (*Pause.*) Or run for state senator.

AMAL: From that day forward, I never slept soundly again. I knew every Arab leader wanted my husband dead. I tried to convince myself that we would be okay if we stayed in non-Arab Muslim countries, where we would always be strangers who spoke in a foreign language and so my husband could never rival local leaders for power or prestige. I had no idea he was planning to attack America itself. I thought he was going to stick to bombing American embassies and the other things I knew he did. None of us thought Osama was capable of doing what he did, not even him. He never spoke to me about his plans for the future, when he spoke to me at all. I never imagined I would grow to feel anything but anxious around him. I never imagined I'd try to take a bullet for him.

AMY: I convinced myself that he loved me, you see. He was the center of my world. I couldn't keep my job. I had to be free to come when I was called for, though I wasn't called for often. I think some men like the idea of having a mistress more than actually having a mistress. I was put on the payroll as an employee of his family's foundation, so I got a regular check that covered all my bills and then some. He would talk to me about his kids. He was proud of them, asked my advice about how to talk to them. He never promised to divorce his wife after he left politics, but it didn't stop me from hoping.

AMAL: I was told by his other wives that I would only know that he truly trusted me when he would confide in me about in his political plans. So, when he told he was going to leave me in Yemen with my family for a while because it would be safer for me, I asked if he was planning another attack on an embassy.

AMY: I asked if I could meet his kids, not as a mistress, but as a friend. I felt close to them. I felt like I should know them. Strange as it sounds, I felt like I was part of their family.

AMAL and AMY: It was a mistake.

AMY: He yelled at me.

AMAL: He got very quiet.

AMY: I think he didn't believe that I wasn't going to try to tell his daughters about our relationship, that I just wanted to meet them. He said he'd kill me if I went near his girls, that a woman like me wasn't fit to be in their presence. He called me names, then he did something worse.

AMAL: When he finally spoke, he said that if I ever asked an inappropriate question again, he would divorce me, which would mean disgrace for me and my family. There are women who can handle disgrace. I was not one of them. That meant I was not allowed to ask anything again, because I never knew what might be deemed inappropriate.

AMY: He left me alone.

AMAL: With my family in Yemen, I watched the towers fall on TV. I watched images of my husband on every channel. I knew I was being watched. But I believed my husband would call for me one day.

AMY: I don't mean to sound arrogant, but I thought he would come back to me, and not simply because the checks kept coming, kept confirming I was still a employee of his family's foundation. There weren't a lot of women who would live like I did, be as discreet as I was. In that time I spent waiting, I made one new friend. I told her that I was fucking the president.

AMAL: I gave one interview with a big Arab newspaper.

AMAL and AMY: It was a mistake.

AMAL: I couldn't help it. Those towers went down, and it felt like the whole world was waiting for me to respond. I knew everyone in Yemen would read my interview. That made me feel important.

AMY: I told her that she'd better not tell anyone else in the way I was told by one of the handlers. He took me by the arm after the first time the president and I met alone and hissed, "Accidents are not always accidents. People disappear all the time. You'd better keep your mouth shut." And that's what I said to her. Word for word. It's funny how original we think we are, when we often just go around repeating to others what was once said to us. In my case, threats were unnecessary. I couldn't stand the thought of being a public person—if my claim to fame was sleeping with a married man. Have people in my face, asking me questions, wanting answers, digging into my past. I couldn't sleep that night.

AMAL: When the reporter asked me if I thought I'd ever be reunited with my husband, I said, "we'll see," and I ended the interview. I felt the reporter was leering at me, asking me to speculate if my husband was yearning for me and me alone, and would do something about that yearning. I knew there was no way my husband could ever contact me and bring me to him without attracting the attention of the people who were watching me, supposedly trying to find him. Part of me wanted to see my husband again, and part of me wished I never met him.

AMY: I called my friend the next day and told her that I was pulling her leg, that—of course—I wasn't having an affair with the president, that I just wanted to see if she was naïve enough to believe me. She never called me again. I stopped going out altogether and waited in that apartment for six months for my president to return to me, and he did.

AMAL: I was smuggled back to him, to a compound in Pakistan. I knew there is no way the people who were looking for him could not have followed my trace, if they were competent and numerous and well-paid, which they were. Was I to believe that these people wouldn't be watching the young wife that my husband left in Yemen, which is what even the most foolish detective would do? No, it was clear we weren't hiding from the Americans. We were hiding from the fools who might actually take seriously the idea that the Americans in charge had no clue where my husband was for several years, at least as many as the five I lived with him after he called for me. Those fools would go running around, alerting everyone that they spotted the elusive Osama bin Laden. They would apparently embarrass the American government into being forced to take my husband's life, which they didn't want to do at the time. This is all my conjecture, of course. I never knew for sure what was really going on. I wasn't allowed to ask inappropriate questions, not even when they concerned my life or the lives of the children I bore in that compound.

AMY: I never asked him about his children again. But he wasn't shy about telling me stuff that I think he probably should have kept secret, stuff you didn't hear on TV. That always surprised me. But, you see, nowadays no one believes anything, except that we don't know what to believe. In an environment where everyone assumes they are always being lied to, it rarely matters if the actual truth gets leaked.

AMAL: All I knew was I was scared because my husband was scared. He knew it would only be a matter of time.

AMY: He told me his advisors had advised him that it was strategic to keep Osama bin Laden alive for the time being, but not in order to justify more war—like so many people believed was the case. Wars rarely need that kind of justification. They could go on and would go on, even after one man was taken off the grid. He said Osama was described to him by his advisors as the head of a snake. If you cut off the head of this snake, a thousand more would grow. It was easier to track the movements of one big snake than fend off a thousand smaller fangs that could come from any direction. It sounded convincing to me. It convinced him.

AMAL: I was almost glad when it was over, when the assassins we knew would come finally came and it was done. Years and years of being afraid that—not only I—but my children would die with him.

AMY: I was surprised that the next president ignored the advice of those same advisors and cut off the head of the snake. I know it must have made him upset that he didn't get the credit for doing that. Of course, I won't bring it up when he calls for me again. Now that he's no longer president, it's even harder for him to get away. I stay home a lot, keep up on the news, wait. I read that the bin Ladens' youngest wife is my age, that she jumped in front of men with guns and tried to shield him—to sacrifice herself for him. I thought to myself, "What a terrible life she must have lived. That poor, poor woman."

END OF PLAY

MODERN ROMANCE

by Bridgette A. Wimberly

World Premiere: Ensemble Studio Theatre, NYC, The River Crosses Rivers II, a Festival of Short Plays by Women of Color. September 14-October 2, 2011. Directed by Chuck Patterson. The cast was Chike Johnson, Trish McCall, and Harvey Gardner Moore.

Bridgette A. Wimberly, an award-winning poet, playwright, and librettist, has been commissioned and produced by a number of prominent theaters off-Broadway, across the U.S., and abroad, including Atlanta Opera, Arizona Opera, English National Opera-London, Opera Philadelphia, Apollo Theatre, Madison Opera, Lyric Opera of Chicago (Charlie Parker's YARDBIRD), Atlanta's Alliance Theatre, The Cherry Lane Theatre, St. Louis Black Repertory Theatre, The Women's Project, and a 2006 collaborative 90th season celebration between Cleveland Play House and Karamu House Theatre (*Saint Lucy's Eyes*, starring Ruby Dee, directed by Billie Allen); Kuntu Repertory Theatre (*The Separation of Blood*, directed by Woodie King Jr.); New York's Ensemble Studio Theatre, where she is a lifetime member (*Rally, Modern Romance, Pluto*, and a commissioned reading of *The Separation of Blood* with James Earl Jones, Brian Stokes Mitchell, Roger Robinson, and Linda Powell); Cleveland Play House (*Forest City*), where she was awarded a Proclamation from the City of Cleveland, Manhattan Theater Club (*The Mark*); and Karamu Theatre (*From Breast Cancer to Broadway*). Her celebrated plays have been published by Samuel French and anthologized in Smith and Kraus' *Best Plays by Women 2001* and *Best Ten Minute Plays 2010*. She participated in the Cherry Lane Theatre Mentor Project 2014 (Mentor: Wendy Keselman). Her article, "The Bird in My Hand: My Journey to Charlie

Parker," about her opera, *Charlie Parker's Yardbird*, was published by *The Guardian,* in June 2017. Bridgette was a 2016 Sundance Ucross Theatre Fellow and received an Appreciation Award in 2009 from Ensemble Studio Theatre's Going to the River. The River Crosses Rivers Festival, for initiating a ten-minute play festival that produced fourteen short plays by women of color, was part of the 2006/08 Women's Projects Producers' Lab. She is an alumni member of Lincoln Center Theatre's Directors Lab, where she initiated four theater projects with the lab, which included programs in collaboration with the Negro Ensemble Company, Cherry Lane Theatre, and Riverside Church Theatre. Her fellowships include Manhattan Theatre Club (The Mark) and Cave Canem, where she is a lifetime member. Her poems are published in six of their anthologies of poetry from 1999 to 2006. Wimberly is Founder and Program Director of From Breast Cancer to Broadway, a program that teaches playwriting to and presents short plays by breast cancer survivors, performed by professional actors at professional theaters in collaborations with medical centers. She is also the recipient of fellowships and awards from the New York Foundation for the Arts and The New York Urban Arts Initiative. She serves on the Board of Directors of off-Broadway's Cherry Lane Theatre. She is a 2018 Audible commissioned playwright.

CHARACTERS

TANYA, 40, attractive.
ROLANDO, a little younger, handsome.
CHARLES, a little older.

SETTING

Tanya's living room.

TIME

The present.

Note

Permission to produce *Modern Romance* does not include the rights to this music. *

• • •

TANYA's *living room in the late afternoon. We see a sofa and chair placed in front of a cocktail table, where a vase of roses, a bottle of red wine, two glasses,* *a romance novel, a television remote, and house keys rest. One of the glasses of wine is half-empty. The other has not been touched. There is a large floor plant behind the sofa and a set of golf clubs between two doors leading to the bedroom and the kitchen, respectively. We hear jazz music, i.e., "My Funny Valentine."* As lights come up on Tanya sitting on Rolando's lap, they are kissing passionately. They stare at each other briefly. He takes her hand.*

ROLANDO: Baby, I've got to go.

TANYA: Come on, be brave and stay the night.

ROLANDO: You know I can't do that.

TANYA: Just this one night. Just one! I'm worth that.

ROLANDO: You know you are sugar, sweet as ripe fruit on a summer vine. You know I love you more than anything You are my heart.

TANYA: But . . .

ROLANDO: Our agreement.

TANYA: Agreement?

ROLANDO: Yeah. It was your idea. A way to keep things uncomplicated. Keep your time free, your options open. Remember?

TANYA: No!

ROLANDO: Tanya!

TANYA: What?

ROLANDO: You can change your mind, but you can't change the truth.

TANYA: (*As she gets up and sits on the couch.*) Fine. Go!

ROLANDO: (*Sings Otis Redding's "Try a Little Tenderness."* Or another song as she walks away.*) "Oh, she may be weary. Young girls, they do get weary, wearing that same ol' shaggy dress. But when she gets weary, try a little tenderness, that's all you gotta do . . ." (*After a beat or two.*) I can stay a little longer. I just can't do all the things you want me to. That's all. I want to. You know that.

TANYA: Yeah, right.

ROLANDO: Don't spoil things. You want some more wine?

TANYA: Whatever.

ROLANDO: Come on. Our afternoons have been great, right?

TANYA: If you say so.

> (*ROLANDO pours more wine, filling TANYA's half-empty glass. TANYA picks up the paperback book from the cocktail table and opens it as ROLANDO hands her the glass.*)

ROLANDO: Here.

> (*She takes it and sits it on the table. Continues paging through the book.*)

Don't do that.

TANYA: Do what?

ROLANDO: Spoil what we have.

TANYA: (*Referring to the book.*) You mean, this old romance novel? I was with you when I bought it. You were right. It's a hot one.

ROLANDO: Put it down, Tanya. Have some wine. Come sit back on my lap.
(*Takes her hand. Tries to pull her off the sofa.*)

TANYA: (*Resisting, she begins to read aloud.*) "He kisses her. His body hard against her soft, moist femininity. How could she resist him? His eyes search her hungry soul. She could not hide her longing for him. He runs his hands through her curly hair, whispers his passions deep in her ear."

ROLANDO: Tanya, this is rude. I'm here for you now.

TANYA: (*Reading.*) "'I'll stay the night,' he promises her. 'I'll stay every night if that's what you want. I can't get enough of your sugar-sweet love. Like ripe fruit hanging on the summer vine.'"

ROLANDO: (*Covering the book with his hand, stopping her from reading.*)
Now I know why men don't read this stuff.

TANYA: Why? Men do it. You seduce, you promise, gain some poor woman's confidence, then steal her heart . . .

ROLANDO: You are no poor, helpless woman. You knew exactly what you were getting into with me. I never lied to you.

TANYA: You seduced me. You knew how vulnerable I was, and you took advantage of that. All these afternoons here in my bedroom, at cafés, on the beach, in the taxi . . .

ROLANDO: You set the rules. *You* set them! Afternoons, no strings, just two people enjoying each other. Remember? You and me, the sun high in the sky, wine, music, the beach, dancing, lying naked in your bed making stupid, hot, passionate love while the rest of the world busied itself with commerce and problems. We had none of that. So, what's changed?

TANYA: Me, Rolando. I've changed. (*Snatching the book from him, reads.*) "He knew how deeply she was falling for him. It was more than just the sex. He knew she could get that from anyone. But he hinted at more. His kisses promised commitment."

ROLANDO: Commitment?

TANYA: (*Turning the open book toward him.*) Commitment!

ROLANDO: What about Charles?

TANYA: Why are you bringing him up?

ROLANDO: Are you serious!

TANYA: This has nothing to do with him, Rolando. This is about you and me. I love you. How many times do I have to say it? I love you!

ROLANDO: More than you love Charles?

TANYA: Do you even have to ask that? You know how unhappy I've been. You made me feel whole again.

ROLANDO: For the afternoons, Tanya. We agreed. I'd make you feel good and wanted, cherished, appreciated . . .

TANYA: Sexy and titillating and desirable and . . .

ROLANDO: Alive! Yes.

TANYA: Yes. And most of all, loved.

ROLANDO: (*Quietly.*) In the afternoons. I haven't let you down.
     (*Pulling her onto his lap.*)
You make me feel the same way. I lust for you. I love the way you handle me. You turn me on. Baby, I don't want this to end. You have to know that.

(He kisses her neck. She tries not to respond.)

TANYA: I want to be the only thing on your mind . . . all day long, Rolando. Why can't we have this all day long?
(Throwing the book on the table.)
Is there someone else? Someone for your evenings? The reason you can't stay?

ROLANDO: *(Kissing her.)* Shhh, baby. Come on, don't spoil it. I love you. Let me taste your love.

TANYA: I envy her, whoever she is. I envy the nights she spends with you. The dinners by candlelight, dancing by moonlight, the walks under the stars.
(She stands, pulling him to his feet.)
Oh my God, Rolando! To be dressed in an evening gown on your dapper arm, twirling to our favorite song.
(She sings Otis Redding as they dance a little.)
"You know she's waiting, just anticipating the things that she'll never, never, never, never possess, yeah, yeah, while she's there without them, try a little tenderness."
(Laughs, looking into his eyes.)
And after an incredible night making hot, passionate love, we greet the morning together. So, stay! There's some spaghetti with my special marinara sauce in the kitchen. Stay for dinner.

ROLANDO: *(Forcing TANYA out of his arms.)* Tanya, I can't do this. This is not like you. It's not me . . . not us, baby, please.

TANYA: It can be.

ROLANDO: I've got to go.

TANYA: *(Walking away from him.)* You're mean. You know that?

ROLANDO: You're married! Did you forget that!

TANYA: When did you become so sensitive?

ROLANDO: *(As he picks up his coat, puts it on.)* Should I come back tomorrow? I'll be here with bells on, if that's what you want.

(TANYA picks up his keys off the table, putting them behind her back. She smiles and runs to the other side of the room, laughing.)

TANYA: You're not going anywhere.

ROLANDO: (*Chasing her.*) Come on, Tanya, this is childish. Look at the time! Charles could come home any minute.

TANYA: Let him! Let him see what his boring wife has been up to all these weeks. Let him see that someone really cares for me. Loves and appreciates me! Someone handsome who doesn't cuss and scream and ignore me. (*Suddenly sad.*) I hate him. I hate myself more.

ROLANDO: Let's not do this.

> (*TANYA throws the keys on the table. They stand, staring at each other. She picks up the glass of wine and sits down. ROLANDO tries to comfort her, but she resists.*)

TANYA: I hate men. I hate you.
> (*She picks up the book. Hands it to him.*)
I chose afternoons because I planned my mornings looking for a new job. I wanted to spend my afternoons enjoying myself. Taking care of me for a change. I told you how depressed I was, being laid off. How impossible my husband was.

ROLANDO: I know. You've been having a hard time.

TANYA: Charles doesn't love me! He hasn't for a long time. It's awful to lie in bed with a man all night and still be lonely.
> (*She stares at him for a reflective beat.*)
It wasn't my intention to meet you or anybody that afternoon. I was just in the bookstore looking for a good book and . . .

ROLANDO: There you were, Miss Sunshine. You looked at me and smiled the biggest, brightest, sweetest smile I think I've ever seen. I knew you were lonely. But you had your head on your shoulders. You knew who you were and what you wanted. Afternoons. That was our agreement. Your mornings were for business. Your evenings for Charles.

> (*TANYA looks away in disagreement, shaking her head. ROLANDO turns her face back toward him.*)

Yes. Your afternoons are for me. And I will love you like no other man ever will, because I love you like no other man can. This is for the best. You're a smart, beautiful woman. You'll find another job soon and . . .

TANYA: I'll die from numbness. Go completely insane sitting right here on this couch. Do you understand? I can't go on without feeling something, not after loving you. You breathed life back into every cell in my body. Charles knows nothing about passion or romance. He thinks a G spot is the sound you get strumming chords on that guitar he plays more than he even talks to me.

(She takes the book, holds it close to her chest.)
And we used to talk all the time, he and I. We used to laugh, used to take long walks and hot baths. We used to be inseparable. Now all we do is argue, if we speak at all.

ROLANDO: It won't be good if Charles knows. He already suspects. I think that's why you're so edgy, so uptight, desperate! Threesomes don't work, baby. Not for me. I think I can safely say it won't work for you either. Okay? Are we cool?

(TANYA opens the book, tries to read, but he stops her.)

TANYA: What if I leave him? Don't you want me to?

ROLANDO: *(Disapproving.)* Tanya!

(Keys are heard in the distance. A door opens.)

ROLANDO: *(Startled, whispers.)* Damn! It's Charles!
(He stands, anticipating trouble.)
Now what? What are we going to do? Baby, you just messed things up bad!

CHARLES: *(Calling offstage.)* Tanya! Tanya, you home? What you got the chain on the door for! Tanya!

TANYA: *(Taking ROLANDO's hand)* I'm worth it, Rolando. Say I'm worth it. *(To CHARLES.)* Hold on, I'm coming!

(She walks offstage to the unseen door as ROLANDO quickly hides behind a standing plant. TANYA reenters, quickly walking back to the couch, turns as CHARLES enters the room.)

CHARLES: *(Puzzled by the way she is dressed, he drops his briefcase.)* Tanya? What's going on?
(He steps toward her.)
You didn't have that on last night. And you sure didn't have that on this morning when I left either!

(TANYA backs away, picks up her robe from the sofa, covers herself, then stands in front of the plant shielding ROLANDO. CHARLES and TANYA stand staring at each other.)

I don't believe this!

(CHARLES turns and walks angrily toward his golf club bag, pulls out a club, and exits into the bedroom, looking for a fight. TANYA follows him to the bedroom doorway.)

TANYA: *(Shouts into the bedroom.)* Believe it!
(She turns toward ROLANDO, who steps out from behind the plant. Staring at him briefly, she whispers.) I'm not sorry.
(ROLANDO puts his finger to his lips, signalling her to be quiet. We hear CHARLES's incoherent tirade from the bedroom. He exits quickly, storming into the kitchen as TANYA follows him. We can hear them in an incomprehensible heated argument as ROLANDO steps from behind the plant. Suddenly, there is a loud crash of a pot or plate hitting the floor. ROLANDO is jumpy, not knowing what to do. He searches for his keys— pant pockets, coat, couch—before retrieving them from the table. He heads for the door. TANYA comes out of the kitchen carrying her book.)

TANYA: *(Calling to him softly.)* Rolando! Are you leaving without your book?

(ROLANDO turns slightly toward her. She walks over to him, turning him completely so they are face-to-face. Opens book, panic fills his face.)

Are you alright, baby? *(Reading from the book.)* "She asked in a comforting but reassuring voice. She knew there was no turning back now. She could feel his heart racing. She wanted him to know she was worth the risk, worth the fight, worth the night."

(CHARLES enters from the kitchen without his jacket, carrying a plate of spaghetti. He looks at her disappointedly.)

CHARLES: Well, well, well!!! Look here, we're having spaghetti with marinara sauce, AGAIN.

TANYA: *(As she leads ROLANDO back to the couch)* Well, well, well!!! It's not like you're here for dinner half the time anyway.

CHARLES: Don't start with that. You know I have to work. What's your excuse?

(Sitting in the chair.)
I'm tired, Tanya. I've had a long week. I don't want to argue, please. What's up with you anyway? Why are you dressed like that? You look like you never got out of bed.

(She ignores him, helping ROLANDO out of his coat.)

CHARLES: (Snatching the book out of her hands.) Is this all you've been doing all day, reading these dumb-ass romance novels again? You find a job!

(He waits for her to answer. TANYA extends her hand for her book, but CHARLES, incredulous, does not respond. She stands behind ROLANDO, rubbing his shoulders comforting him. CHARLES turns the book over and reads the title with exuberance.)
Afternoons with Rolando!!!! That sounds exciting.

(TANYA tries to take the book. CHARLES puts it out of her reach. They stare at each other. CHARLES reads with a dramatic expression.)

"Rolando knew he could not leave her. He was nervous, but without saying, she knew he had agreed to stay. Their agreement had changed." (*To* TANYA.) Now I know why men don't read this stuff.

(TANYA takes the book back. CHARLES picks up the glass of wine, sips it.)

CHARLES: Wine! Are we expecting company, or is this supposed to go with our week-old spaghetti?

(Gives her a suspicious look. They stare uneasily at each other. CHARLES picks up the remote and turns on the television. We hear canned laughter from a mindless sitcom. TANYA, standing behind CHARLES, reaches out as though she is going to massage his shoulders but retracts, folding her arms around herself.)

TANYA: I had a job interview this morning.

(We hear canned laughter. CHARLES laughs with it.)

CHARLES: What's that?
(He continues to eat.)

TANYA: I said, could you turn that thing down please? I can't hear myself think!

CHARLES: Sorry.

(He turns it down. TANYA sits on the couch next to ROLANDO. She looks at Charles, who continues to watch TV. Opens her book.)

TANYA: (*Reading.*) "They ignore him. He is disgusting. (*Looking at* CHARLES.) Rolando kisses her as he rides her with skillful passion enough to melt the North and South Poles. 'New agreement,' she whispers. 'I'm leaving Charles tomorrow.' They continue making passionate, hot love right under his nose. Rolando whispers his passions deep in her ear.

(ROLANDO puts his arms around her. She rests her head on his chest, throws the book on the table.)

"I love you. I'll love you in the mornings, in the afternoons, and all through the night. He promises her, tomorrow, after they've showered and had breakfast together, they would ride horseback off into their glorious future. She could hardly wait."

(We hear canned laughter. TANYA and ROLANDO continue to caress one another passionately as CHARLES watches TV in the glow of the light from the television as lights fade to black and an Otis Redding tune is heard.)

END OF PLAY

MY AIM IS TRUE

by Lucy Wang

Production History:

Staged reading, 365 Women A Year in Los Angeles, September 26, 2015, at Samuel French Theatre and Film Bookshop, Los Angeles, California. This performance was directed by Jean Bruce Scott (then producing executive director of Native Voices at the Autry). Rob Nagle played the role of the FBI director, and Delanna Studi (currently Co-Artistic Director of Native Voices at the Autry) played the role of Anna Mae Aquash.

Two staged readings produced by NO Plays in New Haven, March 10–11, 2017, at the Silk Road Art Gallery directed by Shellen Lubin. John Little played the role of the FBI director, and Alexandra Dehart played the role of Anna Mae Aquash.

HERSTORICAL FIGURES II, Playwrights for Pets Fundraiser, Rescue Dogs for Rescue Soldiers. This staged reading was held at the Producers Club in New York, November 10, 2019. This performance was directed by Sue Yocum. David Lapkin played the role of the FBI director, and Sera Lys played the role of Anna Mae Aquash.

Lucy Wang writes, teaches, and performs. Her plays have been performed all over, and are available from Applause Books, Original Works Publishing, Amazon, and YouthPLAYS. Wang has also written two short films (one of which she directed), and sold a half-hour comedy. Her awards include the Kennedy Center Fund for New American Plays, Best New Political Social Play from the Katherine and Lee Chilcote Foundation, Berrilla Kerr

Foundation, James Thurber Fellowship, CAPE's New Writers TV Award, NATPE Diversity Fellow, William and Flora Hewlett Foundation Honorary Fellow, and Annenberg Community Beach House Writer in Residence. She also won an NEA playwrights initiative fellowship at Djerassi, May/June 2019, and outstanding female artist in Los Angeles, 2020.

CHARACTERS

ANNA MAE AQUASH, Micmac woman, almost 30 years of age. She's a good mimic.
FBI AGENT, male, any age.

SETTING

Pierre, South Dakota, on November 24, 1975. Interrogation room.

• • •

ANNA MAE *is being interrogated by an FBI agent.*

FBI AGENT: We can keep you for as long as you want, you know.

ANNA MAE: You mean for as long as *you* want. Not me.

FBI AGENT: Or you can walk out of here a free woman, Anna Mae. It's up to you.

ANNA MAE: There's no such thing as a free Indian.

FBI AGENT: Tell us about Banks.

ANNA MAE: I'm sure I don't know anything you don't already know.

FBI AGENT: Then you know he's never gonna leave her. Ka-mook.

ANNA MAE: Ka-mook is my friend.

FBI AGENT: Who do you think you're fooling?

ANNA MAE: Fine. Rub it in. More salt, please.

FBI AGENT: He's done you wrong, Anna Mae. Hiding when you and Ka-mook are locked up in jail. Leaves you two behind bars while he runs off scot-free. What kind of man does that to the women he loves?

ANNA MAE: A man in fear for his life.

FBI AGENT: I ask you, is that right? Aren't you his soul mate? Wait, before you answer, I have something profound to share with you.

(Retrieves sheet of paper from his pocket, reads.)

"But the sun is up and you're going?
My heart is filled with tears.
Please don't go, I need you walking by my side . . .
The road is long and weary
And I get so tired."

Oh, Anna Mae, poor Anna Mae, how could he wring your heart dry? Let's get the lying, cheating bastard.

ANNA MAE: Where'd you get ahold of my poem?

FBI AGENT: I can either let you go, or I can let Ka-mook go. Where is he, Anna?

ANNA MAE: You think I know? Nobody tells me anything.

FBI AGENT: And why should I believe you?

ANNA MAE: None of your charges have stuck so far, have they?

FBI AGENT: Even if you knew, I bet you wouldn't tell me.

ANNA MAE: What could I know? The men run the movement.

FBI AGENT: Is that fair? When capable, intelligent women like you and Ka-mook comprise half the movement?

ANNA MAE: I'm doing what I can to change things for the better. To be the change I wish to see in the world. It starts with education.

FBI AGENT: You've stirred up a lot of resentment and jealousy from what I hear. Some people say you can't be trusted. You know too much, do too much. Some people say that makes you the perfect snitch.

ANNA MAE: Trust, like Indian land, is sacred. My aim is true.

FBI AGENT: Hey, the FBI believes you. We're offering to put our trust in you. Full faith and credit.

ANNA MAE: In exchange for some version of the truth and some land.

FBI AGENT: In exchange for valuable information.

ANNA: You want the truth? The truth is, white people think this country belongs to them. Put that in your treaty.

FBI AGENT: Funny. You think your AIM is true, but there are plenty of folks, particularly women, on Pie Patrol who think very, very differently. Now, personally I prefer cake, so I can help you if you cooperate.

ANNA MAE: Oh wait, here's something you might like to know about me and Dennis.

FBI AGENT: Excellent. I'm ready when you are.

ANNA MAE: The first night I met Dennis Banks . . .

FBI AGENT: (*Eager.*) He recruited you at the standoff at Wounded Knee . . .

ANNA MAE: Dennis tried to assign me kitchen duty. Can you believe that? Me?

FBI AGENT: I heard you were a real good cook.

ANNA MAE: Really? Well, my pie is killer.

FBI AGENT: You know just how to turn up the heat.

ANNA MAE: Who would say a ridiculous thing like that?

FBI AGENT: Your buddy Leonard Peltier.

ANNA MAE: Yeah, right.

FBI AGENT: Peltier is spreading rumors you're an informant. He wants you out. You must have something on him for him to feel so threatened.

ANNA MAE: Oh, you know Leonard, he likes to talk. (*Mimicking Leonard.*) "Innocence has a single voice that can only say over and over again, *I didn't do it.* Guilt has a thousand voices, all of them lies."

FBI AGENT: Is Thelma Rios lying when she says you're a turncoat? How about Lorelei DeCora? I bet her name feels like a hard punch to the face.

ANNA MAE: You'll say anything, won't you?

FBI AGENT: I'm trying to save your life, Anna Mae.

ANNA MAE: Are you? I'm *that* important?

FBI AGENT: My aim is true, too.

ANNA MAE: Then please help me save more Indians by giving them a solid education. Training. Jobs. We have the lowest per capita income, the highest unemployment, one of the highest murder rates, and the government blames us for drowning our sorrows in alcohol. What happened to our civil rights, our dignity, our future?

FBI AGENT: What happened to your beautiful daughters? When was the last time you saw Denise and Deborah?

ANNA MAE: I think you know the answer.

FBI AGENT: We know everything. How Jake blindsided you by adopting them, slipping those papers in your coat pocket.

ANNA MAE: Are my girls safe? Please tell me they're safe.

FBI AGENT: Yes. But the question you should be asking is, do you want to live long enough to see them grow up? Get married and give you grandchildren?

ANNA MAE: I pray I live long enough to give my two daughters a brighter future. I want them to be proud to be a MicMac and enjoy the rights to a full life. That's why the night I met Dennis and he tried to assign me to kitchen patrol, I stood up and said, "Mr. Banks, I didn't come here to wash dishes. I came here to fight."

FBI AGENT: You made waves from the beginning.

ANNA MAE: I had to. For my people. For Denise and Deborah.

FBI AGENT: You could've gone to Brandeis. Brandeis offered you a scholarship for your brilliant work at Ruggles Street Day Care, helping low-income Blacks and Indians. How could you refuse? How often does that happen? You were a high school dropout. Think of how different your life would be today. You could be living in Back Bay, catching games at Fenway, wearing Red Sox instead of a "bad jacket."

ANNA MAE: (*Donning a Boston accent.*) Sure, I could've been a chowda-head and parked my car in Harvard yard. (*Normal speech.*) I asked myself the same question. How often does that happen—someone wakes up and says, today, I'm going to help the Indians find good jobs? If not me, who?

FBI AGENT: You can't just come down here and show people up. Men don't like it when you show them their true selves by mimicking what they say, adopting their mannerisms.

ANNA MAE: I swear, it's an unconscious habit. It's why I was so good at community work. I could connect to people quickly. I thought for sure I could do the same for AIM.

FBI AGENT: Pine Ridge ain't Boston. Ain't Maine. You're an outsider. Canadian. Strong, fit, healthy. Last to get sick, first to volunteer. You're bound to make lots of enemies.

ANNA MAE: Yes, I keep having recurring nightmares, where . . .

FBI AGENT: Someone is out to get you.

ANNA MAE: Yes.

FBI AGENT: There are drugs for that, you know. I could get you a prescription. A good night's sleep can do wonders to the brain.

ANNA MAE: Indians who fight the hardest for their people usually end up with bullet holes.

FBI AGENT: In this nightmare, whose face do you see?

ANNA MAE: Different faces.

FBI AGENT: Male, female, animal . . .

ANNA MAE: Every night, it's a different person.

FBI AGENT: No way to live, Anna Mae. If I release you early, promise me you'll go back to Canada. Make yourself scarce.

ANNA MAE: I go where I want because I have nothing to hide.

FBI AGENT: But you just admitted you fear for your life. How old are you?

ANNA MAE: Twenty-nine.

FBI AGENT: A youngster. You have so much to live for. Go home.

ANNA MAE: Indians believe it takes five years for the truth to come out.

FBI AGENT: Five years is a long time to live in fear.

ANNA MAE: The truth always comes out.

FBI AGENT: Fine. Truth is, I got nothing on you. So, my bosses are pressuring me to release you early.

ANNA MAE: But you don't have to, right?

FBI AGENT: Not if you give me a really good reason to keep you here. You can do it. Yes, you can!

ANNA MAE: Perhaps you could give me some stationery and some stamps so I could write a few letters. To my daughters.

FBI AGENT: I suppose you want me to post them too.

ANNA MAE: Please. They're completely innocent.

FBI AGENT: Of course.

ANNA MAE: Thank you.

FBI AGENT: Sure you can't help me help you?

ANNA MAE: I can't. Even if I could, I can't possibly tell everything I know to one person. But if someone follows carefully in my footsteps, they will learn what I know. See how I'm trying to help my people the best way I can.

FBI AGENT: You want me to keep following you?

ANNA MAE: You said you were trying to save my life. Save me.

FBI AGENT: You have to tell me what you know. Everything, or I can't guarantee your safety.

ANNA MAE: I don't expect to live long anyways.

FBI AGENT: We could change that right here. Right now. I'm serious, Anna Mae. Cooperate and live.

ANNA MAE: You know what your people say. The only good Indian is a dead Indian.

FBI AGENT: Hey, I'm not the bad guy here. Our sources indicate the person out to get you is most likely someone within AIM. You never know.

ANNA MAE: The only thing I know is . . .

FBI AGENT: I know, I know, your aim is true. Spare me. That ain't gonna stop anyone from taking dead aim at you. You know it, I know it. Whatcha gonna do, Anna Mae?

ANNA MAE: Maybe I could decide after I write my letters?

FBI AGENT: Sure.

(He exits for stamp and stationery. Short beat. ANNA MAE stands up, faces the audience. Spotlight only on ANNA MAE for her last words.)

ANNA MAE: These white people think this country belongs to them—they don't realize that they are only in charge right now because there's more of them than there are of us. The whole country changed with only a handful of raggedy-ass pilgrims. And it can take a handful of raggedy-ass Indians to do the same, and I intend to be one of those raggedy-ass Indians.

(Blackout.)

END OF PLAY

ON THE CROSS BRONX

by Victoria Z. Daly

First production took place at the New Short Play Festival, New York, NY, March 20 and March 23, 2019. Directed by Andrés Gallardo Bustilo, The cast was as follows:

KATE: Elena Clark
JOE: Anthony DePalma

Victoria Z. Daly's plays have been developed/featured at the Actors Studio, Last Frontier Theatre Conference, ATHE Conference, Warner International Playwrights Festival, Alliance for Jewish Theatre, Berrie Center, Spokane's KPBX-FM (NPR), Gi60 Festivals (NYC and UK), the Edinburgh Festival, and Short+Sweet Festivals in Hollywood, Sydney, and Dubai (where *On The Cross Bronx* won Best Play), among other other venues. She is a faculty member in the Dramatist Guild Institute's Plays in Progress Program and the founder of New York City's 9th Floor Writers and Actors Collaborative. Education: MFA in Dramatic Writing, NYU/Tisch; AB and MBA, Harvard; *Certificat d'Etudes* in theater from L'Ecole Jacques Lecoq. www .victoriazdaily.com.

CHARACTERS

KATE, late 30s to early 40s, from the New York suburbs, frantic and in labor.
JOE, early 30s, Bronx police officer, Bronx accent.

SETTING

A police car parked on the side of the Cross Bronx Expressway.

TIME

Evening rush hour. Now.

Author's Note

It is possible to localize this play, that is, to set it in your geographic vicinity. This would entail changing the title as well as some of the local references This may be done only with the permission of, and in collaboration with, the playwright, mail to: vzdaly@gmail.com.

A "/" within two successive lines of dialogue indicates where those lines overlap.

• • •

Sound of KATE *groaning. Lights dim up on the backseat of a police car. She lies partially upright, her lower half draped in a blanket.* JOE *kneels nearby.*

JOE: BREATHE!

KATE: (*Contraction.*) Aaaah! I don't want to!

JOE: Don't think ya got much choice.

KATE: Aaaah! If I don't breathe, maybe I won't have the baby yet.

JOE: That's not how it works . . .

KATE: If you want to help, all I need from you . . . (*Another contraction.*) is to get me back in my car . . .

JOE: Sorry. Can't do that . . .

KATE: . . . and fix whatever's wrong with it so I can drive myself into Manhattan!

JOE: Your car's not goin' anywhere. Tha engine's seized.

(*A car honks.*)

KATE: (*To car.*) Yeah, you too, jerk! (*To* JOE.) My daughter's supposed to be born in a suite at Mount Sinai Hospital! In a birthing tub!

JOE: That's real nice . . .

KATE: My husband holding my hand! (*Groans.*) Arrrghh! A new start!

JOE: I'm tryin' ta help here!

KATE: Mozart playing! Essential oils, wafting through diffusers! I brought it all with me.
    (*Pulls out her phone.*)
See? Mozart! (*And a bottle.*) Sandalwood oil . . .

JOE: What does sandalwood do?

KATE: CALM you! What do you THINK! (*Contraction.*) Aaah! This is all his fault!

JOE: (*Into radio.*) ETA on that ambulance?

KATE: My husband promised he'd take my car to the shop because the check engine light stayed lit. He promised he wouldn't work late this week. He never keeps his fucking promises!

JOE: Breathe!

KATE: No! A new start! He promised!

JOE (*Into radio.*) Gotcha . . . Gotcha . . . (*To himself.*) Hell. (*To her.*) They're caught in a backup, 'bout three miles down. Traffic's clogging tha shoulder.

KATE: Great! So—I drive in. Get off at the wrong exit . . .

JOE: Mrs. Allisberg, work with me.

KATE: You have any idea what contractions feel like?

JOE: Sorry, ma'am, tha department won't let me talk about my personal life.

KATE: They feel like the worst case of stomach flu you've ever had. (*Contraction.*) Ugghhh! Multiplied by ten.

JOE: Mrs. Allisberg—I gotta take a look.

KATE: At what?

(*He indicates the blanket. She pulls it more tightly around her legs.*)
Forget it! You pervert!
(*She takes some fast "Hee-hee-hee"–style Lamaze breaths.*)
No, no—they're like—pull your intestines straight out of your pelvis, then up over your head like some sort of giant water balloon!

JOE: Listen to me. You give birth here, you don't cooperate . . .

KATE: (*Contraction.*) Aaaahh! Or—like—she's an alien, she's chewing her way through my uterus, just chewing and swallowing her way right out through my pelvis . . .

JOE: You don't cooperate, something bad happens . . .

KATE: Something *bad* happens?

JOE: Not that something bad's gonna happen. But see, I'm here, just me, and I'm responsible.

KATE: So get me to Mount Sinai!

JOE: What am I, Moses?

(*Beat.*)

KATE: Funny. You're funny.

JOE: Yeah? You think so?

KATE: Officer, are you married?

JOE: Like I said, I'm not allowed ta talk personal.

KATE: George lets me down—all the time. Promised he'd meet me at every obstetrics appointment, came to the first, blew off the rest. Didn't even come to birthing class. I don't get what his problem is.

JOE: Don't look at me, I don't know the guy.

KATE: Men. Men just *suck*.

(*A moment.*)

JOE: Yeah. Sure.

KATE: I didn't mean you.

JOE: Right. Whatever. Hey, don't matter. I've already heard it all: Cops suck. Men suck.

KATE: Come on.

JOE: I, Joe, personally, suck. Pick whatever sucks tha most, and for sure, I'm it. Excuse my bad language.

KATE: You said personally.

JOE: (*Firm.*) I meant that professionally.

KATE: (*Her face crumples.*) I'm *not* going to cry. Not going to cry, not going to cry, not going to . . .
(*She wails. The wail turns into a contraction.*)

JOE: Mrs. A . . .

KATE: Aaaahhhh!

JOE: This baby's comin,' I'm pretty sure. Tha baby's comin'.

KATE: Not in the backseat of a cop car, she's not! It was supposed to be gently. Sweetly . . . Mozart playing! Mozart playing! My last shot at having a kid!

(*As she talks, he takes off his long-sleeved shirt and drapes it over the front of her shoulders.*)

What are you, what are you . . . ?

JOE: There you go . . . happy thoughts . . .

KATE: What are you . . . ?

JOE: Think happy thoughts . . .

(*She calms a bit.*)

KATE: Have you ever delivered a baby before?

JOE: Like I said . . .

KATE: AHHHH! Just TELL me!

JOE: No. I never delivered a baby before.

KATE: Great.

JOE: But—I took a birthing class. At the Academy.

KATE: That's good. Terrific . . . How long ago was that?
  (*Beat. He doesn't answer.*)
Oh. Oh no. Was it years ago? Was it years and years ago?

JOE: No! A couple a months ago.

KATE: You're a *rookie*!?

JOE: I switched jobs recently.
  (*Off her look.*)
What of it? I got a divorce. Believe me, men are not the only ones who cheat and lie and hurt people. Women suck, too. Women you've loved and cared for since high school. They can suck real bad. So, let's be an equal-opportunity name caller while we're at it.

KATE: All right.

JOE: New start. Last chance, you get me?

KATE: You're not running out of time to have a child.

JOE: You're not running out of time to be a cop. If they hadn't taken me now, I'd be too old. This is it. I need to do a great job.

KATE: Oh, shit. Shit shit shit . . . !
  (*She groans.*)

JOE: At least in class I got an hour of training.

  (*She does the quick Lamaze breaths.*)

KATE: Terrific.

JOE: I'm gonna raise the hips. I'm gonna clamp the cord.

KATE: What! That doesn't happen yet!

JOE: Breathe! Breathe!

KATE: Your car stinks. It smells like disinfectant and mildew.

  (*He opens the bottle of essential oil.*)

JOE: Mm, that's sandalwood?

(*He blows across the top of the open bottle, tries to disperse it with his hands.*)

KATE: What are you doing!!

(*He shakes it all over her.*)

JOE: Just breathe! Breathe! I'm wafting it! Wafting!

KATE: (*Contraction.*) AAAAH!

JOE: Tha baby's comin', Mrs. A. I know it. Come on, let me take a look. Please!

KATE: No, no, no, no . . .

JOE: Please! Just let me take a look. Please!
(*He takes hold of the blanket, she grabs back. They each pull on opposite ends. A standoff.*)

KATE: No—ok! Fine!

(*He pulls the blanket back down over her legs, steels himself, looks under. Note: feel free to play this as discreetly as you like.*)

JOE: JESUS.

KATE: What!

JOE: Ohhhhh . . . Ohhh . . .
(*He backs away.*)

KATE: Joe! Joe, what! . . . Joe! What!

JOE: The head's crownin'.

KATE: Joe . . . ? Joe! . . . Are you scared?
(*This stops him short.*)

KATE: Are you scared?

(*He doesn't answer.*)

You and George, you're just alike. You talk facts, not feelings.

JOE: Do NOT lump me in with that deadbeat husband of yours!

KATE: He . . . He's not a /deadbeat . . .

JOE: /"Men just suck?" Oh yeah? Well, who's takin' care of you? Here, right now? Me! *I* showed up, and I'm takin' care of you, so don't compare us.

KATE: I'm sorry.
(*A moment.*)

JOE: It's all right.
(*A bigger, longer contraction.*)

KATE: Owwww, it hurts, Joe, it hurts, it hurts so much . . .

(*He groans with her.*)

Ow, ow, ow . . . Make it go away, make it go away! . . . Happy thoughts, happy thoughts . . .

JOE: You know, my ex, she never said sorry to me. Not once.

KATE: No? That's sad.

JOE: Yeah. I'm really scared. I never done this before. I'm petrified. I wish there was an armed robbery going on right now I could be taking care of . . . or, or the ground would open and swallow me up. I'm really scared.
(*A moment.*)

KATE: Thank you.
(*She breathes and lies back.*)
Oh, fuck! I don't want to have a baby! I don't want to be a mother! I don't want to do this alone!

(*He takes her hand.*)

JOE: You got New York.

KATE: What?

JOE: You're not alone. You got tha whole New York City police department behind you right now. They're on their way. Right now, tha NYPD is gonna help you deliver your child. As gently and sweetly as we can. Ok?

(*A moment. Sound of ambulance siren; flashing lights.*)

JOE: Oh, thank God. (*Motioning to the car outside.*) Over here! She's over here!

KATE: All right, I'm ready to push.

JOE: No! No . . .

KATE: I'm going to push now!

JOE: No, hear that? They're comin'! They're here!

KATE: I'm breathing! Joe, I'm breathing!

JOE: Wait! Wait . . .

KATE: Joe? Joe! Just don't let go.

(*Still holding her hand, with his free hand he clicks on her phone. It plays a piece by Mozart.*)

KATE: Ahhh/hhh!!

(*JOE chimes in.*)

JOE: /Ahhhhhh!

(*Lights go to black as the Mozart piece plays.*)

KATE and JOE's VOICES: AHHHHHH!

END OF PLAY

PEACE PLAZA

by Christine Toy Johnson

Originally commissioned by ReImagined World Entertainment with grant support from the California Civil Liberties Public Education Program in 2011.

Premiere staged reading produced by Leviathan Lab (info@leviathan lab.com), as part of their "Dark Night Series" on November 19, 2011, at the Arclight Theatre, New York City, with the following cast:

DOROTHY: Yan Xi
LILY: Dawn Saito
GENIE: Ali Ewoldt

Directed by Christine Toy Johnson.

Christine Toy Johnson is an award-winning writer, actor, director, film-maker, and advocate for inclusion. Her plays, libretti, and screenplays have been commissioned, developed, and produced across the country by such companies as the Roundabout Theatre Company, The O'Neill Theater Center, Prospect Theater Company, Village Theatre, Crossroads Theatre, Theatre Elision, Leviathan Lab, Diverse City Theatre Company, The Barrow Group, Weston Playhouse, Gorilla Rep, CAP21, the New York Film Academy, and the Writers Lab (supported by Meryl Streep and Nicole Kidman) and are included in the Library of Congress Asian Pacific American Performing Arts Collection. She is part of the elected leadership of the Dramatists Guild of America (and chair of the Guild's Diversity, Equity, and Inclusion Committee), founder of the Asian American Composers and

Lyricists Project, and an alum of the BMI Musical Theatre Writing Workshop. Christine is the host of The Dramatists Guild's podcast TALKBACK, distributed on the Broadway Podcast Network. Details: www.christinetoy-johnson.com. Twitter: @CToyJ.

CHARACTERS

DOROTHY LEE, Chinese American, 34.
LILY OKAMOTO, Japanese American, 40.
IMOGENE (GENIE) OKAMOTO, Japanese American, Lily's pregnant
    daughter, 18.

TIME

April 3 and 4, 1968.

PLACE

Peace Plaza in Japantown, San Francisco, and at an Oakland peace rally.

• • •

The rhythmic sound of Taiko drums beats, then fades into a distant echo. Early evening. LILY stares at the Peace Pagoda in Peace Plaza and then sits on the edge of it. She looks up and down the street. DOROTHY, in a flurry of energy, rushes past, then returns to where LILY is sitting.

DOROTHY: Excuse me, ma'am. Do you know that store that makes those squishy little rice balls? Sweet-ish? Sort of. Like dessert, if you like that sort of thing? Oh! Ben-ky-oo-doo, maybe? On Buchanan Street! Oh dear. Maybe I'm not saying it right. Ben-ky-oh-toh? Is that it?
    (She finally looks at LILY's face.)
Mrs. Okamoto! I'm sorry. I didn't realize it was you . . .

LILY: Mrs. Lee.

DOROTHY: Long time, no see!

LILY: But I saw you this morning. At school.

DOROTHY: Right. Um. Never mind. Geez, getting sent to the principal's office never gets fun, does it? Thirty-four years old, and I still feel like I'm the one in trouble when they call our house.

LILY: They call that often?

DOROTHY: What? No! No. That's not what I meant. Look, I know you think it's Jack's fault what happened . . .

LILY: Yes, I do.

DOROTHY: But let's face it! Boys will be boys! And if they get into a fight with other boys . . .

LILY: Black boys.

DOROTHY: So?

LILY: If they get into a fight with black boys, then one of them has a problem that goes deeper than just being a boy. In this neighborhood.

DOROTHY: What are you saying? That my son is a racist?

LILY: You tell me.

DOROTHY: He's five!

LILY: I just know that my son has never had a problem with any of the boys in the Fillmore. Until your son moved into our neighborhood and started being a bad influence.

DOROTHY: Oh, really?

LILY: Really.

DOROTHY: Maybe you're the one who has a problem.

LILY: Maybe I am.
    (She gets up.)
It's pronounced Ben-kyo-doh, by the way. And you're looking for *manju*. Straight through the Buchanan Mall, on the corner. They close at six, so you'd better hurry.

DOROTHY: Oh. Okay. Thanks.

LILY: Why are you even bothering if you don't like it?

DOROTHY: It's for my husband's boss.

LILY: *(Surprised.)* He's Japanese?

DOROTHY: John Sullivan? Heck no! But we're celebrating this big job they just finished. Right where we're standing, as a matter of fact! See, my Tommy worked on the design of this whole trade center here . . .

LILY: The trade center they built on top of my sister's house.

DOROTHY: I beg your pardon?

LILY: But where else were they going to put the Benihana, right?

DOROTHY: (*Not catching her sarcasm.*) I love Benihana! Have you been?

LILY: No. I haven't.

DOROTHY: Anyway, I thought it'd be cute to have something Japanese for dessert!

LILY: I see. Well, then. Enjoy.

DOROTHY: I will! Thanks!

   (*LILY begins to pace, agitated.*)

Are you alright?

LILY: What? Of course. I'm fine.

DOROTHY: No, really.

LILY: No, really. I'm fine. Now, if you'll excuse me . . .

DOROTHY: I know we didn't exactly get off on the right foot. But . . . mother to mother? I know that look. You're way past tired and cranky. What's going on?
   (*Beat.*)

LILY: It's my daughter. Genie. She's late. She's never late.

DOROTHY: I didn't know you had a daughter! Me, too! Abigail's almost two now! Who knows? Maybe someday they'll be friends!

LILY: Not likely.

DOROTHY: Oh?

LILY: Genie's eighteen.

DOROTHY: Hey—free babysitting for you! That's cool!

LILY: And pregnant.

DOROTHY: Hey—free babysitting for her! That's cool!

LILY: I never should have let her go.

DOROTHY: Where?

LILY: To the rally . . .

  (DOROTHY watches as LILY tells her the story.)

Yesterday. *Benkyodo* had just opened, and we were picking up some *manju* for breakfast . . .

DOROTHY: For breakfast? Really?

  (GENIE enters, wearing a "Peace Is Love" T-shirt. She is very pregnant.)

GENIE: For breakfast? Really, Mom, can't we just go to Denny's one day and have some ham and eggs?

LILY: Of course we can.

GENIE: Right on!

LILY: The next time that you're paying.

  (DOROTHY laughs. LILY looks at her appreciatively.)
So tomorrow we'll meet here at 2:30, right? I want you to meet this young man working at the paper, and he . . .

GENIE: Mom. I can't.

LILY: What do you mean, you can't? I thought we said . . .

GENIE: I know we did. But see, there's this thing. In Oakland tomorrow. And Sam really wants me to . . .

LILY: Sam Chang?

GENIE: What other Sam is there?

LILY: What kind of "thing"?

GENIE: Promise you won't get mad.

LILY: Promise you won't say anything to make me mad.

GENIE: There's this rally . . .

LILY: No. Absolutely not.

GENIE: A peace rally. To support Dr. King. While he speaks in Memphis tomorrow. Sam says it will be a chance to meet his other friends and . . .

LILY: You do know that protesting the war won't do any good.

GENIE: Like you would know what that's about.

LILY: Excuse me?

GENIE: Nothing, Mom. I'm sorry. And anyway, this isn't even about war. It's about peace. Look, I can't just sit around while this country goes down the drain. Sam is helping people. Poor people. White people. Black people. The Panthers are . . .

LILY: Don't tell me. The Panthers are all about "serving the people."

GENIE: But they are!

LILY: Oh, Genie! For heaven's sake!

GENIE: No! Mom! They are! They're giving hot breakfasts to poor kids all over the city, every day! And when they talk about our rights, they're talking about our rights, too!

LILY: These people are dangerous, Imogene! And I don't want you near them. Period. End of story.

GENIE: They're my friends, Mom. And I believe in them.

LILY: You can't fight the system without the system fighting back.

GENIE: And you can't base everything in your life on what happened to Uncle Michael twenty-five years ago. That was then, this is now! (*Beat.*) Look, it's just a peace rally. It will be over by 3:00, and I'll be here to tell you all about it an hour later, okay? Maybe an hour and a half. Two. Tops. How 'bout I call you?

(*DOROTHY steps forward.*)

DOROTHY: Oh! See? It's only quarter of six now! Don't worry—she's probably just hanging out with her buddies. Her buddies, the Black Panthers.

(She half-heartedly makes a power fist.)

GENIE: You trust me, don't you?

LILY: Yes. Of course I do.

GENIE: Okay then.
(She kisses her mother on the cheek.)
I'll see ya tomorrow! Don't worry! You worry too much! Peace!
(She runs out.)

LILY: Peace.

(Back to the present.)

DOROTHY: I'm sure she's fine!

LILY: But after what happened today, to Dr. King! Who knows what's happened today?

(GENIE appears again, in another reality, looking at her mother from a distance.)

GENIE: The truth is, I knew my mom would be worried if I told her what was really going on. But she worries about everything. And Sam had this amazing idea! To bring the Panthers together in a big rally at the same exact time when Dr. King was talking to the workers in Mobile! The energy was so powerful! We sang and drank, and well, you don't need to know the rest. It seemed like nothing could go wrong ever again. As long as we were together, united in love and action and dreaming of the better world we were seeing change right in front of our eyes. And then that world fell into the sea. And I started to wonder if she was right. I started to wonder if you really can't change the world. That if Mom and Uncle Michael and all the others had tried to fight back in the camps—it wouldn't have made any difference, like she's always said. Like she's always said, "We're just pawns in the white man's theater of politics." I know it's a mixed metaphor, and I always used to think it was lame. But it suddenly started to make sense. *(Beat.)* Then a fleck of gold from Sam's eyes jumped into my heart, and I realized that I couldn't go down that road. Because if I can't believe in a better world for our baby, what is there to believe in? So, I told him that we needed to stick together. Make a candlelight vigil. And that's what we did. For all the truths we still hold to be self-evident. For all the faith that we still have that we can be the change we want to see, that we can still have a dream, that one day we will overcome. That one day my neighbors will look at me as a human being, not as a "slant-eyed gook" responsible for killing their only son in a jungle ten thousand miles away. But peace was no longer in our grasp by then. Peace had been torn away from us, until there was nothing to do but tear back.

(There is a crescendo of Taiko drumming—and then gunshots. GENIE fades away.)

DOROTHY: I mean, we women worry too much, right? That's what we do.

LILY: If something happens to her, I'll never forgive myself.

DOROTHY: Times have changed. People express themselves differently now.

LILY: And some people don't like it when they do.

DOROTHY: Well, that's nothing different.

LILY: My brother Michael, he fought for what he believed in. But it didn't fight for him. That's what I worry about. That it's the 442, World War II . . . all over again.

DOROTHY: What do you mean?

LILY: You fight too hard, you get killed in battle, and still nothing changes.

DOROTHY: You can't believe that! We can't believe that! And with all due respect, Mrs. Okamoto. That was then. This is now!

LILY: Is it?

(DOROTHY takes LILY's hand. LILY resists at first, then gives in. They sit in silence.)

DOROTHY: You'll see. She'll be okay. And so will we. Robert Kennedy will be our next president, and we'll all be just fine. Right?

(GENIE appears again at the height of the rally. Loud chants of "We shall overcome" give way to the sound of Taiko drumming again, as it gets louder and louder, then ends in a deafening silence.)

(Blackout.)

END OF PLAY

PRIVILEGE

by Susan Kim

Originally produced as part of Ensemble Studio Theatre's 37th Marathon of One-Act Plays (produced by EST in association with Radio Drama Network), May 12–June 1, 2019. Directed by Jose Zayas. The cast was as follows:

A: Laura Gomez
B: Ana Grosse
C: Dalia Davi
D: Satomi Blair

Susan Kim's plays include *The Joy Luck Club*, *The Arrangement*, *Merlin's Apprentice* (lyrics: Stephen Cole; score: Matthew Ward), *Memento Mori, Pandora, Dreamtime for Alice, Rapid Eye Movement, Seventh Word Four Syllables,* and *Death and the Maiden*. Her plays have been produced around the country and are published by Dramatists Play Service and Smith and Kraus. With her husband, Laurence Klavan, she has written YA fiction and graphic novels. Susan has also written fiction, nonfiction, documentaries, and children's TV. She is a winner of a Writers Guild of America award and has been nominated for an Emmy six times. She currently teaches in the low-residency MFA program at Goddard College.

CHARACTERS

A.
B.
C.
D.

Notes

A and B are a couple, as are C and D.

All should be in their 40s–60s and cast with a flexible eye regarding race, ethnicity, and gender/gender preference/gender identification.

SETTING

The upscale living room of A and B.

TIME

The time is now.

• • •

D is looking at a phone.

D: oh my god

B: right?

D: I can't believe that's/you

B: the hair the glasses the whole/look

D: you weigh ninety pounds. Both of you
How old are you?
You two are/babies

　　A and C enter.

C (to A): did you even read it?

A : I don't need to
that's the point

B (to A): When was Take Back the Night?
Was that sophomore year?

A : freshman.

B: wait . . . this is cafeteria workers. Or divestiture?
"Wesleyan out of South Africa/now."

C: but it was in the *Times*

A: oh then of course it's true.
I can't believe you just said/that

D: what are you two fighting about?

A: we're not/fighting

C: We're *talking* about that article. The one I/sent you?

A: Article? You mean blog

C: blog article
what's the difference

A: The difference is an article is researched. It's reported.
This was an opinion

C: yes but he makes good/points

A: No. We live in a
We're *drowning* in opinions. People are getting paid to have opinions.
And we're wasting our lives reading/them.

B: You can't invalidate an argument just because someone has an opinion.

A: Then call it something else. Call it
That's why they have reporting
Like that bullshit piece? It was in the *Atlantic* a few years ago.
Everyone was talking about it

D: what piece?

A: by that guy. That "journalist"?
He says that no one he knows
no one we know
can get their hands on five hundred dollars

B: You mean poor people

A: Not poor people. People like us. Normal, middle-class/ people.

B: compared to the rest of the world, we're rich. Globally speaking, we're
one/percenters

A: Listen. The entire piece was about this. He said that most people he
knows

people like us
could not put together five hundred dollars
in cash
on short notice. His point/being

B: In cash? Who uses cash? Do you guys still use/cash?

A: Listen. Listen. His point being
that between credit card debt and mortgages and second homes and/and

C: college tuition

A: right and tuition
nobody has any money. Right?
which gets back to what I was saying. About a so-called journalist putting
himself into a story/and

B: Or herself/Themself.

A: and acting like that's reporting.

D: I'm sorry. That isn't?

A: It's not factual. It's one man's
sorry one person
one person's experience.

D: Meaning

A: meaning it's not true. It's not journalism. It's not even/anecdotal.

C: It's not true that no one can get their hands on five hundred dollars?
You don't know that

A: Well no. No of course I don't know
I mean
Actually yes. I do know.
Everyone we know
people like us
can get their hands on five hundred dollars./Right?

B: Anyone for dessert? I made/basbousa

A: It's not that much. It's practically what most people have lying around. It's
practically

C: Well actually
Actually
We can't
    (Beat.)

A: Sure you can.

D: that's like Egyptian cake/right?

C: Nope
We can't

A: Five hundred dollars

C: Not unless we broke open a CD

A: Not allowed.

C: or made some calls.
Like if I had a day

A: Not allowed. It's what you have lying/around

B: Oh, so now there are rules?
Let's have dessert. It's from Ottolenghi I found the recipe/online

A: so you're serious?

C: yep. dead serious.

    (Beat.)

D: What are about you?

B: what about
Well
We've been lucky. Right, babe? We've been really really/lucky.

A: Well
sure.

B: I mean we work. Constantly. What's a weekend?
Not that we're special. It's just that we both work
all the time.
Not that other people don't. That's not what I
It's just that we
we've been very very lucky.

A: Wait.

(A reaches into a pocket and pulls out a small plastic box.)

D: what's that?

B: What are you doing with that? I thought you threw it away
    (B tries to take it.)
You still have this? Why do you still/have this?

A: No reason.

D: what is that? Can I/see?

B: I mean it's no big deal
Well actually it is
You said you were going to toss this. You said you were going to throw it/out

A: I lied.
    (To C.)
Here. Take it

(C doesn't take it.)

C: What is it?

A: Take it. Hold it against your heart

D: Why? What is it?

A: Hold it against your heart and empty your mind of conscious thought
Then press the button.
It brings you money
    (Beat.)

C: Money?

D: How much money?

C: Enough for the mortgage? And three more years of Swarthmore?

A: Sure

C: and med school? And senior year at /Collegiate?

B: Med school?

D: she's thinking. We'll see

A: But there's a catch

D: Of course. When isn't there/a catch?

C: Yeah yeah. It's like *The Twilight Zone*, right?
You can only use it three times. But you screw things up with the first two.
So you need the third to undo it./I saw this

A: No no. You can use it as long as you want. Any time you want
But
Every time you use it
. . . it takes someone

D: Takes someone?
Like
to/Disneyland?

A: You know
Every time you use it
Someone dies
      (Beat.)

B: it's not real it was a joke it's just one of those gruesome souvenirs you pick
up somewhere it doesn't mean anything it's just/a joke

C: Can I?
      (C takes it.)
So what am I supposed to do? Put it against my/heart?

B: Stop it. That's not funny that's actually/disgusting.

A: right and empty your mind of all thoughts

D: well that should be easy.
You do that all the/time

C: shhh. And push this thing and I get money. But someone dies.
Someone I know?

      (A shrugs.)

Someone I don't know.
I mean
people die all the time

A: Right

C: It could be some baby in Chad. A peasant in China

A: Villager in India

B: Stop

C: Some third-world plane crash.
Like in Indonesia
they're always going down

A: investigative journalist in Russia.

C: wedding party in Afghanistan.
A drone attack

B: Jesus. Stop it
That's not funny

A: Hey guess what
people die

D: I mean, can you choose who goes? I bet with the right populations

C: you're right
With most parts of the world
No one would care.

A: No one would even/notice

B: Put that down
That's not funny
What's wrong with you? What's wrong with
PUT THAT DOWN NOW
        (Beat.)

D: sorry

A: Jesus
We were just

C: yeah
I wasn't really going to
We were just
        (Beat. C hands the object back to A.)

I'm sorry

B: No. I'm
I'm sorry
I just
I just can't joke about
Don't listen to me. I'm crazy. Just don't
    (Beat.)

D: So.
Did someone say basbousa?

C: I'm sorry.

B: No.
No. I'm

D: It's semolina cake. Right? With rosewater.
I'm dying to try it

    (D and C exit. A beat.)

B: Why didn't you
I mean, we agreed. We fought about it
That even though it was just a
Why did you keep it?

A: No reason

B: But there had to be
I mean, you had it in your pocket
There had to be a reason
There had to
    (Beat.)
You tried it
You tried it, didn't you
You actually

A: So?
It's just a stupid
It's not real. You know that. You don't believe any of that, do you?

B: . . .

A: C'mon.

We work damn hard
and we've been lucky
Right?

B: . . .

. . .

right

A: Look.

>   *(A throws it in the garbage can.)*

It's gone. See?
All gone.
Okay? Okay?
We good?

>   *(Beat.)*

B: We good.

>   *(B exits. A is about to follow. Then A retrieves the object, pockets it, and exits.)*
>
>   *(Blackout.)*

END OF PLAY

TENNESSEE WALTZ

by A.D. Williams

Original Production:
Full Circle Play Festival, Circle East Theater Company At HERE Performing
Arts Center
September 2000. The cast was as follows:

SADIE: Novel Idea
BARTENDER: Charles Reese
TERRY: Forrest McClendon

Directed by Adrienne D. Williams

Artistic Director: Michael Warren Powell
Scenic Design: Eric Renschler
Lighting Design: Brian Aldous
Sound Design: Samuel D, Tresler
Production Stage Manager: Jennifer Moody
Producer: Reed Clark

Adrienne D. Williams is a New York–based writer, director, and actor. She
holds an MFA in Acting from Binghamton University and studied Vocal Performance at Converse College. Her directing credits include *Angela's Mix-
tape, Electra, Bus Stop, Trouble In Mind, Nora, What Now?, Uncle Vanya,
Pipeline, Crumbs From The Table Of Joy, A Limbo Large And Broad, Luck Of
The Irish, Joe Turner's Come And Gone, Antigone, Intimate Apparel, Iphigenia
At Aulis, Zooman And The Sign, The Colored Museum, Before It Hits Home,*

Just Passin' Through, *The Dark String* (opera), and *The Tales Of Hoffman*. She is currently working on a book of monologues for African American women and a television series (working title), *Blues in the Night*. Upcoming projects include the film *Less Than Or Equal To* that focuses on housing discrimination and civil rights. She is a project director at the Juilliard School of Drama and has taught and guest-directed on the faculties of New York University TISCH Graduate Acting, Hunter College, Marymount Manhattan College, City College of New York, NYU Gallatin School, 92nd Street Y, John Jay College, Binghamton University, and New York State Summer School for the Arts. She is a member of SAG-AFTRA, AEA, SDC and the League of Professional Theatre Women.

CHARACTERS

SADIE DOLL, white, 60s from small southern town, an old maid school teacher/ drunk, contemplating suicide at beginning of play, does not carry her Southern accent.
TERRY, African American male, 30s, boyish, troubled, Southern accent.
BARTENDER, 50s, male, any ethnicity, longtime friend of Sadie, protective, no accent.

SETTING

The play takes place in a small town in the north, such as upstate New York. They are in a hotel bar downtown next to the local bus station of nowheresville USA.
A bar, a jukebox. two stools, a table, two chairs. Lighting is a little dark and gloomy, but warms up for the dance.

TIME

About 2006.

Note

Permission to perform this play does not include permission to use this music.*

• • •

In a hotel bar near the bus station. Lights up on SADIE, *an older woman sitting and drinking alone in an empty, darkly lit, small-town bar. She sings as she drinks. She periodically plays with a ring on her left hand.*

SADIE: I remember the night of the Tennessee Waltz, when an old friend I happen to see. I introduced her to my darling, and while they were dancing, my old friend stole my sweetheart from me.

(She hums. A bus sound is heard.)

BARTENDER: *(Entering with ice.)* That must have been the 11:13 pulling off. Looks like it's just you and me again, Sadie.

(SADIE continues to sing.)
That must be the two-hundredth time I've heard you sing that song.

SADIE: Yeah.
(Continues to hum.)

BARTENDER: I guess everybody's got a favorite song.

SADIE: Least favorite. It just reminds me . . .

BARTENDER: Of what?

(SADIE hands him her glass.)

SADIE: Why I prefer Jack.
(Laughs to herself.)
Fill her up.
(Beat.)

BARTENDER: I gotta say you look good tonight, Sadie. Special occasion?

SADIE: Retirement party. Party? Huh. Sixty-two and put out to pasture. They should call it what it is. A so long toots, we don't need you no more party.

BARTENDER: You been teaching there a long time, right?

SADIE: Forty years. Bring the bottle, Ace.

BARTENDER: Forty years. That's some accomplishment, must feel good.

SADIE: Just feels lonely . . . I gotta go.

BARTENDER: Put it on your tab?

SADIE: Nope. Tonight, I pay up. How much?

BARTENDER: The whole week?

SADIE: Yep.

BARTENDER: That is . . . one sixty-seven fifty.

(She gives him money.)

SADIE: I'm gonna hit the can.

BARTENDER: But this is . . .

(SADIE holds up her hand to stop him.)

SADIE: Keep it.

BARTENDER: Thanks, Sadie.

(She grabs a key from the bar—goes in bathroom. On her way in, she makes a music selection. Pause. Door opens and a young man enters with suitcase. He walks to the bar.)

TERRY: Can I get a drink—JD, straight up?

BARTENDER: You got it.

(Jukebox starts to play the "Tennessee Waltz.")*

TERRY: You play that song?

BARTENDER: Nope. One of my regulars. She's in a real mood tonight. Why? You like it?

TERRY: My momma used to sing it all the time—mostly late at night on the porch in the moonlight. She'd just rock and sing, sometimes all night.

BARTENDER: Then your momma would have something in common with Sadie.

TERRY: Sadie?

BARTENDER: Yeah. Sadie Doll. You know her?

TERRY: No! I mean, ah . . . just rang a bell, I guess.

BARTENDER: I didn't think so. Sadie's pretty much a loner, keeps to herself. 'Nother one?

(TERRY nods.)

I see you gotta suitcase. In town on business?

TERRY: Ah. Yeah, family business.

BARTENDER: Oh, you got family here?

TERRY: Not really. I . . . it's complicated.

BARTENDER: Ain't it always. Down the hatch.

(They drink. Beat. SADIE walks out of bathroom, stands by jukebox.)

BARTENDER: Hey Sadie, one more on me in honor of your retirement.

SADIE: One for the road.
(Hums as she makes her way to the bar.)

TERRY: Hey.

SADIE: Hey? (*Mocking his accent.*) Where the hell are you from?

TERRY: Tennessee.

SADIE: Tennessee. Ha, I used to be from Tennessee. Got the hell outta there and never went back.

BARTENDER: Not even to visit family, Sadie?

SADIE: No family. My folks got lucky and died young. I was raised by my daddy's old bitter aunt. She hated my guts. My distant relatives drew straws, and she got the short one.

TERRY: When a person leaves home, they always leave something behind, or someone.

SADIE: Ain't it the truth . . . I gotta get outta here.
(She grabs her purse and heads toward the door.)

BARTENDER: Sadie, you gonna be alright?

SADIE: I just got something to do, and I gotta do it now.

TERRY: (*Trying to get her attention.*) Ms. Doll?

SADIE: Miss.
(She continues to the door without turning around.)

TERRY: Please . . . uhm . . .

(SADIE stops.)

SADIE: Spit it out. I'm in a hurry!

TERRY: I'd like to buy you a drink.

SADIE: Sorry, kid, I've got an appointment.
   (She continues out.)

TERRY: *(More determined to get her to stay.)* Miss Doll . . .

SADIE: That's my name, don't wear it out!

TERRY: I went to Sweetwater High, too. You're quite a legend there. Track team, Drama Club, National Honor Society, Homecoming Court . . .

SADIE: What are you talking . . . ?

TERRY: I heard you were quite the track star.

SADIE: Look, I don't know who you are or what you want, but whatever you're selling, I don't want it. I left Sweetwater forty-four years ago, came north, and never looked back, and that Sadie Doll doesn't exist anymore.

   (They exchange a look.)

TERRY: Miss Doll, I'm sorry. I'm Terry Hill Jr. Turk Hill was my daddy.

SADIE: I'm sorry for you.
   (She goes to open the door—stops.)
Was? When'd he die?

TERRY: Six months ago.

SADIE: Couldn't happen to a nicer guy.

TERRY: Look, I know you're angry.

SADIE: Shut the hell up. You don't know nothing about me, kid.

TERRY: Ms. . . .
   (He stops himself this time.)
He left you something.

SADIE: I'll thank him in hell when I see him.
   (She opens the door. He closes it.)

TERRY: Please! I don't want to do this any more than you do, but I owe it to my daddy. This is something I gotta do.

BARTENDER: Want me to call somebody, Sadie?

(She looks at BARTENDER, then goes back to TERRY.)

SADIE: Look, you seem like a decent kid, but I don't owe you or anybody else on the face of this lousy earth anything. And there ain't a damn thing you could say that would change the past or erase what your daddy did to me.

TERRY: I know.

SADIE: What do you think you know, huh?

TERRY: I know that betrayal's a hard thing to forgive, but not everybody lets it ruin their life.

(She is visibly shaken.)

Ma'am, this apology is fifty years too late, and I'm sure I'm not the person you wanted to hear it from. And yes, ma'am, there are many things I don't know. I don't know why I'm standing here today and Daddy's not. I don't know how to heal a broken heart, and believe me, I wish I did. The only thing I'm sure of is that this is the best I can offer.

(He holds out the box to her. SADIE retreats to the bar.)

SADIE: Give me a drink.

(BARTENDER brings a bottle and a glass.)

BARTENDER: You OK, Sadie?

(She nods. Beat.)

(After a while, TERRY cautiously approaches her. Beat.)

TERRY: Can I have one of those?

(BARTENDER brings a glass. SADIE pours.)

Thanks.

SADIE: Don't think this changes anything. I've been known to drink with worse.

TERRY: No, ma'am.

SADIE: And don't be so damn polite.

TERRY: No, ma . . .

(She stops him with a look.)

No.

(Long pause. They drink in silence.)

My daddy said you were always one of the best-looking gals in school.

SADIE: That was a long time ago.

TERRY: He also said you were sweethearts in seventh grade.

SADIE: I flipped him for it.

TERRY: How's that?

SADIE: He sent me a note saying will you be my girlfriend, yes or no. I walked right up to him and said, Hey, Turk, heads yes—tails no. It was heads.

TERRY: And you stayed friends even after you broke up, right?

SADIE: There are all kinds of friends, kid.

TERRY: You trusted him with the secrets of your heart.
     (He slides her the box.)
That's why he wanted you to have these.

(She slowly takes the box. She opens it, takes out pearls, and touches them to her face. There's a card.)

SADIE: (*Reading.*) "Forever, my love . . . Madeline." What else did he tell you?

TERRY: He said that you had a plan that would rock the town of Sweetwater, and the Senior Dance of 1956 to its knees.

SADIE: That wouldn't have taken much back then.

TERRY: You planned to announce to everybody that the two most popular girls in town, Sadie Doll and Madeline Troy, were really in love . . .

SADIE: Stop.

TERRY: You even had your own private ceremony in Carson's woods.

SADIE: That's enough! Enough! You don't need to tell me this story . . . We said vows. She gave me a ring, and that day I put these pearls around her neck. (*Pause.*) She looked so beautiful that day. For a moment, I really believed we could live happily ever after. Some kind of fool, huh, kid? Did your dad tell you that?

TERRY: He wanted you to know the truth.

SADIE: What truth is that?

TERRY: He was scared, Miss Doll. He was so sure that both your lives would be ruined, maybe even lost, if you made that announcement, so that's when he came up with his own plan.

(*She turns.*)

SADIE: What?

TERRY: The night of the Senior Dance, he spiked Madeline's drinks and told her he had a surprise for her in the parking lot.

SADIE: She would never have left without me.

TERRY: She wanted to wait for you, but he told her you were getting the champagne. He knew that you and her father would come out to show off the new car he had gotten her for graduation—the one that you helped pick out.

SADIE: And when we did . . .

TERRY: He was waiting for you. And you found them together. Just like he'd planned.

SADIE: That son of a bitch!! He more than anyone knew how something like that would affect me. (*Pause.*) I left that night. I was so angry, so hurt. I knew if I stayed there, I would have killed somebody. I packed a bag, went to the bus station, and took the first bus leaving Sweetwater. I've been replaying that night over and over for the last fifty years. And all that pain just keeps starin' back at me from this glass.

TERRY: That's why I'm here, Miss Doll. She eventually found a way to forgive him. Years later, they got married and had me.

SADIE: You're her . . . ?

(He nods.)

Is she . . . ?

TERRY: She died two years ago. He loved her, Miss Doll, and he was good to her all his life. But there was always something between them. When I was young, I always thought it was my fault—that I did something to make my momma seem so sad. I thought if I was just a good boy, they'd be happy.
(Takes letter from his pocket.)
I found this after she died. First, I hated them both, for a while hate was all I felt. Then one day I woke up and knew that I had to find a way to let it go, move on. You weren't easy to find, but I had to do this. I finally stopped blamin' myself, and this is the last thing I have to do to put the hurt behind me.
(Hands her the letter.)
She left this for you.

(She reads the letter. A voice-over is heard.)

MADELINE: (*Voice-over.*) "June 5, 1966. Dearest Sadie Lynn, Today is my wedding day, and you have been in my every thought. I can't say 'I do' until I say I'm sorry. Please forgive me. When you left, I wasn't strong enough to come after you, and for that my heart has grieved. I've watched and waited, and listened for you every day for the past ten years. I see your face in every window and hear the sweetness of your voice whispered on the wind. The warmth of your smile warms my dreams, and everything around me seems to murmur your name. Dearest, please forgive me. I must move on. The warmth and love and care we shared will strengthen my heart always. Today I close one chapter of my life and open another. I do so knowing that no one will ever love me as you have loved me. My sweet, sweet Sadie, thank you. I will always remember the love we shared, and the night we danced in the moonlight to the 'Tennessee Waltz.' Forever, my love. Madeline."

SADIE: (*She hums a little.*)
The "Tennessee Waltz." That was her favorite song.
(She walks to the jukebox. Plays number 116, the "Tennessee Waltz."
TERRY approaches her at her jukebox.)

TERRY: Allow me.

(She hands him the pearls, and he puts them around her neck. They look beautiful. She turns to look at him and touches his face.)

SADIE: You have her eyes . . . and her smile.

(He holds out his hand to her. They begin to dance.)

And her heart.

(They continue to dance.)

(Lights fade to black.)

END OF PLAY

THE WOODPILE

by J. Thalia Cunningham

Originally performed at Living Room Theater
March 2017, New York, New York

Director: Marcus Yi

The cast was as follows:
LACEY RAE: Caitlin Belforti
MARY LOUISE: Laura Ferland

J. Thalia Cunningham is a playwright, travel writer, and photographer. Her work has been commissioned, produced, and developed at the Panndora's Box New Play Festival, New Jersey Repertory Company, Red Fern Theatre, Hit and Run VII Short Comedy Festival, Dayton Playhouse FutureFest, Pittsburgh Short Works Festival, Siena College, Living Room Theatre New Play Incubator, Golden Thread's Re-Orient Festival, Rhinebeck Short Play Festival, Potpourri World Women Works, the WorkShop Theater Company, the Actors Studio, Short and Sweet Festival in Dubai, Australia, the Philippines, and Malaysia, where she won the award for best script. Member of the League of Professional Theatre Women, the WorkShop Theater Company; the Actor's Studio Playwrights/Directors Unit; League of Professional Theatre Women. Education: BA, The Johns Hopkins University. Cunningham has traveled to around 120 of the "official" destinations of the Traveler's Century Club, an organization of people who have visited at least one hundred countries, which she has no intention of joining. She has written for national publications such as the *New York Times* Travel Supplement, Arthur

Frommer, Diversion, and Specialty Travel Index. Her experiences include trekking with mujahedeen in Tora Bora, Afghanistan, after sneaking over the Khyber Pass disguised as an Afghan woman; participating in West African voodoo rituals; crocodile hunting with spear-toting Papua New Guinea natives; and talking her way out of an arrest (erroneous) for prostitution in the tribal area of Pakistan, while Pakistani soldiers aimed the nostrils of their AK-47s at her own. Cunningham's predilection for insurgents proffers continuous opportunities to enter intimate worlds of a broad spectrum of humanity. Her firsthand knowledge of people in crisis influences her work, allowing her to explore society's most challenging issues and serve as a catalyst for further reflection.

CHARACTERS

LACEY RAE CRAWFORD, 45–60, Caucasian. Postmenopausal, quintessential traditional Southern belle. Socialite. Southern accent. Lives her life according to society's expectations and standards, a bigot—but not unkind. Her right-leaning views would plop her somewhere in the vicinity of Tibet.

MARY LOUISA CRAWFORD, Lacey Rae's daughter, late teens, Caucasian, not tall. Spends her life trying to resemble her mother as little as possible. Snarky humor. Only a twinge of her Southern accent remains. Her left-wing attitudes hover somewhere around Samoa. Or maybe Fiji.

SETTING

Blackmore Hall, the Crawfords' historic estate in South Carolina.

TIME

The present. Lacey Rae's bedroom at Blackmore Hall.

• • •

Bedroom. Table with mirror and a chalk-white Kabuki or Peking opera mask—or any white mask. LACEY RAE CRAWFORD *is partially dressed for a formal affair, fussy dress unzipped, elaborate coiffure, still barefoot. One shade of lipstick on the left of her lips; a completely different shade on the right.*

LACEY RAE: Mary Louisa? Drat, where has that girl got to? MARY LOUISA!!

(MARY LOUISA enters wearing earphones, tattered jeans, no makeup, clutching several papers.)

MARY LOUISA: So much for your mantra that a lady never raises her voice.

LACEY RAE: When you wear those things on your ears . . . when do you plan to fix yourself up for tonight?

MARY LOUISA: There's plenty of time.

LACEY RAE: Momma always said if you can be ready in thirty minutes, then you shouldn't go.

MARY LOUISA: Granny hates being wrong, so I won't go.

LACEY RAE: Honey, please. They're honoring me with an award.

MARY LOUISA: And all folks had to do was shell out $1,000 each to watch you get it.

LACEY RAE: It's a UDC fund-raiser for . . . I forget . . . some disease or other . . .

MARY LOUISA: UDC. Sounds like a racist birth control device.

LACEY RAE: Since 1894, United Daughters of the Confederacy was a hereditary society of Southern women. Our mission statement says the United Daughters of the Confederacy will not associate with any organization identified as being militant, unpatriotic, or racist.

MARY LOUISA: If they're listing things in order of importance, notice they put racist at the end. (*Singing.*)
"Oh, I wish I was in the land of cotton
Old times there are not forgotten, look away . . ."

LACEY RAE: Change those clothes. Fix your hair. You need lipstick . . .

MARY LOUISA: Like yours, Mommy dearest?

LACEY RAE: (*Peering in mirror.*) What's wrong with my . . . ? Oh. I couldn't decide which shade looked best with my dress . . .

MARY LOUISA: While the *whole world* is imploding, your only concern is matching your lipstick to your dress?

LACEY RAE: When a lady looks her best, the *whole world* takes her more seriously.

MARY LOUISA: Better warn Marie Curie before she commits fashion suicide, and no one takes her seriously. Want to hear some interesting news?

LACEY RAE: Can't this wait until . . . ?

MARY LOUISA: I think you'll want to know. So will all your United Daughters of the Confederacy ladies.

LACEY RAE: What is all this?

MARY LOUISA: (*Handing her papers and prancing around in what could only be called a victory dance.*) I had my DNA done. I'm officially 12 percent African. From Ghana, West Africa. That's where they kept the slaves in slave forts on the coast before shipping them . . .

LACEY RAE: You . . . what? That's impossible!

MARY LOUISA: DNA tests don't lie.

LACEY RAE: They're wrong. I don't believe it. They . . . this . . . you couldn't . . . why?

MARY LOUISA: After I read about Craig Cobb . . .

LACEY RAE: Craig who?

MARY LOUISA: Craig Cobb is—was—that white supremacist who went on a TV reality show and found out he had 14 percent sub-Saharan African blood. But he stuck to his principles and lynched himself. I figured if he had black blood, maybe our family with ancestors who were slave-owners could.

LACEY RAE: You hush this very minute! Our family . . .

MARY LOUISA: "Our family, our family." I hoped if the results showed some black, maybe you'd shut up.

LACEY RAE: I refuse to believe it.

MARY LOUISA: That's because you're in the Denial stage. You know, Kübler-Ross's stages of death and dying? Once you navigate through Anger, Bargaining, and Depression, you'll disembark at Acceptance.

LACEY RAE: I could just *die.*

MARY LOUISA: Kübler-Ross advises holding off dying until you go through the other four stages.

LACEY RAE: What would I do if she found out?

MARY LOUISA: Who? Dr. Kübler-Ross? She's dead, so I don't think she'll care.

LACEY RAE: Our UDC chapter president.

MARY LOUISA: If I'm 12 percent sub-Saharan African with slave roots, you must be even blacker than me.

LACEY RAE: Than *I*. For your information, our ancestors . . .

MARY LOUISA: Will you shut up about our goddamned ancestors? Wait 'til I tell everyone I'm biracial.

LACEY RAE: Don't tell anyone! I don't have anything against them, but oil and water just don't mix.

MARY LOUISA: Evidently, they did. We're a regular genealogical marble cake. And aren't you already wearing enough makeup to give a drag queen stiff competition?

LACEY RAE: (*Staring at herself in mirror, grabs foundation and powder, applies them frantically.*) This is a lighter shade. I just decided I don't want a healthy glow.

MARY LOUISA: So, you're going for pernicious anemia?
  (*Rummages around, finds paper bag, and holds it up to her mother's face and her own.*)
Not to worry. See? We can pass the paper bag test.

LACEY RAE: (*Futzing with her makeup.*) We . . . the what?

MARY LOUISA: The paper bag test. If your skin is lighter than a brown paper bag, they'll accept you.

  (*LACEY RAE holds chalk-white up to her face, comparing.*)

LACEY RAE: Why did you do it?

MARY LOUISA: I told you. And if you wear that, I'll make sure to write it down in the family Bible.

LACEY RAE: How do I look? Zip me up, will you?

MARY LOUISA: (*Zipping up the dress, imitating Mammy from* Gone with the Wind.) Now, Miz Scarlett, you' stays ain' laced tight enough. Hole otter sum pin' an' suck in yo' breaf." Why do you like the UDC, anyway? Bitches living in the past.

LACEY RAE: (*Parroting.*) We preserve our cultural heritage. Honor Southern women for their hardship during the struggle.

MARY LOUISA: Y'all honoring Harriet Tubman? She struggled more than white Southern womenfolk.

> (*LACEY RAE tries on different earrings, shoes, still attempts to keep her temper under control.*)

LACEY RAE: We volunteer at VA Hospitals in gratitude to those who served our country in conflicts abroad.

MARY LOUISA: Which wouldn't be necessary if we never got involved in "conflicts abroad" in the first place. (*Reading.*) In addition to being African, I'm also British, French, and German; Northern European.

LACEY RAE: Well, of course.

MARY LOUISA: And I've got some Neanderthal.

LACEY RAE: We. Have. Always. Been. Presbyterian . . .

MARY LOUISA: (*Still reading.*) Says here even though Neanderthals vanished 40,000 years ago, they interbred with humans. One of our great-great-whatever ancestors fucked a Neanderthal. That in the family Bible?

LACEY RAE: Stop using that vulgar language.

MARY LOUISA: (*Still reading.*) Neanderthal DNA is associated with short stature. No wonder I didn't make the basketball team.

LACEY RAE: You are not . . .

MARY LOUISA: All that from saliva in a tube. Who needs a family Bible when you can just spit?

LACEY RAE: (*Holding mask to face again.*) Honey, does it . . .

MARY LOUISA: Stop comparing yourself to a mask.

(LACEY RAE dabs her face once more with white powder.)

LACEY RAE: Maybe I should change? Does my dress look too . . . too . . . ?

MARY LOUISA: Like a black lady dressed up all fancy for church?

LACEY RAE: There's nothing wrong with presenting your best self before God.

MARY LOUISA: You invited God to see you get that award, too? Did they make Him pay a thousand bucks?

LACEY RAE: It's obvious you didn't inherit any of my pride in our heritage.

MARY LOUISA: Maybe now I'm now eligible for affirmative action opportunities.

LACEY RAE: You are not. Those things are for . . .

MARY LOUISA: Black people? Remember the one-drop rule? If you've got even a single drop of black blood . . .

LACEY RAE: I suppose I shouldn't be surprised that you did this.

MARY LOUISA: If my DNA says I'm black, that means you or Daddy are black, too. Your daughter isn't the only one hiding in the woodpile.

(At this reference to "woodpile," the lava simmering underneath finally erupts.)

LACEY RAE: How dare you!

MARY LOUISA: But Mother dear, I wanted to know more about our illustrious heritage.

LACEY RAE: *(Escalating.)* That is bullshit, and you know it.

MARY LOUISA: Such vulgar language. I declare, I'm shocked.

LACEY RAE: *(At full Mount St. Helens pitch.)* Shut up, missy. I have had enough of this. Even when you were in diapers, you showed how much you hated me. You'd shit in your diapers the minute I finished changing them. Only with me. Never your father. Or your nanny. And you'd look up at me, smiling and giggling. Like you knew exactly what you were doing.

MARY LOUISA: Why, Mother, I thought you always said a lady never raises her voice.

LACEY RAE: Maybe it's time I did.

MARY LOUISA: Maybe I *will* see if I'm eligible for affirmative action scholarships, dammit. Then you won't have to pay my college tuition, and I'll be completely independent from you.

LACEY RAE: Might be a good thing for you to find out what it's like to manage on your own.

MARY LOUISA: Fine. Apparently, I carry one copy of the HIV-resistance allele. In case I convert to a drug-addicted, hemophiliac homosexual, I suppose you'll be disappointed if it doesn't kill me?

LACEY RAE: (*Cooling down.*) You'll be independent from me, so I won't know . . . Does it say . . . anything else?

MARY LOUISA: Like what?

LACEY RAE: About diseases; or . . . ?

MARY LOUISA: What? What is it?

LACEY RAE: (*Crying.*) Oh God! Please tell me you didn't inherit any diseases. Your aunt Lucinda . . . her breast cancer . . . what if . . . do you . . . ?

MARY LOUISA: I'm negative for the BRCA gene, if that's what you're asking.

LACEY RAE: Honey, I'm so sorry, so sorry. Daddy and I always wanted children. We tried for years, but . . .

MARY LOUISA: So, I'm illegitimate as well as black?

LACEY RAE: Daddy couldn't . . . he . . . so I . . . we . . .

MARY LOUISA: What? I'm adopted? What are you saying?

LACEY RAE: We went to a fertilization clinic. I was artificially inseminated.

MARY LOUISA: My real father is a turkey baster? Not Daddy?

LACEY RAE: Daddy *is* your father.

MARY LOUISA: Whose sperm was it?

LACEY RAE: We don't know his name, but the clinic was very selective. We looked through a catalogue of donors and chose someone with the same hair and eye color as ours. He's educated, healthy.

MARY LOUISA: Did you happen to take note of his race while you were catalogue-shopping?

LACEY RAE: His ancestry is English and French. Like ours.

MARY LOUISA: Did they check his DNA? Or believe what he told them?

LACEY RAE: I don't know. But I do know that no parent ever loved a child as much as Daddy and I love you.

MARY LOUISA: Is that why I'm an only child?

LACEY RAE: Once we got you, we didn't want anyone else.

MARY LOUISA: You don't know whether my 12 percent African blood comes from him or from you?

LACEY RAE: . . . No.

MARY LOUISA: You lied! My whole life is a lie. No wonder I've always felt like the proverbial square peg.

LACEY RAE: Maybe we should have told you sooner, but we . . . I'm sorry . . . I don't know . . .

MARY LOUISA: Why didn't you?

LACEY RAE: I'm not sure . . . We wanted you to feel secure . . . loved . . . it doesn't matter.

MARY LOUISA: (*Escalating.*) It doesn't matter? Black lives matter. *My* life matters. I'll never trust you again.

LACEY RAE: Darling . . .

MARY LOUISA: My reason for existence is nothing but a business deal. Some college student figured jerking off in a clinic's bathroom was an easier way to earn tuition money than working at Burger King.

LACEY RAE: What do you want from me?

MARY LOUISA: It wasn't supposed to work this way. Now I know even less about who I am.

LACEY RAE: You're our daughter. Do you want me to help you find your genetic father, your records?

MARY LOUISA: Are you still going to accept an award from those racists?

LACEY RAE: I love the UDC.

MARY LOUISA: I know, I know, but do you love your daughter?

LACEY RAE: The two aren't mutually exclusive.

MARY LOUISA: It's dishonest. What if we're both black? How can you be gracious to those people knowing . . . ?

LACEY RAE: Southern women always rise to the occasion. I'll charm dew off the honeysuckle if I need to. Momma always said, "Be pretty if you can, be witty if you must, but be gracious if it kills you."
    (Grabs tissue and begins wiping off makeup.)
Dear Lord, I've got to take off this face and start over.

MARY LOUISA: I think it's about time you did that.
    (She exits. LACEY RAE stares at herself in the mirror. She reaches for the paper bag, holds it up to her face, comparing . . .)

(Lights fade.)

END OF PLAY

TINDER . . . SUCKA

by Inda Craig-Galván

Tinder . . . Sucka was originally produced by SkyPilot Theatre (Los Angeles) in February 2018. Directed by Cynthia Kaye McWilliams. The cast was as follows:

CANDY: Morgan Dixon
LEONA: Trishia Iheonye
SAMUEL: Mike Polidore
MAX: Chris Aikens
WAITRESS: Trishia Iheonye

Inda Craig-Galván is a Chicagoan living in Los Angeles, where it's warm. Her playwriting dwells in Chicago stories that explore the breadth and multiplicity of intraracial conflicts, allegiances, and politics within the African American community. Female protagonists and a dose of magic/realism are prominent in her work. Plays include *Black Super Hero Magic Mama* (Geffen Playhouse) and *I Go Somewhere Else* (Playwrights' Arena, Los Angeles). Her work has been developed at Eugene O'Neill National Playwrights Conference, Ojai Playwrights Conference, OSF's Black Swan Lab, San Francisco Playhouse, and others. Honors include Kesselring Prize, Jeffry Melnick New Playwright Award, Kilroys List, Kennedy Center Rosa Parks Playwriting Award, Steppenwolf's The Mix, Blue Ink Playwriting Prize, and Humanitas Prize. Television writing credits: *How to Get Away with Murder*, *The Rookie*. MFA in Dramatic Writing, University of Southern California.

CHARACTERS

CANDY, a foxy lady. Runs the South Side. 30s, Black.
LEONA, her henchwoman. 30–40, any ethnicity.
SAMUEL, a groovy cat. Runs the West Side. 30s, Black.
MAX, his henchman. 30–40, any ethnicity.
WAITRESS, self-explanatory. Played by same actor as Leona.

SETTING

Present day, but with '70s Blaxploitation language and feel. All locations can be suggested with lights, a chair, whatever minimal props you have available. No need for cross fades or blackouts between bedroom scenes, to keep everything fluid and groovy, baby. Please, add music where appropriate.

Note

The author would like to thank your fine-ass mama for making you. Also, thanks for not being a humorless jive-turkey . . . it's a comedy.

● ● ●

A warehouse EXPLOSION. CANDY, aka South Side Mama, and her hench-woman, LEONA, dust away the rubble, smoke.

CANDY: That West Side Sucka has meddled in my turf for the last time.

LEONA: Are you going to retaliate, South Side Mama?

CANDY: Have you ever known me to not retaliate?

LEONA: Yeah . . . maybe not your best trait. I'm sorry, South Side Mama, but if you continue being reactionary . . .

CANDY: But he . . .

LEONA: You. What about you? Hmm?

CANDY: "Whose actions can I control?"

LEONA: Right. Breathe.

CANDY: I am.

LEONA: Really breathe.

CANDY: Fine.

LEONA: Ground yourself . . . ?

CANDY: Am I okay? Am I still standing? What's the real damage?

LEONA: Good. You're doing the work.

CANDY: The real damage . . . (*Shouting.*) . . . is that West Side Sucka blew up my mother-loving warehouse! I want revenge!

LEONA: I get that you're angry, South Side Mama. But if you hit back now, it'll mean an all-out war against the West Side.

CANDY: War? No, Leona. This means MASSACRE!!!
(*DING.*)
Hold up. Tinder. (*Checking phone.*) Oh, he is so adorable.

LEONA: Please tell me you two finally hooked up.

CANDY: No way.

LEONA: No action?!

CANDY: Haven't even met in person yet. First step in changing my outcome, is changing how I handle / the initial interactions. You of all people . . .

LEONA: Initial interactions. I know, I know. But even I didn't expect you to wait this long.

CANDY: We've both been busy. I've got work, that new Pilates class, racketeering, drug smuggling . . .

LEONA: What does he do?

(*Lights cross to a diner.*)

(*SAMUEL [aka West Side Sammy] and his henchman, MAX, plot over coffee.*)

SAMUEL: What do I do now?

MAX: Hit 'em again. Harder. We took out South Side Mama's biggest warehouse. Next, we get our smack into her territory, knock down that damn orphanage she's so proud of . . .

(*SAMUEL pounds his fist onto the table.*)

SAMUEL: NO!

(He shows his phone to MAX.)

I meant with my Tinder date. Flowers seem like I'm trying too hard, but you should see some of her messages. We've really connected. So . . . I don't know.

(MAX waits for SAMUEL to focus. It takes a while.)

Sorry.

MAX: Sam. You know what the lames in the streets are calling you, right? West Side Sucka.

SAMUEL: (*Unfocused.*) Okay, no flowers.

MAX: Sam? Big Sam. West Side Sammy. You're the man. You're the baddest cat to run these ghetto streets since you stole the turf from King Jeremiah. You did that. You're a bad mother.

(Waitress ducks in to offer:)

WAITRESS: Coffee?

(SAMUEL, his West Side badness shining through, freezes her with an icy stare. She slinks away.)

MAX: See? That's what I'm talking 'bout! You put the fear of god in these squares. You better let these jive turkeys know!

SAMUEL: Yeah. Yeah!

MAX: You're cold-blooded. Righteous.

SAMUEL: Show you right!

MAX: The fly-est cat . . .

SAMUEL: A dozen roses!

MAX: Alright, then.

(Lights cross to CANDY's crib. She checks her makeup. Positions a white rose in her 'fro. LEONA's there, too.)

LEONA: You know West Side Sammy's going to go after the orphanage soon. We've got be tactical. Strategic. I'm saying, maybe now's not the time to be worried about your 'fro.

CANDY: Don't think that just because I'm focusing on my foxy, that I've lost my edge.

LEONA: You sent the troops to reinforce the joint?

CANDY: Even better.
(She opens her skirt to reveal a large gun strapped to her leg.)

LEONA: How's that going to help the kids in the orphanage if you're off on your hot date?

CANDY: I told my mystery man to meet me at that little café right across the street from the orphanage. So, when West Side Sammy and his men show up . . .
(She mimes blasting them with her big gun.)

LEONA: Aww, sooky-sooky now!

CANDY: I'm killing two birds with one stone.

LEONA: Two turkeys, you mean.

CANDY: Gobble, gobble.

(She turns up the volume on the radio and the two get down, get funky wit it. Um . . . they dance.
In SAMUEL's abode, SAM clips a white rose to his jacket lapel. Same song plays on his radio. He dances in the mirror. Max turns down the volume.)

SAMUEL: I'm telling you, Max. This lady is B-A-D, bad! Did I show you her Tinder picture?

MAX: Lay it on me, blood.

(SAMUEL passes his cell phone to MAX.)

SAMUEL: She's hot stuff, huh?

MAX: Hot, alright. This is a cartoon drawing of that cookin' little feline that Pepé Le Pew is always trying to mack to.

SAMUEL: Pretty far out, ain't she? Love a woman with a sense of humor.

(LEONA looks at Candy's phone.)

LEONA: You're jiving me. Blood has been using this bogus picture of Pepé Le Pew? And you swiped right on that?

CANDY: Can you dig it? I can dig it.

LEONA: You mean to tell me that you've never actually . . .

MAX/LEONA: . . . seen her face?/ . . . seen his face?

SAMUEL: Um . . .

CANDY: No.

LEONA: He could be a lame-ass dud.

MAX: She could be a pimple-faced trick.

LEONA: He could be . . .

CANDY and SAMUEL: Stop!

CANDY: On the real tip, it doesn't matter. This is some heavy stuff. Deep.

SAMUEL: Isaac Hayes deep.

CANDY: I've never felt this connected to a dude.

SAMUEL: This in tune with a lady's vibes.

CANDY: This comfortable.

SAMUEL: This easy.

CANDY: This free.

SAMUEL: This outta sight.

CANDY: This . . .

SAMUEL and CANDY: Groovy, baby!

LEONA: Yeah, no.

MAX: I'm outta here.

> (*Lights up on the café. CANDY sits at a table. Alone. SAMUEL sits at another. Alone. Their backs to each other. They keep barely missing sight of each other as they glance around the café. They drain their cups, and with that, give up. They've been waiting a long while. They stand and, at once, turn to face each other.*)

CANDY: (*Snarls.*) You!

SAMUEL: (*Also snarls.*) You!

CANDY: West Side . . . (*Notices his rose.*) . . . Wait. Hold up.

SAMUEL: Why? So you can attack my . . . (*Notices her rose.*) Oh.

CANDY and SAMUEL: Oh . . . OH!

CANDY: Pepé Le Pew?

SAMUEL: That cat he chases?

CANDY: Penelope. The cat's name is Penelope.

SAMUEL: Yeah, okay, yeah. You?

CANDY and SAMUEL: (*Softening.*) You . . .
  (*They're melting into each other's eyes. But, no. CANDY pulls out her gun.*)

CANDY: This is a trick. I knew you were a dirty, low-down jive turkey, West Side Sammy—shit. Your name's really Samuel—doesn't matter. You West Side Sucka. This is a long-con, even for you. I didn't think you were smart enough.

SAMUEL: Me? I have to hand it to you, South Side Mama. You cooked up this heavy, freaky-deaky plan and you never let on. Not even once. Had me thinking you actually had feelings. But turns out you really are the cold, heartless snake everybody says you are.

CANDY: I could have never cared about you, West Side.

SAMUEL: And it'd be a cold day in hell before I ever even thought about you.

CANDY: Enough talk.

SAMUEL: Let's rumble, baby.
  (*They kick/throw the chairs aside.*)

CANDY: I'll even make this a fair fight.

  (*She puts down her gun. They fight, seventies movie–karate style. He gets her in a headlock.*)

SAMUEL: Your hair smells like heaven.

CANDY: That's Afro-Sheen, daddy.

(She back-headbutts him. They keep fighting. She gets him pinned down, gazes down at him.)

You've got the foxiest eyes I've ever seen.

SAMUEL: They're hazel, baby.

(They continue fighting. She snatches his rose from his lapel. They stop fighting. He gingerly approaches her and plucks the rose from her hair. They stand there, a beat. They kiss.)

CANDY: This can't be.

SAMUEL: This has to be.

CANDY: How can we possibly make this work?

SAMUEL: You're South Side Mama.

CANDY: And you're West Side Suck—Sammy. West Side Sammy.

SAMUEL: Samuel. Call me Samuel.

CANDY: Candy.

SAMUEL: Enchanté, Candy.

CANDY: Eau de Pew, Samuel.

(They resume kissing. Groovy music plays.)

END OF PLAY

WAYLAY MAKEOVER

by Donna Latham

Original Production
Houston Scriptwriters 10 × 10 Play Festival, Houston, Texas
Artistic Director: Devan Wade
Director: Dabrina Sandifer

The cast was as follows:

DOMINIQUE ANGELLE: Erica Young
BETH: Kimberly Hicks
ABNER FABULOUS: Dabrina Sandifer

Donna Latham is an award-winning playwright based in Houston. Her plays have been produced from coast to coast and in Northern Ireland, Ireland, England, France, Scotland, and Indonesia. A resident playwright at Rising Sun Performance Company in New York City, a member of Honor Roll Playwrights, and a script reader for Houston's Alley Theatre, she's a proud member of the Dramatist Guild.

CHARACTERS

DOMINIQUE ANGELLE, smarmy stylist, any age.
ABNER FABULOUS, flamboyant makeup artist, any age.
BETH, exhausted new mother, 30s.

SETTING

City street.

TIME

Present.

• • •

ABNER *and* DOMINQUE, *coiffed to within an inch of their lives and dressed to the nines.* ABNER *wears a toupee. They hold microphones and speak into an unseen camera. As they prowl the street looking for unsuspecting victims, they speak in the highly caffeinated fashion of early-morning talk show folks.*

ABNER: Good morning, America! Happy Monday!

DOMINIQUE: And welcome to Waylay Makeover!

ABNER: I'm your host, Abner Fabulous. With me as ever is my stunning co-hostess . . .

DOMINIQUE: Dominique Angell.
    (Blows a kiss to camera.)

ABNER: We're roaming the streets to waylay one lucky layday . . .

DOMINIQUE: To take from drab to fab!

ABNER: From wannabe to queen bee!

DOMINIQUE: From fashion don't to glamour do!

ABNER: From lump of clay to work of art! Look, Dominique. A hideous specimen is lumbering our way.

    (BETH hurries by, carrying a briefcase. Her hair is wet, and her clothes are rumpled. She's been up all night with a colicky baby.)

DOMINQUE: Oh, miiiiss!

BETH: What?

DOMINIQUE: Yes, you! Harried mama who's let herself go to hell.

BETH: Excuse me. I'm in a hurry.

DOMINIQUE: And clearly allergic to morning.

ABNER: Ah-choo!

BETH: Ah, no. I'm allergic to crazy.

DOMINIQUE: Is that baby spit-up on your collar?

BETH: Colic's not for sissies.

DOMINIQUE: Unkempt is so last winter.

ABNER: Washed out is washed up.

BETH: Hey, you're invading my personal space.

DOMINIQUE: We're your rescue squad. What's your name, sugar?

BETH: None of your damned beeswax.

DOMINIQUE: We'll take you from grumpy frumpy . . .

ABNER: To yummy mummy.

BETH: Beat it, creeper.

DOMINIQUE: You need fresh color. Some razzle dazzle!

ABNER: Espresso with caramel highlights.

DOMINIQUE: Right? And a dash of red!

ABNER: Love, love, love, Dominique! How about a spicy cut?

DOMINIQUE: With bold texture!

ABNER: Piecey!

DOMINIQUE: Choppy!

ABNER: Beachy waves! Right?

BETH: Do not touch me again.

DOMINIQUE: You'll be sexy!

ABNER: Sassy!

DOMINIQUE: Sophisticated!

ABNER: Kicky!

DOMINIQUE: Dramatic!

ABNER: Outrageous!

DOMINIQUE: Say hi to the folks at home.

BETH: Get that mic out of my face.

ABNER: Let's snap a before picture.

BETH: No pictures!

ABNER: Girl, you're wash and wear.

DOMINIQUE: You need to buff and fluff.

BETH: Quit following me.

DOMINIQUE: We're hot on your trail. You'll never escape.

BETH: Stalker!

ABNER: Admit it. You're desperate for a blowout.

DOMINIQUE: Your roots have roots.

ABNER: What did you think? You'd just pray the gray away?

DOMINIQUE: Let's ditch that horrid polyester . . .

ABNER: And tart you up in a kicky new frock.

BETH: Let go of me!

DOMINIQUE: Ab Fab will strap you in his magical chair. Whip out his cashmere brushes.

ABNER: Cheekbones! Where aaaare you?

DOMINIQUE: He's the contour queen.

ABNER: Let's make those sleepy eyes pop with a smoky lid. And a pale lip.

DOMINIQUE: Sex, sex, sexy!

ABNER: Sass, sass, sassy!

BETH: Back off.

DOMINIQUE: Oh, come on. You don't want to disappoint the folks at home.

BETH: I don't need to be fixed.

DOMINIQUE: *Au contraire.*

BETH: This is who I am. This is how I look. My own work of art.

ABNER: You look rough, girl. That's why we're here to help.

BETH: Who are you to judge me?

ABNER: I'm Abner Fabulous, makeup artist to the stars!

BETH: Grandiose much? Seek treatment for clinical hysteria.

DOMINIQUE: You're a fright!

BETH: You're a Barbie. Now, step the hell back. Or I'll jam that lipstick up your nostril.

DOMINIQUE: Pucker up.

BETH: Scram! Before I rip out your weave and feed it to you.

DOMINIQUE: Just one itsy-bitsy dab.
   (Goes at BETH with lipstick.)

BETH: Mace to the faces, bitches!

   (She whips out Mace and sprays DOMINQUE and ABNER. There is a tussle as they try to disarm her and she eventually prevails. ABNER feels around to find his lost toupee. He tosses it on. DOMINIQUE crawls to her mic and staggers to her feet. She yanks ABNER up and adjusts his toupee. DOMINIQUE wipes her nose with her lace hanky and blots blood from her blouse.)

DOMINIQUE: Bloody noses are so medieval. Well, America!

ABNER: That's all the time we have today!

DOMINIQUE: I'm Dominique Angell.

ABNER: And I'm Abner Fabulous.

DOMINIQUE: Roaming your street to waylay one lucky lady.

ABNER: Until tomorrow, America!

DOMINIQUE: Get waylaid!

(BETH chases DOMINIQUE and ABNER off.)

END OF PLAY

YOU HAVEN'T CHANGED A BIT

by Donna Hoke

You Haven't Changed a Bit was first produced in 2013 at Barrington Stage in Sheffield, Massachusetts. Director: Kristen van Ginhoven. The cast was as follows:

LEN: Matt Neel
LOTTIE: Peggy Pharr

Donna Hoke's work has been seen in forty-seven states and on five continents, including at Barrington Stage, Barrow Group, Celebration Theatre, Gulfshore Theatre, Queens Theatre, The Road, Writers Theatre New Jersey, Phoenix Theatre, Atlantic Stage, Purple Rose, Skylight, Pride Films and Plays, New Jersey Rep, Hens and Chickens (London), The Galway Fringe Festival, and Actors Repertory Theatre of Luxembourg. Plays include *Brilliant Works of Art* (Kilroys List), *Elevator Girl* (O'Neill and Princess Grace finalist), *Safe* (winner of the Todd McNerney, Naatak, and Great Gay Play and Musical Contests), and TEACH (Gulfshore New Works winner). She has been nominated for the Primus, Blackburn, and Laura Pels prizes, and is a three-time winner of the Emanuel Fried Award for Outstanding New Play (*Seeds, Sons & Lovers, Once In My Lifetime*). She has also received an Individual Artist Award from the New York State Council on the Arts to develop *Hearts Of Stone*, and, in its final three years, Artvoice named her Buffalo's Best Writer—the only woman to ever receive this distinction. Donna also serves on the Dramatists Guild Council, is an ensemble playwright at Road Less Traveled Productions, and is a blogger, a moderator of the 12,000+-member Official Playwrights of Facebook, a *New York Times*-published crossword puzzle constructor; children's and trivia book author; and founder/ co-curator of BUA Takes 10: GLBT Short Stories. Speaking engagements include Citywrights, Kenyon Playwrights Conference, the Dramatists Guild National Conference, Chicago Dramatists, the Austin Film Festival, and a live Dramatists Guild webinar. Her commentary has been seen on #2amt, howl-round, The Dramatist, the Official Playwrights of Facebook, *Workshopping the New Play* (Applause Theatre and Cinema Books, 2017), and at www.donna hoke.com.

CHARACTERS

LEN, old man, 88.
LOTTIE, old woman, 88.

Note

The playwright realizes, of course, that eighty-eight-year-old actors are in short supply, so please cast with the actors you have available.

SETTING

The lobby of a restaurant/banquet hall.

TIME

The present.

• • •

LEN *paces anxiously, watching the door.* LOTTIE *enters, looks around, spots* LEN. LEN *lights up.*

LOTTIE: Are you here for the . . .

LEN: Seventieth high school reunion? You bet I am, Lottie.

LOTTIE: You recognize me!

LEN: You haven't changed a bit.

LOTTIE: Oh, you. I'm sorry—I don't . . .

LEN: Len. Len Bennett?

LOTTIE: Len. My apologies. I'm a little nervous. I haven't been to any of the reunions.

LEN: I know. I've been to all of them.

LOTTIE: I guess I just never felt the need.

LEN: I always hoped you would.

LOTTIE: The letters would come, and I'd put them aside to think about later, and somehow . . .
(*Shrugs.*) I did keep in touch with a few friends, and I was always so busy that the past just didn't seem—I don't know. But those friends are gone now, so I thought . . .

LEN: I'm glad you did.

LOTTIE: The reunion committee was very insistent. It was hard to ignore all those letters.

LEN: It could be our last chance.

LOTTIE: That's what the reunion committee said. So, here I am.

LEN: You've been missed.

LOTTIE: Really? I haven't thought about high school in so long. Or the people—
Hey, do you remember Howie Peters? We voted him class clown. He made me laugh so.

LEN: He's gone. Emphysema.

LOTTIE: Oh, that's awful! Silly, funny Howie—You know who I'd love to see? Patsy Parker. She used to sit next to me in homeroom. Parker, Parkman. We joked about that all the time, how our names would keep us joined for life. I haven't seen her since high school.

LEN: She died. Just recently, actually.

LOTTIE: Oh no! Now I suddenly miss her. That big, toothy smile, remember that? I wish we'd kept in touch. Mary Albright? She was . . .

LEN: Liver cancer. About twenty years ago.

LOTTIE: Twenty years already?

LEN: She ended up marrying Carmine Jackson. Remember him, from the football team?

LOTTIE: That smoothie! I never thought he'd settle down. Is he here?

LEN: (*Shakes head.*) Before Mary, actually. He had Alzheimer's.

LOTTIE: Oh, that's the worst. I thank God for my mind.

LEN: If you've got your mind, you've got your life. Mary had a tough time with him.

LOTTIE: I should have sent her a note, but I didn't know.

LEN: She got the cancer shortly after.

LOTTIE: Poor thing. My husband died from cancer. Pancreas. It's been nearly five years now.

LEN: I heard. I'm so sorry. I wanted to send a note, but I didn't know if it would be . . . appropriate.

LOTTIE: I never thought it would start getting hard to remember that life, the one with him in it. Maybe my mind really is going. And high school seems so many lives before that. The reunion committee must have had some time trying to round people up.

LEN: A lot came all along, so we could kind of keep track.

LOTTIE: I've missed a lot, haven't I?

LEN: Oh, you know how they go.

LOTTIE: Not really. Tell me.

LEN: Well, at the first one, ten years . . . it was a lot of remember this and remember that. And catching up. Do you have kids? What kind of work do you do? Who made it and who didn't dare show up. Who got fat. Ten years later, we were all fat. And we counted divorces and remarriages until Carmine started talking about the big game, like he always did, and there was a slide show, and we just ended up remembering a lot more of this and that. I think the next one is when we started talking about how old we were all getting, and thinking it might not be so bad to be back in high school. Then we started losing people, and I don't know . . . after that, I think we were just happy to have each other . . . and memories to share with people who knew us when we didn't walk so slowly, when our lives were full of promise, when we first fell in love . . .

LOTTIE: Benjamin Brack! He had a name for the pictures, didn't he? I don't suppose . . .

LEN: '98. Lou Gehrig's.

LOTTIE: I wish I'd known that. I really wish I'd known that.

LEN: I talked to him a few times over the years. If it helps, he remembered you fondly.

LOTTIE: As I remember him. Where did the time go?

LEN: Fluttered by like a butterfly. Beautiful. Fleeting.

LOTTIE: That's very poetic, Len. And sad. Sad for Ben, and Patsy, and Mary. I remember them so young. And it's sad that there's no one who sees me like that, that fresh-faced girl and not this old woman.

LEN: I do.

LOTTIE: But I . . .

LEN: You liked blue sweaters/

LOTTIE: /Yes/

LEN: /and I liked you in your blue sweaters.

LOTTIE: Len! You're making an old woman blush.

LEN: And you wore your hair in braids on Fridays.

LOTTIE: It always got dirty by then.

LEN: Do you remember when I interviewed you for the school paper? You were protesting that girls should be able to play sports. The war was over, and you said you needed a new cause.

LOTTIE: I said that? How self-important you must have thought me.

LEN: Not at all. I took great pride in sharing your views in the *Trumpeter*.

LOTTIE: The *Trumpeter*? My goodness! I haven't thought about that in years.

LEN: You were busy even then.

(*He reaches into his pocket and pulls out two clippings.*)

LOTTIE: You saved them!

LEN: My earliest bylines. I don't like to let things go.

LOTTIE: (*Reading them.*) "By Leonard Bennett." Len Bennett. Oh! Oh my! You're Lenny Benny!

LEN: Nobody's called me that since the last reunion.

LOTTIE: You sat behind me four years in a row in English class. You always asked me how my weekend was.

LEN: Yes!

LOTTIE: And smelled like Mennen.

LEN: I borrowed my dad's.

LOTTIE: And . . . and you asked me to the senior ball before you knew Benjamin had asked me already.

LEN: Yes.

LOTTIE: I can't believe I didn't recognize you. Lenny Benny.

LEN: It's been a long time.

LOTTIE: But you recognized me.

LEN: You haven't changed a bit.

LOTTIE: (*Suddenly struck by a thought.*) What if I don't recognize anybody? You've seen them over the years, but I . . .

LEN: Lottie . . .

LOTTIE: That would be so embarrassing if everybody recognized me and I didn't . . .

LEN: Lottie . . .

LOTTIE: I . . .

LEN: We're it.

LOTTIE: What do you mean?

LEN: We're it. We're all that's left of our class.

LOTTIE: That can't be true.

LEN: It's true. But they insisted I come, that it might be my last chance. It is our last chance.

LOTTIE: The reunion committee . . .

LEN: Lottie, I was the reunion committee.

LOTTIE: Just you?

LEN: All by myself.

LOTTIE: You sent all those letters?

LEN: I wanted you to come.

LOTTIE: We're the only ones left. How could I not have known that?

LEN: You've been busy.

LOTTIE: (*Gestures toward the door.*) So, there's no reunion . . .

LEN: Yes, there is.

LOTTIE: But you just said . . .

LEN: I've made dinner reservations for two. Will you join me, Lottie, for the 70th reunion of our class at P.S. 92?

LOTTIE: Just us?

LEN: Just us. And our memories.

(*LOTTIE looks at LEN, who extends his arm. She takes it, and they go through the door to dinner.*)

END OF PLAY

10-MINUTE PLAY PRODUCERS

Actors Studio of Newport
TASN Short Play Festival
http://www.newburyportacting.org/
Contact Marc Clopton, info@newburyportacting.org

Acts on the Edge, Santa Monica, CA
mariannesawchuk@hotmail.com

American Globe Theatre Turnip Festival,
Gloria Falzer
gfalzer@verizon.net

The Arc Theatre
arciTEXT Ten-Minute Play Festival
contact Natalie Sallee: natalie@arctheatrechicago.org

Artistic Home Theatre Co.
Cut to the Chase Festival
Kathy Scambiatterra, Artistic Director
artistic.director@theartistichome.org

Artist's Exchange
One Act Play Festival
Jessica Chace, Artistic Director, OAPF
jessica.chace@artists-exchange.org
www.artists-exchange.org

The Arts Center, Carrboro, NC
10x10 in the Triangle
Jeri Lynn Schulke, Director
theatre@artscenterlive.org
www.artscenterlive.org/performance/opportunities

A-Squared Theatre Workshop
My Asian Mom Festival
Joe Yau (jyauza@hotmail.com)

Association for Theatre in Higher Education New Play Development Workshop
Charlene A. Donaghy
charlene@charleneadonaghy.com
http://www.athe.org/displaycommon.cfm?an=1&subarticlenbr=70

Auburn Players Community Theatre Short Play Festival
Bourke Kennedy
bourkekennedy@gmail.com

The Barn Theatre
www.thebarnplayers.org/tenminute/

Barrington Stage Company
10X10 New Play Festival
Julianne Boyd, Artistic Director
jboyd@barringtonstageco.org
www.barringtonstageco.org

Belhaven University, Jackson, Mississippi
One Act Festival
Joseph Frost, Department Chair
theatre@belhaven.edu

Black Box Theatre
FIVES New Play Festival
Nancy Holaday, Producer
(719) 330-1798
nancy@blackboxdrama.com

Blue Slipper Theatre, Livingston, Montana
Marc Beaudin, Festival Director
blueslipper10fest@gmail.com
www.blueslipper.com

Boston Theatre Marathon

Boston Playwrights Theatre
www.bostonplaywrights.org
Kate Snodgrass (ksnodgra@bu.edu)
(Plays by New England playwrights only)

Boulder Life Festival, Boulder, Colorado

Dawn Bower, Director of Theatrical Program (dawn@boulderlifefestival.com)
www.boulderlifefestival.com

The Box Factory

Judith Sokolowski, President
boxfactory@sbcglobal.net
www.boxfactoryforthearts.org

The Brick Theater's "Tiny Theater Festival"

Michael Gardner, Artistic Director
mgardner@bricktheater.com
www.bricktheater.com

Broken Nose Theatre

Benjamin Brownson, Artistic Director
Bechdel Fest
www.brokennosetheatre.com/bechdel-fest-3
ben@brokennosetheatre.com

The Brooklyn Generator

Erin Mallon (contact)
email: brooklyngenerator@outlook.com
website: https://www.facebook.com/TheBrooklynGenerator/info

Camino Real Playhouse

Show!Off Playwriting Festival
www.caminorealplayhouse.org
kathyfischer@cox.net

Celebration Theatre

WriteHer Festival
Women Playwrights
www.celebrationtheatre.com
Alli Miller, festival@celebrationtheatre.com

Chagrin Valley Little Theatre
10-10 New Plays Festival
www.cvlt.org
cvlt@cvlt.org

Chalk Repertory Theatre Flash Festival produced by Chalk Repertory Theatre
Ruth McKee
ruthamckee@aol.com
www.chalkrep.com

Chameleon Theater Circle, Burnsville, MN 55306
www.chameleontheatre.org
jim@chameleontheatre.org

Changing Scene Theatre Northwest
Pavlina Morris
changingscenenorthwest@hotmail.com

Cherry Picking
cherrypickingnyc@gmail.com

Chicago Indie Boots Festival
www.indieboots.org

City Theatre, Miami, FL
www.citytheatre.com
Susan Westfall (susan@citytheatre.com)

City Theatre of Independence
Powerhouse Theatre
Annual Playwrights Festival
Powerhouse Theatre
www.citytheatreofindependence.org

The Collective New York
C10 Play Festival
www.thecollective-ny.org
thecollective9@gmail.com

Colonial Playhouse
Colonial Quickies
www.colonialplayhouse.net
colonialplayhousetheater@40yahoo.com

Company of Angels at the Alexandria
Box 3480
Los Angeles, CA 90078
(213) 489-3703 (main office)
armevan@sbcglobal.net

Core Arts Ensemble
coreartsensemble@gmail.com

Darkhorse Dramatists
www.darkhorsedramatists.com
darkhorsedramatists@gmail.com

Darknight Productions
4 Women Only and 4 Men Only
www.darknightproductions.com

Distilled Theatre Co.
submissions.dtc@gmail.com

Driftwood Players
www.driftwoodplayers.com
shortssubmissions@driftwoodplayers.com
tipsproductions@driftwoodplayers.com

Drilling Company
Hamilton Clancy
drillingcompany@aol.com

Durango Arts Center 10-Minute Play Festival
www.durangoarts.org
Theresa Carson
TenMinutePlayDirector@gmail.com

Eastbound Theatre 10 Minute Festival (in the summer: themed)
Tom Rushen
ZenRipple@yahoo.com

East Haddam Stage Company
Kandie Carl
Kandie@ehsco.org

Eden Prairie Players
www.edenprairieplayers.com

Emerging Artists Theatre
Fall EATFest
www.emergingartiststheatre.org

En Avant Playwrights
Ten Lucky Festival
www.enavantplaywrights.yuku.com/topic/4212/Ten-Tucky-Festival-KY-deadline-10-1-no-fee#.UE5-nY5ZGQI

Ensemble Theatre of Chattanooga Short Attention Span Theatre Festival
Garry Posey, Artistic Director
garryposey@gmail.com
www.ensembletheatreofchattanooga.com

Fell's Point Corner Theatre 10 × 10 Festival
Richard Dean Stover (rick@fpct.org)
www.fpct.org

Fem Noire (plays by New England women playwrights)
Image Theatre
www.imagetheater.com
imagetheaterlowell@gmail.com

Fine Arts Association
Annual One Act Festival-Hot from the Oven Smorgasbord
ahedger@fineartsassociation.org

Firehouse Center for the Arts, Newburyport, MA
New Works Festival
Kimm Wilkinson, Director

www.firehouse.org
Limited to New England playwrights

Flush Ink Productions
Asphalt Jungle Shorts Festival
www.flushink.net/AJS.html

The Fringe of Marin Festival
Annette Lust
jeanlust@aol.com

Fury Theatre
katie@furytheare.org

Fusion Theatre Co.
http://www.fusionabq.org
info@fusionabq.org

Future Ten
info@futuretenant.org

Gallery Players
Annual Black Box Festival
info@galleryplayers.com

Gaslight Theatre
www.gaslight-theatre.org
gaslighttheatre@gmail.com

GI60
Steve Ansell
screammedia@yahoo.com

The Gift Theater
TEN Festival
Michael Patrick Thornton
www.thegifttheatre.org

Good Works Theatre Festival
Good Acting Studio
www.goodactingstudio.com

The Greenhouse Ensemble
Ten-Minute Play Soiree
www.greenhouseensemble.com

Heartland Theatre Company
Themed 10-Minute Play Festival Every Year
Mike Dobbins, Artistic Director
boxoffice@heartlandtheatre.org
www.heartlandtheatre.org

Hella Fresh Fish
freshfish2submit@gmail.com

Hobo Junction Productions
Hobo Robo
Spenser Davis, Literary Manager
hobojunctionsubmissions@gmail.com
www.hobojunctionproductions.com

The Hovey Players, Waltham, MA
Hovey Summer Shorts
www.hoveyplayers.com

Image Theatre
Naughty Shorts
jbisantz@comcast.net

Island Theatre 10-Minute Play Festival
www.islandtheatre.org

Ixion Ensemble, Lansing, MI
Jeff Croff, Artistic Director
Ixionensemble@gmail.com

Kings Theatre
www.kingstheatre.ca

Lake Shore Players
www.lakeshoreplayers.com

ATTN: Joan Elwell
office@lakeshoreplayers.com

Lee Street Theatre, Salisbury, NC (themed)
Original 10-Minute Play Festival
Justin Dionne, Managing Artistic Director
info@leestreet.org
www.leestreet.org

Little Black Dress Ink
Tiffany Antone.
info@LittleBlackDressINK.org
www.LittleBlackDressINK.org

Little Fish Theatre
Pick of the Vine Festival
holly@littlefishtheatre.org
www.littlefishtheatre.org/wp/participate/submit-a-script/

Live Girls Theatre
submissions@lgtheater.org

Luna Theater
New Moon Short Play Festival
lunatheater@gmail.com
www.lunatheater.org

Madlab Theatre
Theatre Roulette
Andy Batt (andy@madlab.net)
www.madlab.net/MadLab/Home.html

Magnolia Arts Center, Greenville, NC
Ten Minute Play Contest
info@magnoliaartscenter.com
www.magnoliaartscenter.com
Fee charged

Manhattan Repertory Theatre, New York, NY
Ken Wolf

manhattanrep@yahoo.com
www.manhattanrep.com

McLean Drama Co.
www.mcleandramacompany.org
Rachel Bail (rachbail@yahoo.com)

Miami 1-Acts Festival: two sessions—Winter (December) and Summer (July)
Steven A. Chambers, Literary Manager (schambers@new-theatre.org);
Ricky J. Martinez, Artistic Director (rjmartinez@new-theatre.org)
www.new-theatre.org
Submission Requirements: No more than 10–15 pages in length; subject is not specific, though plays can reflect life in South Florida and the tropics and the rich culture therein. Area playwrights are encouraged to submit, though the festival is open to national participation. Deadline for the Winter Session is October 15 of each year; deadline for the Summer Session is May 1 of each year.

Milburn Stone One Act Festival
www.milburnstone.org

Mildred's Umbrella
Museum of Dysfunction Festival
www.mildredsumbrella.com
info@mildredsumbrella.com

Mill 6 Collaborative
John Edward O'Brien, Artistic Director
mill6theatre@gmail.com

Monkeyman Productions
The Simian Showcase
submissions@monkeymanproductions.com.
www.monkeymanproductions.com

Napa Valley Players
8 × 10: A Festival of 10 Minute Plays
www.napavalleyplayhouse.org

Newburgh Free Academy
tsandler@necsd.net

New American Theatre
www.newamericantheatre.com
Play Submissions: JoeBays44@earthlink.net

New Jersey Rep
Theatre Brut Festival
Their yearly Theatre Brut Festival is organized around a specified theme.
njrep@njrep.org

New Short Play Festival
https://www.newshortplayfestival.com/

New Urban Theatre Laboratory
5 & Dime
Jackie Davis, Artistic Director
jackie.newurbantheatrelab@gmail.com

New Voices Original Short Play Festival
Kurtis Donnelly (kurtis@gvtheatre.org)

NFA New Play Festival
Newburgh Free Academy
201 Fullerton Ave, Newburgh, NY 12550
Terry Sandler (terrysandle@hotmail.com)
(may not accept electronic submissions)

North Park Playwright Festival
New short plays (no more than 15 pages, less is fine)
Submissions via mail to:
North Park Vaudeville and Candy Shoppe
2031 El Cajon Blvd.
San Diego, CA 92104
Attn: Summer Golden, Artistic Director
www.northparkvaudeville.com

Northport One-Act Play Festival
Jo Ann Katz (joannkatz@gmail.com)
www.northportarts.org

Northwest 10 Festival of 10-Minute Plays
Sponsored by Oregon Contemporary Theatre
www.octheatre.org/nw10-festival
NW10Festival@gmail.com

The Now Collective
Sean McGrath
Sean@nowcollective@gmail.com

NYC Playwrights
Play of the Month Project
http://nycp.blogspot.com/p/play-of-month.html

Nylon Fusion
nylonsubmissions@gmail.com
www.nylonfusioncollective.org

Onion Man Productions Summer Harvest
onionmanproductions@gmail.com

Open Tent Theatre Co.
Ourglass 24 Hour Play Festival
opententtheater@gmail.com

Otherworld Theatre
Paragon Festival—sci-fi and fantasy plays
Elliott Sowards, Literary Manager of Otherworld Theatre and Curator of the
Paragon Play Festival (elliott@otherworldtheatre.org)
www.otherworld.org

Over Our Head Players, Racine, WI
www.overourheadplayers.org/oohp15

Pan Theater, Oakland, CA
Anything Can Happen Festival
David Alger (pantheater@comcast.net)
http://www.facebook.com/sanfranciscoimprov

Pandora Theatre, Houston, TX
Vox Feminina

Melissa Mumper, Artistic Director
pandoratheatre@sbcglobal.net

Paw Paw Players One Act Festival
www.ppvp.org/oneacts.htm

Pegasus Theater Company (in Sonoma County, north of San Francisco)
Tapas Short Plays Festival
www.pegasustheater.com/html/submissions.html
Lois Pearlman (lois5@sonic.net)

Philadelphia Theatre Company
PTC@Play New Work Festival
Jill Harrison (jillian.harrison@gmail.)
www.philadelphiatheatrecompany.org

PianoFight Productions, LA
ShortLivedLA@gmail.com

Piney Fork Press Theater Play Festival
Johnny Culver, submissions@pineyforkpress.com
www.pineyforkpress.com

The Playgroup LLC
Boca Raton, FL
theplaygroupllc@gmail.com
www.theplaygroupllc.com

Playhouse Creatures
Page to Stage
newplays@playhousecreatures.org

Play on Words Productions
playonwordsproductions@gmail.com
Megan Kosmoski, Producing Artist Director

Playpalooza
Backstage at SPTC (Santa Paula Theatre Co.)
John McKinley, Artistic Director
sptcbackstage@gmail.com

Playwrights' Arena
Flash Theater LA
Jon Lawrence Rivera (jonlawrencerivera@gmail.com)
www.playwrightsarena.org

Playwrights' Round Table, Orlando, FL
Summer Shorts
Chuck Dent (charlesrdent@hotmail.com)
www.theprt.com

Playwrights Studio Theater
Milwaukee Chamber Theatre
http://www.milwaukeechambertheatre.com/
5210 W. Wisconsin Ave.
Milwaukee, WI 53208
Attn: Michael Neville, Artistic Dir.

Renegade Theatre Festival
www.renegadetheatre.org

Salem Theatre Co.
Moments of Play
New England playwrights only
mop@salemtheatre.com

Santa Cruz County Actor's Theatre
Eight Tens at Eight
Wilma Chandler, Artistic Director
ronziob@email.com
http://www.sccat.org

Secret Room Theatre
Alex Dremann (alexdremann@me.com)
www.secretroomtheatre.com

Secret Rose Theatre
www.secretrose.com
info@secretrose.com

Secret Theatre (Midsummer Night Festival), Queens, NY
Odalis Hernandez (odalis.hernandez@gmail.com)
www.secrettheatre.com/

She Speaks, Kitchener, Ontario
Paddy Gillard-Bentley (paddy@skyedragon.com)
Women playwrights

Shelterbelt Theatre, Omaha, NB
From Shelterbelt with Love
McClain Smouse (associate-artistic@shelterbelt.org)
submissions@shelterbelt.org
www.shelterbelt.org

Shepparton Theatre Arts Group
"Ten in 10" is a performance of 10 plays each running for 10 minutes every
year.
info@stagtheatre.com
www.stagtheatre.com

Short+Sweet
Pete Malicki, Literary Manager (Pete@shortandsweet.org)
http://www.shortandsweet.org/shortsweet-theatre/submit-script

Short Play NYC
https://shortplaynyc.com
admin@shortplaynyc.com

Silver Spring Stage, Silver Spring, MD
Jacy D'Aiutolo
oneacts2012.ssstage@gmail.com
www.ssstage.org

Sixth Street Theatre
Snowdance 10-Minute Comedy Festival
Rich Smith
Snowdance318@gmail.com

Source Festival
jenny@culturaldc.org

Southern Repertory Theatre
6 × 6
Aimee Hayes (literary@southernrep.com)
www.southernrep.com/

Stage Door Productions
Original One-Act Play Festival
www.stagedoorproductions.org

Stage Door Repertory Theatre
www.stagedoorrep.org

Stage Q
www.stageq.com

Stillwater Short Play Festival
Town and Gown Theatre (Stillwater, OK)
Debbie Sutton, Producer
snobiz123@aol.com

Stonington Players
HVPanciera@aol.com

Stratton Summer Shorts
Stratton Players
Rachel D'onfro, President
www.strattonplayers.com
info@strattonplayers.com

Subversive Theatre Collective
Kurt Schneiderman, Artistic Director
www.subversivetheatre.org
info@subversivetheatre.org

Ten Tuckey Festival
doug@thebardstown.com

The Theatre Lab
733 8th St., NW
Washington, DC 20001
https://www.theatrelab.org/
Buzz Mauro (buzz@theatrelab.org, 202-824-0449)

Theatre Odyssey
Sarasota, Florida
Tom Aposporos, Vice President
www.theatreodyssey.org

Theatre One Productions
theatreoneproductions@yahoo.com

Theatre Out, Santa Ana, CA
David Carnevale (david@theatreout.com)
LGBT plays

Theatre Oxford 10 Minute Play Contest
http://www.theatreoxford.com
Alice Walker
10minuteplays@gmail.com

Theatre Roulette Play Festival
Madlab Theatre Co.
andyb@mablab.net

Theatre Three
www.theatrethree.com
Jeffrey Sanzel (jeffrey@theatrethree.com)

Theatre Westminster
Ten Minute New (And Nearly New) Play Festival
ATTN: Terry Dana Jachimiak II
jachimtd@westminster.edu

Theatre Works 10-Minute Play Festival
https://theatreworks.us/playfestival-event.php

Those Women Productions
www.thosewomenproductions.com

TouchMe Philly Productions
www.touchmephilly.wordpress.com
touchmephilly@gmail.com

Towne Street Theatre Ten-Minute Play Festival
info@townestreet.org

Underground Railway Theatre
www.undergroundrailwaytheatre.org
Debra Wise, Artistic Director (debra@undergroundrailwaytheatre.org)

Unrenovated Play Festival
unrenovatedplayfest@gmail.com

Walking Fish Theatre
freshfish2submit@gmail.com

Weathervane Playhouse
8 × 10 Theatrefest
info@weathervaneplayhouse.com

Wide Eyed Productions
www.wideeyedproductions.com
playsubmissions@wideeyedproductions.com

Winston-Salem Writers
Annual 10 Minute Play Contest
www.wswriters.org
info@wswriters.org

Write Act
www.writeactrep.org
John Lant (j316tlc@pacbell.net)